A Quick Index to Twenty Essential Questions

BUILDING TYPE BASICS FOR

research laboratories

Other titles in the
BUILDING TYPE BASICS
series

HEALTHCARE FACILITIES
Michael Bobrow and Julia Thomas; Thomas Payette;
Ronald Skaggs; Richard Kobus

ELEMENTARY AND SECONDARY SCHOOLS
Bradford Perkins

MUSEUMS
Arthur Rosenblatt

HOSPITALITY FACILITIES
Brian McDonough; John Hill and Robert Glazier;
Winford "Buck" Lindsay; Thomas Sykes

BUILDING TYPE BASICS FOR

research laboratories

Stephen A. Kliment, Series Founder and Editor

DANIEL WATCH
Perkins & Will

Watkins College
of Art & Design

JOHN WILEY & SONS, INC.

New York, Chichester, Weinheim, Brisbane, Singapore, Toronto

Dedicated to the researchers, administrators, facility engineers, fellow architects, and engineers who strive each day to create better research environments, and thus contribute to new scientific discoveries that improve the quality of all our lives

Library of Congress Cataloging-in-Publication Data:

Watch, Daniel.
    Building type basics for laboratories / Daniel Watch
        p. cm.
    Includes index
    ISBN 0-471-39236-7 (cloth : alk. paper)
        1. Laboratories—Design and construction. 2. Architecture, Modern—20th century.
    I. Title.

NA6751 .W38 2001
727'.5'000222—dc21

Printed in the United States of America.

10 9 8 7 6 5 4 3 2 1

CONTENTS

CONTENTS

EDITOR'S PREFACE

STEPHEN A. KLIMENT, *Series Founder and Editor*

This book on laboratory facilities is another in Wiley's "Building Type Basics" series. It is not a coffee-table book lavish with color photography but meager in usable content. Rather, it contains the kind of essential information to which architects, consultants, and their clients need ready access, especially in the crucial early phases of a project. As architectural practice becomes more generalized and firms pursue commissions in an expanding range of building types, the books in the series provide a convenient, hands-on source of such basic information.

Like the others in the series, this volume is tightly organized for ease of use. The heart of the book is a set of twenty questions most frequently asked about a building type in the early stages of its design. These cover such concerns as programming and predesign, project process and management, design concerns unique to the type, and site planning. Also included are building code and ADA matters, engineering systems, energy and environmental challenges, as well as special equipment, interior design and materials issues, lighting and acoustic concerns, wayfinding, and renovation/ upgrading. The final questions take up international challenges, operation and maintenance, and cost and feasibility concerns.

To explore any of the twenty questions, start with the listing on the endpapers (inside the front and back covers), locate the category you want, and turn to the pages referenced.

This book is designed to serve three types of user: architects; their engineering and other consultants; and private, government, and academic bodies planning a laboratory and eager to acquaint themselves with the issues before interviewing and selecting an architect. Architecture students will also find the volume useful in getting a head start on a studio problem in this building type.

Laboratory design is crossing a divide marking permanent changes in the space program, form, and use of these facilities. As author Daniel Watch points out, three conditions are driving laboratory design:

- The global marketplace. A global research marketplace is emerging, with the United States and many other nations investing huge sums in research intended to advance the state of the art in science and technology and to make them more competitive. The proliferation of global alliances between the private and public sectors will spur the design and construction of facilities ranging from single buildings to great research parks.

- Research by team. The era of the isolated researcher burning midnight oil in pursuit of a scientific grail has been replaced by that of scientists and engineers in academe, government, or private industry working in teams, and often in mega-alliances that cross institutional boundaries. The team concept has stood facilities design on its head, as laboratory structures now must provide attractive locations throughout the building for researchers to gather and talk. Who knows what scientific breakthroughs are spawned in such informal settings?

- Applied computer technology. New software is able to crunch huge numbers at unheard-of speeds, communicate documents across any distance in a few seconds, and create real-time forums for researchers in far distant parts of the world. The implications for laboratory design are immense, demanding access to electronic communications systems throughout the building. The arrival of the wireless web may well simplify these systems, but at this writing a number of uncertainties concerning this emerging technology keeps wired systems at the forefront of design.

A manifest outcome of these trends is the need to design flexibility into lab facilities. While they cost more to construct than single-purpose laboratories, flexible labs are proving themselves more economical over the long run. Consequently, designs will increasingly be oriented not to a single specialty but to a range of disciplines. A general laboratory may be outfitted to afford a research team all available resources, including even pilot manufacturing facilities.

Dan Watch has organized his material into five chapters. Chapter 1 describes the new laboratory design model as it emerges from the various influences just described. Chapter 2 defines the three main laboratory categories, according to type of owner, operator, and objective—namely, private industry, academe, and government. This chapter includes space guidelines. Chapters 3 and 4 cover architectural and engineering design issues, respectively. Chapter 3 focuses especially on planning the lab module, key adjacencies, casework, ergonomics, fume hoods, and security. Chapter 4 deals with the four main engineering systems—structure, mechanical, electrical, plumbing—along with communications and renovation. Chapter 5 offers useful cost guidelines.

I hope this book serves you well—as guide, reference, and inspiration.

PREFACE

DANIEL WATCH

In my early years as an architect, I worked on a wide variety of buildings, including custom houses, multifamily housing, high-rise condominiums, large transportation projects, urban design and city planning projects, a football stadium, corporate office buildings, medical office buildings, and several design competitions. In 1990, when I was employed by the Philadelphia firm of KlingLindquist, I had the opportunity to work on my first laboratory project, for Glaxo in Stevenage, England. The program was 1.8 million GSF for phase 1 alone. It was a wonderful project and a valuable experience. The people at Glaxo taught me the importance of designing high-quality laboratories. After that project, I knew I wanted to design more laboratories, because of the complexity of the work, because of the opportunity to work with researchers, and, not least, because there was a construction boom in laboratory facilities.

From then on, each time I went to a new city, I spent time visiting academic and corporate labs. I even spent portions of my vacation touring lab facilities. On a few occasions, I found myself using a frequent flyer ticket to fly across the country over a weekend to study a lab project that had just been published. I ended up seeing quite a few labs, all over the United States. The more I saw, the more I understood the wide range of labs and the wider range of design solutions. I began writing down the lessons I'd learned, photographing the buildings, and developing an extensive library of resources.

Now I have the opportunity to share my research with clients and with other architects. I find myself giving clients and architects tours of labs to show them what works well and to get them in the habit of doing their own research. It is especially enjoyable to take clients on site visits. If a client asks me a question for which I do not have a complete answer, I take time to do the research and find the answer. Finding the answers to questions that clients and other architects and engineers have asked me is a large part of the genesis of this book.

As I work on each project today, I focus on creating new and unique solutions that are appropriate for the researchers, administrators, facility engineers, and architectural and engineering design team that I am working with. When I put the plans and elevations of each project that I have been responsible for on the wall, I am pleased to see that no two are alike. I am always asking myself, the client, and the design team to be creative and to think "outside the box" to develop quality laboratory environments with the money and program available. I will continue to ask others what is working well in their lab facilities, and I hope people will continue to be gracious and share their knowledge with me.

The sources of information for this book include the projects I have completed while employed by Perkins & Will and other architectural firms, as well as resource books, conferences, and the lessons I have learned from touring more than 150 lab facilities over the past five years. The photos, drawings, and other images in the book—which clarify and reinforce key issues throughout—come from approximately 50 research laboratory projects in the United States (about half the states are represented in the projects illustrated here), United Kingdom, South Korea, and China.

ACKNOWLEDGMENTS

I would like to thank the hundreds of researchers, administrators, facility engineers, and clients who have shared with me the lessons they have learned. I appreciate their comments, suggestions, and time. Touring approximately 150 research buildings in the last five years and talking with these experts has helped me to understand the many options and details of laboratory facility design.

I am thankful to those who have given me permission to show photographs or drawings of their projects.

I am deeply indebted to several experts who have coauthored portions of this book: John Nelson, CEO of Affiliated Engineers, Inc. (mechanical, electrical, and plumbing); Philip Lofgren, Director of Communication Technologies for Shooshanian Engineering Associates, Inc. (information technology); Mike Fletcher of Walter P. Moore (structural); Steven Sharlach and Bevan Suits, signage and graphic designers at Perkins & Will; Richard Price, Sustainable Design at Perkins & Will; Joseph Wagner, Private Sector Labs at Perkins & Will.

I would like to thank Rick Johnson and Fisher Hamilton for information, drawings, and illustrations on the latest in casework design.

I wish to express my appreciation to the following people at Perkins & Will for their production, graphic, and moral support: Alice Angus, Deepa Tolat, Gary McNay, Kimberly Polkinhorn, Lance Kirby, Marcy Snyder, and Reese Frago.

I would also like to thank my wife, Terrie, and daughters, Megan and Kalie, for their patience and understanding during the time I spent putting this book together.

INTRODUCTION

Early labs, such as Thomas Edison's facility in Fort Myers, Florida, were simple work areas, with basic casework and straightforward operational procedures. Technology was limited, and there was little equipment to support the research.

The first major shift in laboratory design in the 1960s, with the development of interstitial space at the Salk Institute in La Jolla, California. Jonas Salk led the effort to create the first laboratory facility that encouraged change, allowing scientists to design spaces that were appropriate for their research.

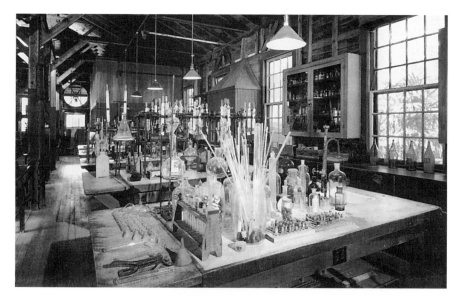

◀ Thomas Edison's chemical research laboratory, Fort Myers, Florida, 1928.

▼ The development of interstitial space. The Salk Institute and Institute of Biological Studies, La Jolla, California. Louis I. Kahn, architect.

We are now witnessing the next major shift in laboratory design. The three key drivers of this change are the development of the competitive global marketplace, the move toward team-based research, and the use of computer technology to accelerate the research process.

The global marketplace is changing the face of research. Many countries, including the United States, are investing in financial and human resources for science and technology (S&T), recognizing that such investment is the essential underpinning for social and economic well-being. Individual scientists and engineers, industrial firms, and academic institutions are taking advantage of the increasingly international character of S&T, as witnessed by the enhanced international mobility of the S&T workforce, the international coauthorship of scientific publications, the development of international industrial alliances, and the global flow of technological know-how. The global marketplace has spurred the merger and consolidation of several large research companies. Research parks are being constructed and growing at a rapid pace because of the partnering of the private and public sectors.

Major strides are increasingly likely to be made by research teams, both domestic and international, rather than by individuals. The globalization of science is reflected in a pervasive trend in scientific publishing—greater and greater collaboration. In 1995, half the articles in the science journals had multiple authors, and almost 30 percent of these involved international collaboration. Teamwork is necessary for sharing information efficiently and speeding up the discovery process. Partnering and the sharing of resources are becoming the norm. Less time is being spent in the lab, and more in meetings, both face-to-face and teleconferenced. Researchers are requiring breakout areas within their lab areas to encourage spontaneous as well as planned work sessions for exchanging information and ideas. In addition, lab teams have to be able to change their work spaces quickly and with little cost. Lab layouts are changing to allow for interactive research. Flexible furniture that incorporates the use of the computer, casework that can be easily moved, and engineering systems that can be cost-effectively modified are becoming more important to the long-term success of a research facility.

As in any business today, the computer is a way of life and a necessity in the laboratory. The marketplace is demanding more "discoveries" in less time than ever before, and companies are in heavy competition to be first with a new discovery. Computer technology is speeding up the entire research process, from discovery to market. Computers are encouraging researchers to reinvent their laboratory environments.

The burgeoning use of computers in research means that more dry labs—fitted with mobile casework for stacking computer hardware and research instruments—are required. The demand for and the production of more discoveries creates the need to upgrade existing labs, construct new laboratory facilities, and provide support functions such as pilot plants and manufacturing facilities.

These three factors—the global marketplace, team-based research, and the increasing use of computers—provide the context for the development of a new laboratory model, and it is to that subject that we first turn our attention, in chapter 1.

CHAPTER 1
A NEW DESIGN MODEL

A new model of laboratory design is emerging—one that creates lab environments that are responsive to present needs and capable of accommodating future demands. Several key needs are driving the development of this model:

- The need to create *"social buildings"* that foster interaction and *team-based research*
- The need to achieve an *appropriate balance between "open" and "closed" labs*
- The need for *flexibility* to accommodate change
- The need to *design for technology*
- The need for *environmental sustainability*
- The need, in some cases, to develop *science parks* to facilitate partnerships between government, private-sector industry, and academia

In the fall of 1998, the American Society of Interior Designers (ASID) completed a survey that identified five key principles for creating a productive workplace. Although these principles are applicable to workplaces in general, all make sense as bases for good laboratory design. These principles translate into the following imperatives for design and management:

- Improve people's performance by creating a team atmosphere in which communication and interaction are facilitated.
- View the designed environment as a tool rather than just another expenditure. Provide adequate access to resources, including team members and equipment. Accommodate ergonomic needs, such as comfortable seating and flexible workstations. Create an inviting, pleasant office atmosphere. Reduce distractions and disruptions that hinder employee concentration by designing acoustically sound work environments that provide appropriate levels of privacy.
- Redesign work processes and the physical environment to improve workflow within workstations and throughout the office building. Implement process efficiencies and reduce disruptions in workflow.
- Update and maintain technology so that employees work at their highest efficiency. Supply the right tools—computers, software, and other appropriate equipment. Make purchasing and planning decisions with an eye to accommodating future needs.
- Offer training and education opportunities. Maintain adequate support staff levels. Provide competitive salaries, bonuses, rewards, and other incentives. Adopt flexible policies, such as flextime and telecommuting.

SOCIAL BUILDINGS FOR TEAM-BASED RESEARCH

Despite popular images of scientists toiling in isolation, modern science is an intensely social activity. The most productive and successful scientists are intimately familiar with both the substance and style of their colleagues' work. They display an astonishing

▲ *Stair landings offer opportunities for people to interact. Boyer Center for Molecular Medicine, Yale University, New Haven, Connecticut. Cesar Pelli & Associates, architect.*

◥ *Top of stair as lounge area. Stevenson Center Complex Chemistry Building, Vanderbilt University, Nashville, Tennessee. Payette Associates, Inc., architect.*

capacity to adopt new research approaches and tools as quickly as they become available. Thus, science functions best when it is supported by architecture that facilitates both structured and informal interaction, flexible use of space, and sharing of resources.

A "social building" fosters interaction among the people who work there. With the advent of a new research model that deemphasizes departmental divisions and stresses the pursuit of research projects by teams (which change as projects change),

lab designers must pay increased attention to the social aspects of laboratory buildings.

Meeting Places

A critical consideration in designing such an environment is to establish places— such as break rooms, meeting rooms, and atrium spaces—where people can congregate outside their labs to talk with one another. Even stairways—fire stairs or stairs off an atrium, with built-in window seats—can provide opportunities for people to meet and exchange ideas.

Designers must look for such opportunities in public spaces, making optimal use of every square foot of the building.

In designing meeting spaces—whether formal or informal—care should be taken to use a variety of colors and materials that are pleasing to the eye. Studies have shown the use of color to create interior spaces can support the health and well-being of all who live and work in them. Daylighting, an equally important consideration, is dealt with in the section on sustainability.

The sharing of equipment and space can create further opportunities for people to meet each other and exchange information. Recognizing this, designers can plan instrument rooms to act as cross corridors, saving space and money as well as encouraging researchers to share equipment. Common support spaces, such as cold rooms, glassware storage, and chemical storage, can be situated in a central location in the building or on each floor, and alcoves can be created for ice machines and deionized water. Planning central locations for lab support

▼ *Properly executed, exposed piping reads as "high-tech." Chemistry Addition, University of Virginia, Charlottesville. Ellensweig Associates, Inc., architect.*

▲ *A variety of colors and materials is pleasing to the eye. Boyer Center for Molecular Medicine, Yale University, New Haven, Connecticut. Cesar Pelli & Associates, architect.*

▲ *Tile patterns add visual interest. Stevenson Center Complex Chemistry Building, Vanderbilt University, Nashville, Tennessee. Payette Associates, Inc., architect.*

◥ *Shared equipment rooms promote both a social building and efficient use of resources. Storm Eye Institute, Medical University of South Carolina. LS3P Architects, Ltd.*

▶ *Ice machine located in common area increases opportunities for interaction. Stevenson Center Complex Chemistry Building, Vanderbilt University, Nashville, Tennessee. Payette Associates, Inc., architect.*

▶▶ *Large gathering spaces are needed for special events and otherwise serve to welcome users into the building. Vernal G. Riffe, Jr., Building, Ohio State University, Columbus. Perkins & Will, architect.*

areas can help achieve a more social building as well as a more affordable design.

In academic laboratories, social opportunities can be provided by pre-function areas leading into large lecture halls, outdoor spaces on campus, break rooms, mailbox and locker areas, "living rooms" near faculty offices, student lounges, atriums, large-volume spaces, and along corridors—all areas where students and faculty might meet outside the classroom to discuss new ideas.

Team-Based Labs

The basic lab, oriented to the individual researcher, is becoming increasingly less important. Collaborative research requires teams of scientists with varying expertise, who together form interdisciplinary research units. As data are shared throughout the team and with other teams, and as networks connect people and organizations around the world, designers are organizing space in new ways. Laboratory designers can support collaborative research by:

• Creating flexible engineering systems and casework that encourage research

▶ New construction creates a strong gateway to a campus and well-defined exterior spaces that encourage informal interactions. Chemistry and Life Sciences Building, University of Illinois, Urbana. Perkins & Will, architect.

▼ Seating at entry. McDonald Medical Research Center, University of California at Los Angeles, California. Venturi Scott Brown with Payette Associates, Inc., architects.

teams to alter their spaces to meet their needs

- Designing offices and write-up areas as places where people can work in teams

- Creating research centers that are team-based

- Creating all the space necessary for research team members to operate properly near each other

- Minimizing or eliminating spaces that are identified with a particular department

- Establishing clearly defined circulation patterns

Today, design strongly influences an organization's ability to recruit and retain

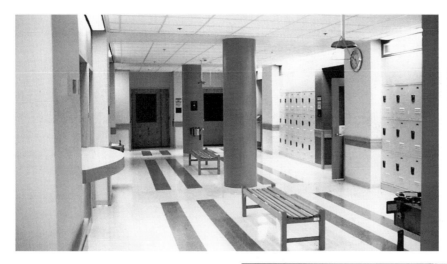

◀ *Mailrooms and lockers are also common areas that provide for casual encounters. Stevenson Center Complex Chemistry Building, Vanderbilt University, Nashville, Tennessee. Payette Associates, Inc., architect.*

▼ *Break-out rooms allow researchers to meet outside their labs. Biochemistry Building, University of Wisconsin, Madison. Flad & Associates, Inc., architect.*

top talent. In an ever more competitive environment, an organization looking to recruit research staff must provide more than just a laboratory to work in. Candidates will want to know who their coworkers will be, how they will work together, and how the team will be supported. And most researchers are looking for laboratory environments that accommodate and encourage interactive, interdisciplinary approaches to research.

"OPEN" VERSUS "CLOSED" LABS

An increasing number of research institutions are creating "open" labs to support team-based work. The open lab concept is significantly different from that of the "closed" lab of the past, which was based on accommodating the individual principal investigator. In open labs, researchers share not only the space itself but also equipment, bench space, and support staff. The open lab format facilitates communication between scientists and makes the space more easily adaptable for future needs. A wide variety of labs—from wet biology and chemistry labs, to engineering labs, to dry computer

science facilities—are now being designed as open labs. A conceptual floor plan of an open lab is shown on page 10.

Most laboratory facilities built or designed since the mid-1990s possess some type of open lab, and the trend is evident in government, private-sector, and academic labs. The National Institutes of Health, in Bethesda, Maryland, and the Centers for Disease Control, in Atlanta, Georgia, emphasize open labs in their biological safety laboratories. An example

▲ New research labs allow the central space to be fitted out by the researcher with floor-mounted equipment, computers, and mobile casework. Technology Enhanced Learning Center, State University of West Georgia, Carrolton. Perkins & Will, architect.

▼ One hundred percent open lab.

focus on separate research projects. The architectural and engineering systems should be designed to affordably accommodate multiple floor plans that can easily be changed according to the research teams' needs.

There is still a need for closed labs for specific kinds of research or for certain equipment. Nuclear magnetic resonance (NMR) equipment, electron microscopes, tissue culture labs, darkrooms, and glass washing are examples of equipment and activities that must be housed in separate, dedicated spaces.

Moreover, some researchers find it difficult or unacceptable to work in a lab that is open to everyone. They may need some dedicated space for specific research in an individual closed lab. In some cases, individual closed labs can directly access a larger, shared open lab. When a researcher requires a separate space, an individual closed lab can meet his or her needs; when it is necessary and beneficial to work as a team, the main open lab is used. Equipment and bench space can be shared in the large open lab, thereby helping to reduce the cost of research. The diagrams on the following pages

from the private sector is provided by Biogen, where open labs are designed for the drug development process. At Biogen, in Cambridge, Massachusetts, some open labs support the drug development process, while others (the Bio6 and Bio8 buildings) primarily support discovery research. Academic laboratory facilities are combining smaller labs to create larger spaces that accommodate interdisciplinary teams and that permit lectures and research to occur in the same room.

There can be two or more open labs on a floor, encouraging multiple teams to

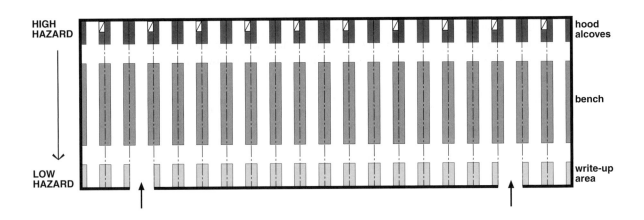

HIGH HAZARD

LOW HAZARD

hood alcoves

bench

write-up area

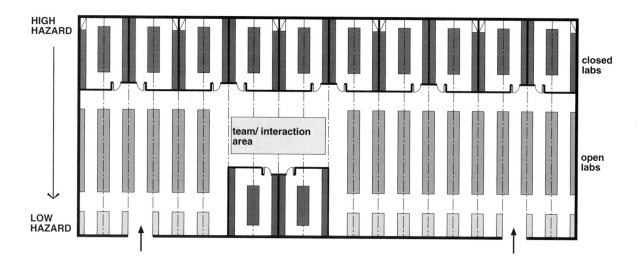

illustrate a combination of open and closed labs. This concept can be taken further to create a lab module that allows glass walls to be located almost anywhere. The glass walls allow people to see each other easily while also having their individual spaces.

The old approach of providing closed labs throughout a facility will still be necessary for some facilities.

FLEXIBILITY

Maximizing flexibility has always been a key concern in designing or renovating a laboratory building, but this has never been more true than today, when competitive pressures and changing research concepts require organizations to be as flexible as possible. Flexibility can mean several things, including the ability to expand easily, to readily accommodate reconfigurations and other changes, and to permit a variety of uses.

Flexibility for Churn

When a research facility and/or its laboratories are designed for flexibility, the problem of churn can be addressed by facility managers in a timely, cost-effective manner. Churn can be accommodated in several different ways.

If churn simply entails moving people from one lab to another—keeping the existing casework and modifying only the equipment—it can usually be accommodated inexpensively because the renovation requirements are often minimal. The facility manager at the 3M Research Complex in Austin, Texas, explained that although his facility has a churn rate of almost 35 percent each year, most of that churn simply involves moving researchers and equipment, with very little change to the casework or walls.

Sometimes churn requires the renovation of a laboratory within the existing walls. Casework is modified, engineering services are changed, and equipment is relocated. Some institutions may, on average, change up to 10 percent of their space in this way each year. The photo on page 11 illustrates an open lab that is designed to allow the research team to bring in its own casework and equipment and locate these items as

Fifty percent open–fifty percent closed lab.

11

▶ *Open/closed lab.*

▶ *Closed lab.*

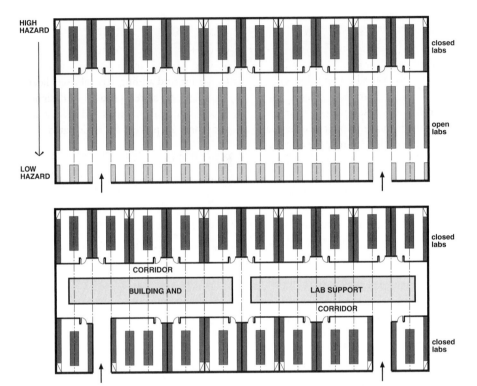

needed. The engineering services are provided from the ceiling and along the walls.

Sometimes, however, churn necessitates the demolition and reconstruction of walls and engineering systems. Basically, an area of the building is emptied and the space is reconstructed. This strategy, requiring significant construction and a staging area to relocate people and equipment, is usually expensive and is implemented less often than the simpler approaches described above.

Finally, churn, combined with changes in the kind of research being conducted and the ways in which research is performed, may require the construction of a new facility and the relocation of people and equipment to that location. This, obviously, is the most expensive

option of all. Maximizing flexibility means reducing the chance that significant renovation or new construction will be needed to accommodate change.

Flexible Engineering Systems

Flexible engineering services—supply and exhaust air, water, electricity, voice/data, natural gas, vacuum systems—are extremely important to most labs. Labs must have easy connects/disconnects at the walls and ceiling to allow for fast, affordable hookups of equipment. The engineering systems may need to be designed to enable fume hoods to be removed or added, to allow the space to be changed from a lab environment to an office and then back again, or to allow maintenance of the controls outside the lab.

From the start, mechanical systems need to be designed for a maximum number of fume hoods in the building. Ductwork can be sized to allow for change and vertical exhaust risers provided for future fume hoods in the initial construction. When a hood is required, the duct can simply be run from the hood to the installed vertical riser. When a fume hood is added or deleted, the mechanical systems will need to be rebalanced to efficiently accommodate the numbers of hoods in use and the air changes necessary through each room. The dedicated individual risers are primarily used for the hoods that exhaust special chemicals (such as radioactive and perchloric fumes) that cannot be mixed into the main laboratory exhaust system.

Installing vertical risers during initial construction takes little time and approximately a one-third the cost of retrofiting and adding vertical risers later.

Engineering systems should be designed to service initial demands and at least an additional 25 percent for anticipated

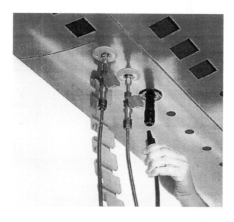

◀ Easy connection and disconnection of engineering services allows for ready reconfiguration of the lab. Courtesy Fisher Hamilton.

◀ An open lab allows the research team to position casework and equipment for each project. College of Medicine, Northwestern University, Evanston, Illinois. Perkins & Will, architect.

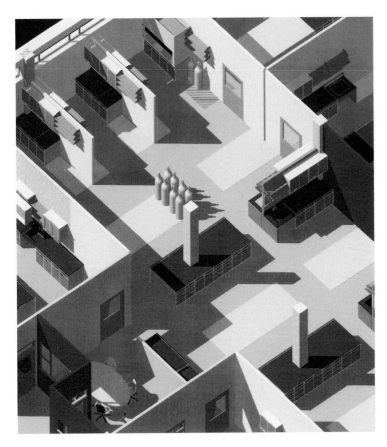

▲ *Laying out casework within an equipment zone. Colored floor tiles identify the zones for equipment and casework.*

as the number of individual research labs declines and that of team-based labs grows, this is no longer the best approach. Casework has to be moveable to meet a team's changing needs.

Equipment zones

It typically takes about three years for a lab to be designed and built. During this time, an organization's research needs may change or the people doing the research may leave and be replaced by others. In either case, there is a good chance that the purpose of the lab will change. If the entire lab is fitted with new casework, the casework may have to be changed before anyone occupies the new laboratory.

To minimize this problem, equipment zones should be created in the initial design. An equipment zone is an area that can be fitted with equipment, movable furniture, fixed casework, or a combination of any of these. Equipment zones are usually fitted out when the research team moves into the lab—that is, when the team knows exactly what will be needed to do the work. The creation of equipment zones that accommodate change easily is a cost-effective design opportunity. The lab can be generic, with 50 percent fixed casework initially and the rest of the lab fitted out later. The fixed casework is usually located on the outside wall, with islands defined as equipment zones. It may also be helpful to locate 3 ft to 6 ft equipment zones on the outside walls to accommodate cylinders near fume hoods and refrigerators at the perimeter.

Generic labs

When a laboratory facility is designed generically, most of the labs are the same

future programs. Space should be allowed in utility corridors, ceilings, and vertical chases for future heating, ventilation, and air conditioning (HVAC), plumbing, and electrical needs. Service shutoff valves should be easily accessible, located in a box in the wall at the entry to the lab or in the ceiling at the entry. All pipes, valves, and clean-outs should be clearly labeled to identify the contents, pressure, and temperature. (Engineering systems are discussed in much greater detail in chapter 4.)

Flexible Lab Interiors

In the past, many labs were fitted with as much fixed bench space as possible. Today, size and are outfitted with the same basic engineering services and casework. Generic labs are a sensible option when it is not known who will occupy the space or what specific type of research will be conducted there. Generic lab design may also make sense from an administrative standpoint, since each team or researcher is given the same basic amenities. The best generic labs have some flexibility built in and can be readily modified for the installation of equipment or for changes to the engineering services or casework. The following are three possibilities among many variations:

- 100 percent fixed casework.

- 50 percent fixed casework, 50 percent open area, allowing researchers to bring in tables, equipment, carts, or more casework to fit out their lab.

- 33 percent sit-down casework, 33 percent stand-up casework, with the rest of the space open. The sit-down casework is for work areas, computer imaging, and other types of research that require the researcher to be sitting down for long periods of time.

Mobile casework

Another benefit of creating equipment zones is that the initial budget for casework and construction can be reduced significantly. Casework can account for 10 percent or more of a construction budget. But, by purchasing only what is initially needed, a facility can reduce casework costs to as little as 6 to 8 percent of the overall budget. Of course, the money saved will have to be spent later, when mobile casework is purchased. But it should be remembered that mobile casework and equipment may be funded through other budgets or grants. This is a very important consideration for many new lab projects where budgets are limited and where the specific research that will be undertaken, and who will be using the labs, will not be determined until construction is completed. Purchasing mobile casework will create an inventory of pieces that can be moved from one lab to another.

Technological advances allow for more research procedures to be automated. In the past equipment was often squeezed into an existing lab setup; today's labs must be designed to accept the needed equipment easily. There are several types of movable casework to consider. Lab tables with adjustable legs, which allow for flexibility in height, can meet the requirements of the Americans with Disabilities Act (ADA) and be ergonomically correct for sit-down and stand-up bench work. Storage cabinets that are 7 ft tall allow a large volume of space for storage and can be very affordable, compared to the cost of multiple base cabinets. Mobile write-up stations can be moved into the lab whenever sit-down space is required for data collection.

Mobile carts make excellent equipment storage units. Often used in research labs as computer workstations, mobile carts allow computer hardware to be stacked and then moved to equipment stations as needed. Data ports are also located adjacent to electrical outlets along the casework. Instrument cart assemblies are designed to allow for the sharing of instruments between labs. Carts are typically designed to fit through a 3 ft wide doorway and are equipped with levelers and castors. Many mobile carts are load tested to support 2,000 lb. Mobile carts can be designed with 1 in.

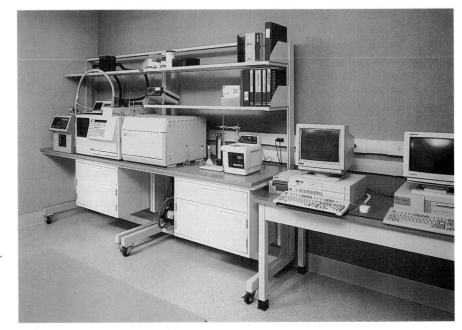

▶ Mobile cart for instruments. Courtesy Fisher Hamilton.

▼ Mobile carts for equipment storage. Courtesy Fisher Hamilton.

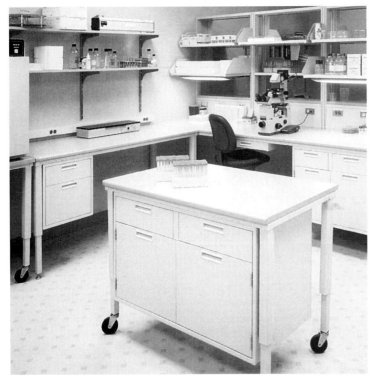

vertical slots to support adjustable shelving. The depth of the shelving can vary to allow efficient stacking of equipment and supplies.

Mobile base cabinets are constructed with a number of drawer and door configurations and are equipped with an anti-tipping counterweight. The drawer units can be equipped with locks. The typical height of mobile cabinets is 29 in., which allows them to be located below most sit-down benches. Also, mobile tables are now available for robotic analyzers. The tables are designed to support 800 lb. A mobile cabinet can also be designed to incorporate a computer cabinet, which can be hooked up to the robotic analyzers. Mobile computer carts incorporate a pullout shelf for the server and a pullout tray for the keyboard in front of the monitor. Wire management is designed as a part of the cart.

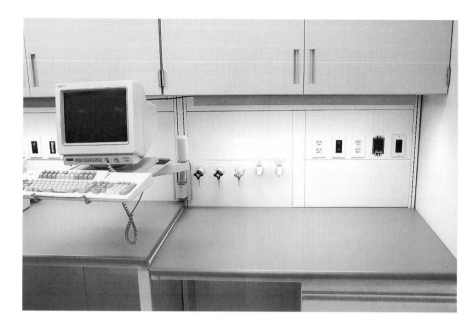

◀ Monitor arm. Courtesy
Fisher Hamilton.

Using the full volume of the lab space

Many labs today are equipment intensive
and require as much bench space as
possible. Using the full volume of the
lab space to stack equipment and
supplies can be very helpful and cost-
effective. Mobile carts, as mentioned
earlier, can be used to stack computer
hardware as well as other lab equipment.
Overhead cabinets allow for storage
above the bench, making good use of
the volume of a space. Flexibility can
also be addressed with adjustable
shelving instead of cabinets. Adjustable
shelving allows the researcher to use the
number of shelves required, at the height
and spacing necessary. If tall equipment
is set on the bench, the shelving can be
taken down to allow space for the
equipment. The bottom shelf should be
19 in. to 20 in. above the benchtop and
should stop 18 in. below the ceiling to
permit appropriate coverage by the
sprinkler system.

Flexible partitions

Flexible partitions, which can be taken
down and put back up in another
location, allow laboratory spaces to be
configured in a variety of sizes. The
accordion wall systems used in the past
were flimsy and had acoustical problems.
Today, manufacturers are producing wall
systems that are very sturdy and avoid
many of the acoustical problems.
Movable walls are being developed that
can accommodate the engineering
services as well as the casework in a
modular design. The system can be a
solid, full-height wall with open shelving
or overhead cabinets above the bench, or
a low wall hidden behind the base
cabinets. It can have slotted vertical
standards to provide an adjustable system
for the casework components. The wall
system can support electrical and
communications wiring, gas distribution
systems, plumbing, and snorkel exhausts.
Although the first cost of mobile walls are

A NEW DESIGN MODEL

▶ *Movable walls. Courtesy Fisher Hamilton.*

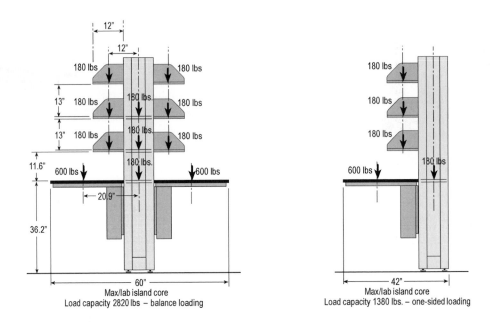

Max/lab island core
Load capacity 2820 lbs – balance loading

Max/lab island core
Load capacity 1380 lbs. – one-sided loading

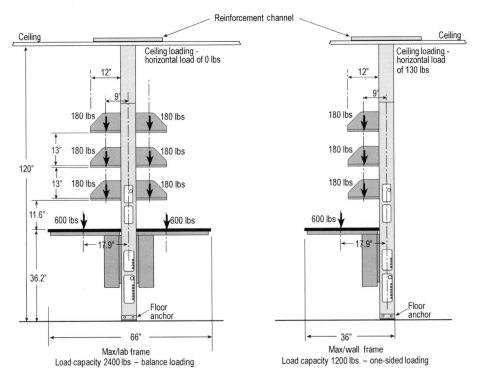

Max/lab frame
Load capacity 2400 lbs – balance loading

Max/wall frame
Load capacity 1200 lbs. – one-sided loading

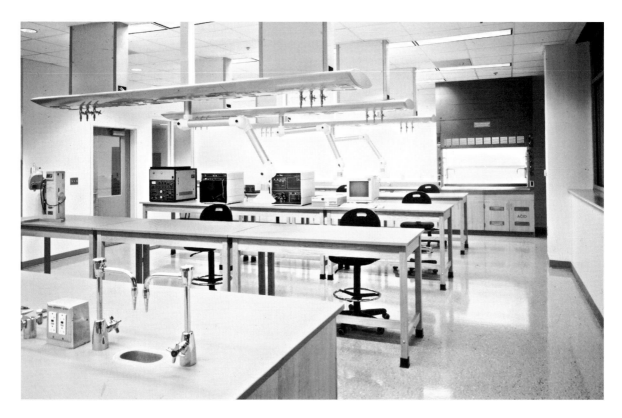

higher than those of dry walls, a cost benefit should be realized with the first renovation and/or reconfiguration.

Overhead service carriers

An overhead service carrier is hung from the underside of the structural floor system. The utility services are run above the ceiling, where they are connected to the overhead service carrier. These services should have quick connect and disconnect features for easy hookups to the overhead service carriers. Overhead service carriers come in standard widths and accommodate electrical and communication outlets, light fixtures, service fixtures for process piping, and exhaust snorkels.

Docking stations

Floor-mounted docking stations can include all utility feeds and a sink. Ceiling-mounted docking units incorporate all utilities. An overhead service carriage is similar to a docking station, minus the sink.

Wet and dry labs

Research facilities typically include both wet and dry labs. Wet labs have sinks, piped gases, and, usually, fume hoods. They require chemical-resistant countertops and 100 percent outside air, and are outfitted with some fixed casework. Dry labs are usually computer intensive, with significant requirements for electrical and data wiring. Their casework

▲ *Overhead service carriers. Technology Enhanced Learning Center, State University of West Georgia, Carrolton. Perkins & Will, architect.*

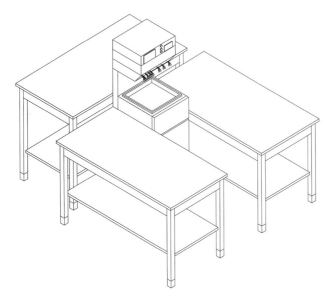

▲ Docking station.
Courtesy Fisher Hamilton.

is mobile; they have adjustable shelving and plastic laminate counters. Recirculated air is sufficient. (Dry lab construction is, in fact, very similar to office construction.) A key difference is the substantial need for cooling in dry labs because of the heat generated by the equipment.

Wet labs cost approximately two times more than dry labs. A building can be zoned for wet labs and non-wet areas (dry labs, offices, meeting rooms, restrooms), thereby saving money in initial construction as well as long-term operational costs. There is a trade-off, however. When a building is zoned in this way, it will be very difficult and expensive to change dry areas into wet labs later on. One option is to decide with the client how much space initially used for dry functions may eventually have to be converted to wet labs. Most laboratory facilities do not need 100 percent flexibility, nor do most organizations have the budget to pay for that degree of flexibility. The trick is to design for the appropriate amount of flexibility while balancing the initial and long-term costs.

DESIGNING FOR TECHNOLOGY

Technology plays an ever larger role in research and in the exchange of scientific information. To accommodate audiovisual, communications, and computer technologies, today's lab designers must

- Create state-of-the-art conferencing, education, and presentation center(s) to provide high-level, multi-use access to advanced interactive computer systems.
- Establish a flexible, reliable, and accessible voice/data network infrastructure that can readily respond to the rapid incorporation of computers within the facility.
- Implement telecommunications distribution design methods that allow the network to be flexible, manageable, and expandable, providing the ability to adapt to changing user and technology environments to meet demands for increased bandwidth or services.
- Ensure the efficient use of telecommunications utility spaces and optimize the ability to accommodate future changes in equipment and/or services.

Presentation and Conferencing Spaces

Teleconferencing

Teleconferencing allows companies to talk to one another as often as necessary. Its use is increasingly evident today, and the technology is becoming better. For most companies, the typical conference room of the future will have teleconferencing capability—giving local participants the sense that they are in the same room as their faraway counterparts and saving a

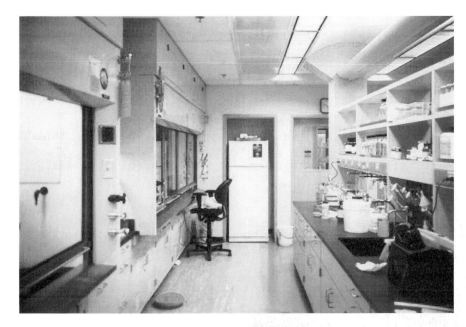

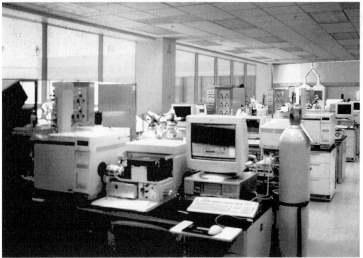

◀ Wet lab. DuPont, Wilmington, Delaware. The Hillier Group, architect.

▼ Dry lab. DuPont, Wilmington, Delaware. The Hillier Group, architect.

tremendous amount of time and cost once used for travel.

Lecture areas

Furniture for lecture areas should accommodate information technology. The furniture should either be pre-wired to allow a laptop to be plugged in or incorporate a raceway to accommodate wiring. Locate a front row of lights near a marker board to allow lights to wash over the board and for zoning of different types of fixtures to serve the different activities that will occur in the room.

Mobile Audiovisual Equipment

In some instances, installation of instructional presentation systems in every room may not be affordable. In these cases, with proper preparation and infrastructure provision, transportable systems can be used. A transportable system should have the audio, video, and control equipment installed in a wheeled

equipment rack, with a video projector installed on top of the rack. The transportable rack should have retractable cables for connecting the rack equipment to a power source, to external media sources (such as the campus CATV system, instructor's computer, document

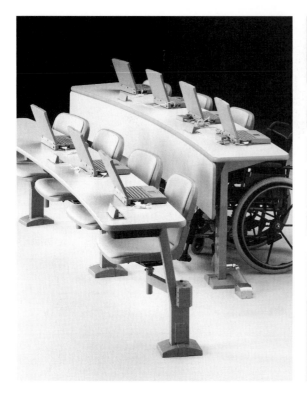

▲ *Auditorium seating.*

◥ *Multimedia seating.*

camera, etc.), and to equipment components installed in the room (e.g., program playback speakers). Rack connections should be provided in recessed floor boxes at the speaker's desk or presentation location. The floor box should have power, data, control, and audio and video tie-line connections to the rack floor box (to avoid having to lay cables on the floor).

The total height of the transportable rack, with the projector installed on top, should not exceed 48 in. Care should be taken to maintain sight lines to the screen for people seated in back of the transportable rack.

Computer Technology

A number of computer-related developments are now influencing laboratory design:

- Computer utilization in the lab is increasing as the ability to research within "virtual" modeling environments increases.

- Traditional experimentation is being augmented or replaced by computer simulations.

- The scope of information technology is expanding to a global network as the speed of voice and data transmissions improve and visual communication is enhanced.

Because of these developments, communication technologies must be considered early in the design process. Data, audio, visual, and computational capabilities should be integrated to facilitate new analysis techniques.

Furniture considerations

One important change that has occurred in the design of research facilities is that furniture must be designed with computer use in mind. For example, furniture must accommodate the cabling necessary for PCs or laptop computers. Tables should be modular so that they can be added to or rearranged consistently with the fixed casework and the lab equipment. Ports and outlets should be located to accommodate multiple furniture layouts. Write-up stations should be at least 4 ft wide to allow for knee space and hardware under the countertop.

Workstations should be 48 in. wide and 30 in. deep, at a minimum. If a computer will be shared, the workstation should, at a minimum, be 72 in. wide and 30 in. deep. In wet labs, computer keyboards must be placed away from spill areas, ideally in separate write-up areas. Laptop computers should be considered for their compact size, mobility, and ease of storage. Electrical outlets must be accessible for plugging in adapters. Designers should consider stacking hardware vertically on mobile carts. Laptops with voice-activated microphones are being developed for use in fume hoods, where use of standard laptops can create safety hazards (or where laptops might be damaged by chemical spills).

Computer labs should provide flexibility, allowing faculty and students to create different teaching and learning environments.

Following are three options in computer furniture:

1. Specialized equipment enclosures.

2. Computer hardware enclosures. There are hardware enclosures that are fully

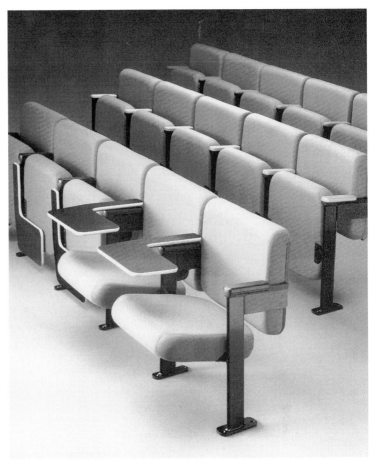

▲ Classroom seating.

ventilated and secure. Security for computers in a lab is a management and design issue, and designers should consider mobile cabinets with adjustable shelving that can be locked.

3. Monitor arms, server platforms, and keyboard drawer solutions. Monitor arms are capable of holding up to 100 lb and can support computer monitors of up to 21 in. Mobile server platforms are designed with adjustable shelving to allow stacking of computer hardware. Keyboard platforms can be adjusted vertically and can be mounted under the work surface.

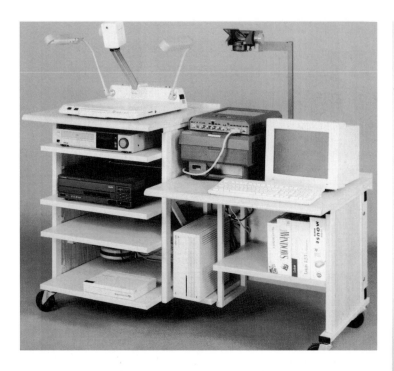

▲ *Mobile electronic equipment furniture. Courtesy Fisher Hamilton.*

◥ *Hardware enclosure. Courtesy Fisher Hamilton.*

Wireless technology

Wireless information technology systems are around the corner. Networks will take on new meaning when high-speed untethered communication becomes a reality. Ironically, it is difficult to determine how much high-speed cable should be installed for "future-ready" computing, if indeed the future is to be wireless. Currently, there are many difficult obstacles to overcome due to frequency limitations that are regulated by the Federal Communications Commission (FCC) and other agencies. Today, just as 8Mbps (megabits per second) wireless networks are beginning to emerge, most hard-wired networks are migrating from 10Mbps to the desktop to 100Mbps or higher. Barring a major technological breakthrough, advanced networks will require physical cabling for quite some time to come.

Robots

Today the laboratory use of robots is commonplace and has resulted in research that can be completed faster, more efficiently, more safely, and at lower cost than was previously possible. Robots are helping industry to address key issues such as competition and quick response time. The research environment, especially in the private and government sectors, will see the development of more sophisticated robots and significant growth in their use in automated labs.

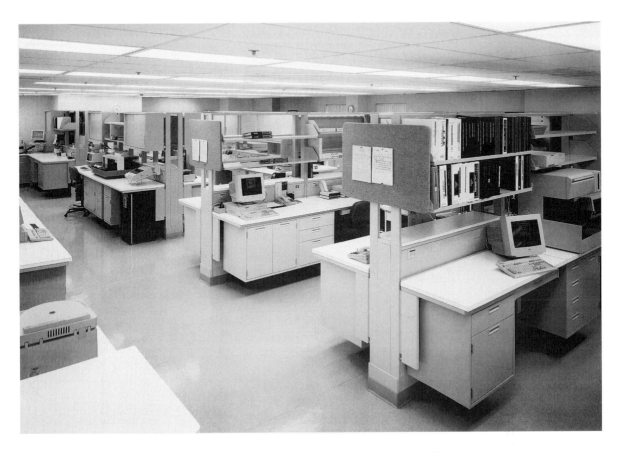

Tasks robots can do cost-effectively are arc welding, assembly, drilling, food processing, inspection, material handling, packaging, grinding, palletizing, pharmaceutical research and development, spot welding, spraying/dispensing, testing, and water-jet cutting. In 1998 there were 80,000 robots at work in the United States; it was estimated that 10,000 robots would be added to the workforce each year. As has been documented by the Robotic Industries Association, the typical robot pays for itself in two years.

Robots are usually custom-fit in a lab, requiring special space and engineering. Leonard Mayer has written, "Space requirements for robots may consist of a series of partially overlapping circular, semi-circular, or linear workstations. The reach or radius may be 3–4 ft and as much as 8–12 ft or more, depending on the scope of the activity. The robotic system may also include a mechanical rail or transport system connecting a series of robotic workstations with human workstations. Space must be provided for the computer hardware components and peripherals, maintenance and repair of the machines (workshops or bioengineering facilities), sufficient access and clearances for adjustments and repair during operations, and space for equipment and spare parts" (Mayer 1995).

▲ Write-up stations at least 4 ft wide. Courtesy Fisher Hamilton.

Automated Labs

Today's research environment requires the generation and analysis of enormous quantities of laboratory-based information. The information avalanche is here and has led to the development of high-throughput automated laboratories. Today, most laboratory activities are carried out by technicians using various labor-saving devices that are semi-automated.

One factor driving the development of automated labs is the triple threat of infectious diseases, foodborne pathogens, and bioterrorism. Discovering solutions to these problems, which threaten to affect large numbers of people, requires (1) large quantities of data; (2) access to appropriate samples—often in great numbers—for testing and analysis; (3) reproducible laboratory procedures; and (4) sufficient quantities of supporting reagents.

The model of semiautomated/semi-manual laboratories has three shortcomings. First, because such facilities require significant human involvement, they scale linearly in cost with the overall size of the problem. Second, such facilities demand people to perform highly repetitive tasks, which are prone to human error. Third, facilities can be overwhelmed by large surges in demand. Such acute surges in demand could occur, for example, during a rapidly spreading epidemic or a bioterrorist attack. Fortunately, a critical number of scientific disciplines and powerful technologies can be combined to address this triple threat:

- Molecular biologists and biochemists have developed a variety of laboratory-based assays that are powerful and readily available to large-scale efforts.

- Engineers have developed innovative robotic and automation technologies that permit an enormous, rapid rise in the number and variety of laboratory experiments.

- Computer scientists have developed programming languages and database management systems that provide the basic building blocks for improved environments for scientific collaboration.

- Physicists have catalyzed the development of the Internet, which is literally transforming the ways in which scientific and technical collaboration take place. Automated systems are flexible, modular, and remotely accessible, thereby enabling a convenient means of "mass customized testing" via the Internet.

Other key design issues in semi-automated labs involve the handling of samples to be tested and the disposal of wastes.

Virtual Labs

Throughout the research industry today, one constantly hears the phrases "virtual labs" and "virtual reality." Virtual labs will become more common each year. Some of the areas in which virtual reality will play a key role in future research are these:

- Virtual manufacturing
- Three-dimensional calibration for virtual environments
- Assembly path planning using virtual-reality techniques
- Virtual assembly design environment
- Knowledge-based systems
- Virtual environments for ergonomic design
- Telerobotics

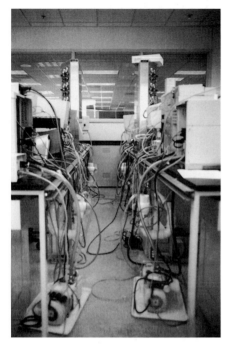

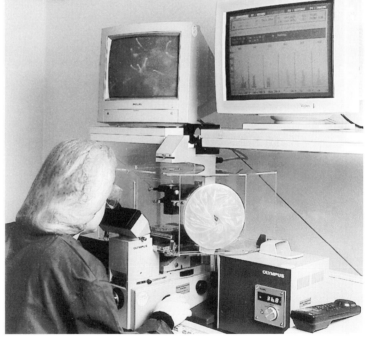

SUSTAINABILITY

A typical laboratory currently uses five times as much energy and water per square foot as a typical office building. Research laboratories are so energy-demanding for a variety of reasons:

- They contain large numbers of containment and exhaust devices.

- They house a great deal of heat-generating equipment.

- Scientists require 24-hour access.

- Irreplaceable experiments require fail-safe redundant backup systems and uninterrupted power supply (UPS) or emergency power.

In addition, research facilities have intensive ventilation requirements—including "once through" air—and must meet other health and safety codes, which add to energy use. Examining energy and water requirements from a holistic perspective, however, can identify significant opportunities for improving efficiencies while meeting or exceeding health and safety standards. Sustainable design of lab environments should also improve productivity.

▲ Computers for research. *Glaxo Wellcome Medicines Research Center, Stevenage, England. Kling Lindquist, architect.*

SUSTAINABLE DESIGN CRITERIA

Parameter	Code Minimum	Code Reference	Standard Practice	Design Target
Ventilation	10 cfm/person	ASHRAE 62/89	same	Maximize outdoor air in the breathing zone
Filtration	none		35–80%	65% per filter / 85% final filter
Indoor design Temperature	75°F summer 72°F winter		same	
Humidity control	uncontrolled		uncontrolled	60% RH summer 40% RH winter
Equipment heat dissipation	NA		3–4W/sq ft	1.5W/sq ft or 2W/sq ft with 75% diversity factor
Toilet exhaust	50 cfm/fixture	ASHRAE 62/89	same	2 cfm/sq ft
Connected lighting heat load	NA		2W/sq ft	0.5-0.75W/sq ft Total task/ambient with occupancy sensors and daylight sensors
Lighting levels	100 ft candles all direct		same	20–30 ft candles with ambient and task lighting
Building shell infiltration	6 in./100 sq ft	ASHRAE guideline	3 in./100 sq ft	1.5 in./100 sq ft (Canadian Standard)
Building shell Infiltration (alternate)	0.60 cfm/sq ft		0.30 cfm/sq ft	0.10 cfm/sq ft
Exterior wall insulation	U = 0.28 btu/sq ft/hr	BOCA energy code	U = 0.10 btu/sq ft/hr	U = 0.15 btu/sq ft/hr (S) / U = 0.05 btu/sq ft/hr (N, E, W) AIB - with insulation both sides
Exterior wall moisture control	none			
Roof insulation	U - 0.07 btu/sq ft/hr	BOCA energy code	U - 0.05 btu/sq ft/hr	U - 0.05 btu/sq ft/hr with low albedo surfacing
Windows				
Glazing type	single/clear		double/clear	heat reflecting clear
Visible transmittance	0.80		0.78	0.70
Shading coefficient	1.00		0.80	0.43
U value	1.04		0.48	0.30
Heat degree days	6,155 btu	ASHRAE	same	determined by DOE 2 analysis of TMY data

Key aspects of sustainable design are as follows:

- Increased energy conservation and efficiency
- Reduction or elimination of harmful substances and waste
- Improvements to the interior and exterior environments, leading to increased productivity
- Efficient use of materials and resources
- Recycling and increased use of products with recycled content

Private-sector CEOs see sustainable building design as providing an opportunity to reduce long-term operating costs while becoming better corporate citizens. The federal government is advocating sustainable building design that is based on resource efficiency, a healthy environment, and productivity. Many government agencies are adopting the LEED (Leadership in Energy and Environmental Design) Green Building Rating System, a self-assessing system designed for rating new and existing buildings that has been developed by the U.S. Green Building Council and the U.S. Department of Energy. It evaluates environmental performance from a "whole building" perspective over a building's life cycle, providing a definitive standard for what constitutes sustainable building design. LEED is based on accepted energy and environmental principles and strikes a balance between known effective practices and emerging concepts. Opposite is an example of a criteria chart set up for a specific project. Each criterion must be reviewed for each specific project.

Architectural Considerations

The design of the building envelope—including overhangs, glazing, insulation, and (possibly) the use of photovoltaic panels—is critical to the building's energy efficiency.

Overhangs

Overhangs for shading windows are often designed as part of the wall system. Though many people believe that adding overhangs to shade windows will reduce energy costs enough to justify the additional cost of the overhang, this is not the case. There is no real energy-savings payback, but overhangs do improve the quality of the natural light entering the interior space. The south elevation should have a horizontal overhang; east and west elevations usually require both horizontal and vertical overhangs.

Glazing

The glazing material for exterior windows should have a thermal break and an insulating section between the inner and outer sections of the frames. Wood or fiberglass frames will give much better thermal performance than aluminum. Low-E windows with at least a R-3 insulation value should be used. "Superwindows" that incorporate multiple thin plastic films can have an R value as high as 12. The problem is that such windows cost up to four times as much as low-E glass. Operable windows generally will not reduce energy costs; in fact, they may increase energy usage, but they usually enhance the quality of the indoor environment and are therefore preferred by most clients.

Roofs and walls

The use of light-colored roofing with a high-albedo coating to reflect light and heat is recommended. The amount of wall and roof insulation needed will vary depending on the climate and the type of lab. For example, equipment-intensive labs will generate a lot of heat and in certain parts of the country will not require as much roof insulation as elsewhere. All electrical outlets and all plumbing and wire penetrations into the building should be sealed, since air leakage can be a significant source of energy waste in some parts of the country.

Today, there is quite a bit of discussion about using photovoltaic panels both to enclose a building and to generate electricity. Photovoltaic panels can be integrated into the building envelope as metal roofing, spandrel glazing, or semitransparent vision glazing. But the panels are difficult to justify in traditional applications because the electricity they generate can cost more than electricity purchased from the grid. To be economically feasible, the panels must cover an area large enough to generate enough electricity to make a difference.

Engineering Considerations

Sustainable engineering addresses civil engineering concerns as well as the design of mechanical, plumbing, and lighting systems. First and foremost, the design team and client should contact the local utility company to explore opportunities for rebates to assist in the purchase of high-efficiency equipment or the use of other energy conservation measures.

Civil engineering

Civil engineering issues to consider include the use of pervious materials wherever possible. In preparing a site for new construction, designers should consider transplanting existing trees instead of removing them.

Mechanical, plumbing, and water-conservation strategies

For the HVAC system, it is most important to simulate the operation of the whole system and to analyze assumptions using whole-building systems analysis software such as DOE-2. Reducing building loads is critical to improving energy efficiency, and one key way to reduce loads is to reduce the amount of outside air used for ventilation. This raises a design challenge, however, since air supplied to laboratories is exposed to chemical contaminants and therefore cannot be returned to the central air handling system and must be exhausted. The volume of ventilation air required for the laboratories is typically greater than that for classrooms, lecture halls, and offices. To utilize outside air efficiently, a mechanical unit introduces 100 percent outside air into classrooms and lecture halls. Return air from these areas is reconditioned through the mechanical system and then ducted to the laboratories as supply air. The supply air to the laboratories is exhausted. In this way, the outside air is used twice before being exhausted.

Electronic air cleaners help minimize air resistance from filters. Maintenance is also important. Effective filter-replacement schedules help keep indoor air quality high and conserve energy. Control systems for variable speed drives on pumps, fans, and compressors should be used only if the controls will be regularly maintained and calibrated.

Numerous strategies can be employed for improving the energy efficiency of cooling, heating, and plumbing systems:

- Insulate hot water, steam, and chilled water piping.

- Maintain condenser water as cool as possible, but not less than 20 degrees above chilled water-supply temperature.

- Reuse wasted heat with a heat recovery system.

- Install an economizer at the boiler. (The water-side economizer will help with humidity controls.)

- Maintain hot water for washing hands at 105 degrees F. Consider using local hot water tanks at kitchens, restrooms, and other areas instead of central hot water.

- For plumbing systems, use ultra-low-flow toilets (0.5 gallons per flush) and automated controls such as infrared sensors for faucets.

- Harvesting rainwater and reusing "gray water" from sinks for irrigation may help reduce water costs.

Sustainable lighting design

Sustainable lighting design reduces energy use while enhancing employee comfort and productivity. Sustainable lighting strategies include the use of compact fluorescents (CFLs) rather than incandescent lamps, maximizing natural daylighting throughout a facility, and employing various photosensing technologies to conserve energy.

Incandescent lamps are extremely inefficient, using only 10 percent of the energy they consume to produce light (the rest is given off as heat). CFLs should be used instead. Research office lighting can be less than .75 watts/sq ft connected load, and with lighting controls it may consume less than 0.5 watts/sq ft. Where functional requirements permit, lighting design should combine task and ambient lighting to reduce the high overall light levels. Good task lighting lessens glare and eyestrain.

Daylighting

Daylight is an important component of sustainable design. Not only does it reduce energy use, but it increases comfort and enhances productivity. Designers should strive to direct natural light into most laboratory spaces and public areas so that, from almost anywhere in the building, people have the opportunity to look outdoors to see what the weather is like and orient themselves to the time of day. Wherever possible, daylighting should be the

▼ Natural light into lab spaces. Biomedical Research Building II, School of Medicine, University of Pennsylvania, Philadelphia. Perkins & Will, architect.

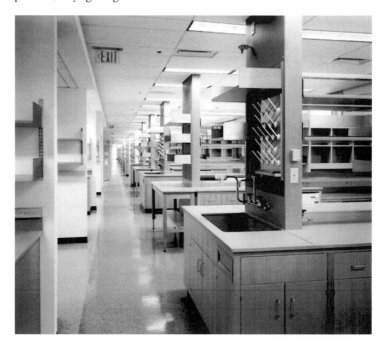

▲ Labs on the exterior offer views of the environs. Manufacturing Related Disciplines Center, Georgia Institute of Technology, Atlanta. Perkins & Will, architect.

photosensing techniques. Photosensing devices can control off-on for exterior lights, triggering fixtures to add light to a particular area when light levels decline. Also, a number of new fluorescent and metal halide fixtures are available that employ daylight harvesting—storing solar energy in the fixture during daylight hours and then using that energy to run the lamp when daylight diminishes. Outdoor lighting systems can easily be retrofitted for these fixtures.

Other photosensing technologies include programmable low-voltage control systems and occupancy sensors. The programmable low-voltage systems can control individual areas of the building or an entire building with one switch. These systems interface with the building automation and dimming systems. They are flexible, can easily accommodate building changes, have a local override capability, and can be used for large or small systems.

Occupancy sensors typically have a one-to-two-year payback. The sensors are designed with adjustable sensitivity levels and timing. There are two technologies: passive infrared and ultrasonic. Passive infrared sensors detect movement of heat between zones. They must have "a line of sight" to detect people in the lab. Ultrasonic occupancy sensors work by broadcasting ultrasonic sound waves, analyzing the returning waves and detecting movement through Doppler shifts. They are effective for larger rooms and can cover a 360-degree area. One problem is that air turbulence can trigger their operation. All occupancy sensor systems must be designed correctly to avoid nuisance operation.

primary source of illumination; artificial lighting should be thought of as a supplement to, rather than a replacement for, daylighting.

Typically, the first 15 ft of depth at the perimeter of the building can be lit entirely by daylight during the daytime. The use of light shelves can extend the daylight zone as far as 45 ft into the building. Clerestory windows and skylights can be used to get even more natural daylight into the building.

Daylighting control systems determine the amount of light available in a given space and switch off one or more banks of lights whenever there is enough sunlight. Both full-range and step fluorescent dimming systems work well.

Photosensing technologies

A key principal to remember in regard to lighting control systems is "simpler is better." Some systems employ

"Green" products

Some casework products now being manufactured are considered "green." Examples include hardwood, veneer, and plywood products that originate from certified sustainable forests. Steel products can also be "green"—for example, steel laboratory casework and fume hoods made of sheet metal that contains 20 to 25 percent scrap steel. (Sixty percent of the scrap steel comes from old cars and appliances, the other 40 percent from manufacturing fall-off.) There is one problem with recycled steel's "greenness," however: recycling steel is highly energy-intensive, which raises the question whether energy conservation or resource conservation is the better environmental/sustainable strategy.

Other sustainability issues

Other sustainable design issues include commissioning the entire building to ensure that building systems are operating as efficiently as possible. The engineers should review the latest ASHRAE energy code requirements. The ASHRAE codes are very conservative—simply meeting codes is not a recipe for an energy-efficient building. Direct digital control energy management systems are seen in many new laboratory facilities.

Buildings should be designed with long-term flexibility options, such as the lab module for all architectural and engineering systems, easy connects and disconnects to the engineering systems, and flexible casework. Computers that turn themselves off during nonworking hours reduce energy use and cost by reducing cooling loads and electrical demands. Laptop computers use one-tenth the energy of desktop PCs.

All the architectural and engineering issues should be studied on a project-by-project basis. Factors such as the client's specific goals, the type of lab being designed, the part of the country where the lab is located, and its position on the site will lead to different solutions. The U.S. Environmental Protection Agency (EPA) and the U.S. Department of Energy (DOE) have launched a new, voluntary program to improve the environmental performance of U.S. laboratories—the Laboratories for the 21st Century (Labs21) initiative. For more detailed information on this initiative, see the appendix to this book.

SCIENCE PARKS

The partnering of research between the public and private sectors has been the main reason for the development of science parks (research parks). Bruce Haxton has summarized the history of science parks: "Science parks first appeared at Stanford Research Park in Menlo Park, California (1951); Research Triangle Park, North Carolina (1959); and Cummings Research Park in Huntsville, Alabama (1962). During the 1980s, the number of science parks dramatically increased by approximately 600 percent worldwide—from 39 parks in 1980 to more than 270 in 1990" (Haxton 1999).

The Bay-Dole Act, passed by the U.S. Congress in 1980, allowed educational institutions in the United States to profit from research previously funded by the U.S. government, and it spurred even more dramatic growth. The number of science parks increased 180 percent worldwide in the 1990s, from270 parks in 1990 to more than 473 in 1998. Four major trends that will impact science and technology parks of the future are:

▶ *Virginia Tech Corporate Research Center EDC, Blacksburg, Virginia. SMBW Architects.*

- Networking relationships with other science parks with similar interests around the world
- Increased use of Internet communication
- Increased focus on corporate incubator facilities
- Increased globalization of trade

There are several reasons to consider developing and expanding research parks. Usually, the first reason has to do with local or regional economic development. The second is closely related: with economic development comes job creation. A third reason for developing research parks is that they provide the opportunity for technology transfer from the academic environment to the marketplace.

Almost 50 percent of developers of science parks are nonprofit corporations; 25 percent are government authorities; 17 percent are academic institutions; and less than 10 percent are for-profit corporations. Though most science parks are started by nonprofit organizations, more than 70 percent of the organizations that move into the parks are private, for-profit companies.

Several key issues affect the choice of a science park's location:

- Proximity to research universities (almost 90 percent of research parks are located immediately adjacent to a university)
- Availability of a highly educated workforce
- Quality of life of the nearest city
- Proximity to a major airport
- Types and variety of research-based companies in the area
- The amount of wet laboratory space available at nearby universities and companies
- Cooperation among economic development groups
- Ability to expand at the same site

◀ *Facility lab in a research park. SMBW Architects.*

Developing strategic alliances with other private or public entities can benefit both academia and private industry because physical infrastructure and individual expertise can be shared. Project-driven instructional and research approaches can make such alliances productive and profitable if the appropriate facilities exist or are developed. Benefits include sharing of equipment and resources, reduction in space requirements and costs resulting from collaboration, financial support of students and faculty by private industry, and the opportunity for private industry to hire the brightest young minds coming out of academia.

The growth of partnerships between academia and industry in research has, however, created a set of difficult professional issues that educational institutions must address, such as conflicts of interest or commitment on the part of academic researchers. Often, faculty members find themselves with less time available for their institutional responsibilities as they attempt to live up to their private-sector commitments.

Nevertheless, private industry is becoming a good neighbor to academic institutions across the country. Researchers can reduce costs for the private sector by establishing some "hits" (leads) in their academic research, which are then developed and brought to market with the help of private industry.

Attracting top employees is likely to continue to be a concern for most companies. By locating laboratories on or next to academic campuses, private-sector industries that may have problems attracting top researchers are more easily able to draw some of the best young talent to their companies. Also, two-year technical colleges are now constructing computer science and general research buildings to provide young employees for the research market. The private sector will need to partner more with the technical colleges to be able to tap into that potential workforce.

Science park lab design—whether the park is founded by a private corporation or a nonprofit organization—resembles speculative office building design. During initial construction, basic engineering systems are put in place, but little or no casework is installed. When a research team leases space, it upgrades its portion of the building with additional engineering systems, casework, and equipment.

The initial cost of the building can be less than $100 per gross sq ft (GSF). The additional cost for outfitting can range from as little as $25 to more than $100 per GSF. Building size typically ranges from 20,000 to 100,000 GSF. The buildings are stand-alone structures that generally look like spec office buildings, and there is minimal site development. The base building allows companies to get started and to add casework and upgrade the engineering systems later, when funding becomes available.

CHAPTER 2
LABORATORY TYPES

There are three lab sectors: private, government, and academic. Design of labs for the private sector, run by corporations, is usually driven by the need to enhance the research operation's profit-making potential. Government laboratories—including those run by federal agencies and those operated by state governments—do research in the public interest. Academic laboratories are primarily teaching facilities but also include some research labs that engage in public-interest or profit-generating research. This chapter focuses on the design issues that differentiate each type of lab.

PRIVATE-SECTOR LABS

Companies in the private sector are focused on making discoveries, creating innovations, and bringing them to market and making a profit from their research for their shareholders. Because private labs are more driven to make a profit than government or academic labs, they tend to be more innovative and willing to explore new research environments. "Speed to market" is an essential characteristic of research companies in the private sector. Reduction of cycle time is critical, requiring organizational dynamics and technical solutions. Sharing information, generating knowledge, and team-based research are some of the ways companies are addressing the marketplace.

The Competitive Marketplace

Because of the current competitive marketplace, many private-sector companies are investing more money in creating high-quality spaces outside the labs. Companies feel the strong need to attract new employees to their campuses and to keep the employees they have. In addition to constructing gracious public areas (such as atriums, well-lit and finished corridors, and break rooms) and providing the latest computer technology in conference areas, private research companies are supplying such amenities as central cafeterias, child-care centers, fitness centers, walking trails, dry cleaners, and on-site banking. These amenities support employees and allow them to do their work more efficiently each day. The competition to keep top researchers and the need to develop more discoveries each year are the main differences between private-sector companies and government and academic facilities.

Many private-sector companies are involved in the discovery-to-market phases of research. For example, in the pharmaceuticals industry, getting drugs to market requires that a company's marketing work closely with its scientists. Marketing experts are now part of many research teams, with offices located nearby.

Teams are created to focus on specific discoveries each year. Because of the competitive market and the utilization of computers and robots in research, more discoveries are necessary each year to meet a company's goals and satisfy its shareholders. In the past, teams were almost always organized around a principal investigator and composed of a more or less permanent set of individuals. Today, principal investigators are collaborating more, individuals are moving from one team to another to

▲ Atrium space helps create a sense of community in this building. 3M, Austin, Texas. HOK, Inc., architect.

systems, and vivarium facilities. Private-sector companies are more likely than others to invest in technical support for the scientists' work. Most private corporations tend to implement extensive facility management to address churn and maintain the facilities. Facility management is important to minimize any downtime for a specific researcher and to keep all researchers happy. Initial cost is always a consideration, but long-term operational costs and return on investments are also key to the design and operation of a laboratory facility.

Mergers and Consolidations

Mergers and consolidations have been a main part of the corporate research industry in the past five years, and this trend is likely to continue. Mergers, most evident in the large pharmaceutical companies, are intended to reduce cost and competition and to allow the merged firms to be more competitive with the remaining larger research companies. On completion of mergers, companies must address concerns such as evaluating existing buildings for their highest and best use, consolidation of facilities, and leasing or selling of real estate.

Startup Companies and Developer-Owned Buildings

Among the results of the recent mega-mergers of pharmaceutical companies has been the emergence of many startup companies. A startup, regardless of its research mission, has a different outlook on facilities. The way in which a startup company obtains services to design and construct its facilities is in most cases different from the traditional design, bid, and build process.

provide their specific expertise, and the boundaries are becoming less defined within the research environment.

Other key attributes of private-sector labs include centralization of services such as glassware storage, engineering

Generally, startup companies do not want to spend their own money on facilities. The money they do have must be used to fund and obtain their research and business goals, and they are not interested in building corporate headquarters per se. Companies that are in the first and second rounds of venture capital do not construct research buildings but lease existing space and upfit to meet their minimum requirements. Companies that are in the third round of funding are now creditworthy and have the business and science credibility to attract investors. Still, in many cases these companies do not want to use their own capital to build facilities but often seek a developer to fund the project with a leaseback option. Most projects at this level come into being through some form of the design-build process, bringing together a developer, a designer, and a builder.

Because of the participation of the developer, planning and design of startup facilities are unlike planning and design for established companies' research facilities. In a few cases, the facility may be programmed and designed to meet the individual requirements of the user group, but in most cases the laboratories will have to be made as generic as possible in case the initial company is not successful and leaves the space. Another consideration— a challenge for the designer—is that in the future the building may have to accommodate multiple tenants.

Where the developer owns the building, it also typically owns much of the equipment: fixed casework, fume hoods, autoclaves, and glass washers. The developer wants to have a leasable, functional laboratory building if the original users leave.

In general, the concept of developer-driven projects works well in the realm of life sciences and general sciences research. If extensive clean rooms, sterility suites, nuclear magnetic resonance machines, or pilot plant applications are required, however, the "fit" will not be as attractive to a developer, as the building and its central utilities become too specialized. As in the design of any laboratory facility, good laboratory planning principles and sound life-safety practices—including the

▲ An atrium also adds visual connectivity to the building. Dupont, Wilmington, Delaware. The Hillier Group, architect.

▲ Open lab with defining boundaries diminishing. Sigma Coating Laboratory, England. Courtesy Fisher Hamilton.

39

provision of clear circulation paths, clear and concise laboratory zones, and laboratory support and office zones—should be followed.

International Clients

The United States accounts for roughly 44 percent of the industrial world's total research and development (R&D) investment and continues to outdistance, by more than 2 to 1, the total research investments made by Japan, the second-largest performer. Many countries, however, have put fiscal incentives in place to increase the overall level of R&D spending and to stimulate industrial innovation.

Architects and engineers in the United States have had many opportunities to provide design services for research companies overseas. American architects' and engineers' fee structures can be competitive, especially in Europe. For example, over the past ten years U.S. rates, when calculated for the European market, have been much lower than those charged by European firms. American firms stand a good chance of getting commissions for major projects in Europe because of their expertise and lower fees (based on the exchange rate). On such projects it is typically necessary to affiliate with a local firm, which manages the agency approvals, contract documents, and construction administration. (A laboratory project in France may require the approval of more than two dozen agencies!)

In Asia, however, U.S. firms' rates are much higher than those of local architects and engineers. Nevertheless, in China, the government may hire a Western firm to design and construct a building with a Western image. A U.S. firm may receive a commission in any of the following ways:

- It can win a design competition, which usually requires an invitation. Competitions are widely used on most major projects in China today.

- It can team with a local firm that is responsible for the construction documentation and construction administration. This approach saves the Chinese government money, lets it employ its own people, and incorporates the U.S. expertise at the U.S. billing rates.

- If a project is too large and complex for the Chinese to complete the contract documents and construction administration, then an American firm may be commissioned to do the entire project based on U.S. billing rates.

A key difference in designing and building outside this country is that all calculations are done in the metric system. The designer must have a clear understanding of the typical room construction methods, materials, and details of the country in which he or she will be working. It is also extremely important to understand the capabilities of the local construction industry. For example, for a large research project in England, pre-cast concrete panels were fabricated by a company in the United States. No concrete company in all of Europe could produce the concrete panels for less than it cost to make and ship the product from the United States. In China, it is common to see granite flooring and interior walls because it is difficult to obtain good gypsum wallboard construction, carpeting, or ceiling tiles. At the beginning of the design phase it is important to understand what can be built locally, at what quality, and at what cost.

A noteworthy international project is the Jahwa Research Facility, in Shanghai, China, which demonstrates the Chinese government's new desire to provide researchers with safe, world-class labs to enhance China's position in the international R&D market (see pages 43–44).

Space Guidelines

In most cases, private-sector research labs are slightly more expensive and larger than government or academic labs because competitive markets require more discoveries each year and because private-sector companies must spend more on facilities to retain their employees.

Benchmarking is used to estimate the cost of a laboratory or research building as well as the amount of space and casework to be provided to each researcher. It is a risky and very difficult process, in part because it is hard to acquire solid, relevant benchmarking data. With the development of the computer and team-based research labs, benchmarking data will change significantly over the next ten years.

It is sometimes necessary to make broad assumptions of scope and cost well before any predesign investigations begin. The following examples are presented for use in such a situation. They are not intended as

▼ The equivalent linear footage of bench (ELF) factor depends on the kind of research.

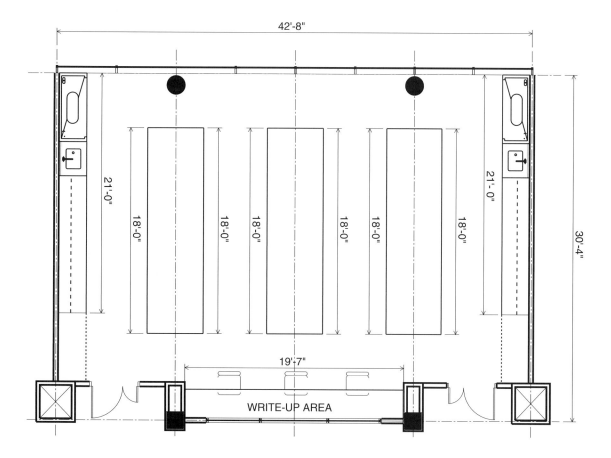

a substitute for programming and should always be superseded by more accurate information, as it becomes available.

Abbott Laboratories estimates $250,000 per scientist for a facility built on its campus. It typically includes shell space for new and remodeled construction projects so that it can affordably address growth in the organization. At its recently completed laboratory facility, Chiron spent $158,200 per scientist (see pages 48–50).

Benchmarking labs can be done by calculating the equivalent linear footage of bench (ELF) factor. Typically, the ELF is based on anything that occupies floor area in the lab, such as casework, equipment, and storage. Today's concern for safety and environmental protection dictates the basic minimum allocation for an organic chemist's benchtop as being no less than 21 ELF. The space consists of 8 ft of fume hood, 8 ft of bench, 2 ft of sink, and 3 ft of refrigerator/freezer. A biologist, on the other hand, needs far less fume hood space but has a significantly greater need for ancillary equipment such as refrigerators, incubators, centrifuges, and environmental rooms. Therefore, an individual biologist's bench need can easily exceed 30 ELF.

The following values and square footages are drawn from the May 2000 issue of Earl Wall Associates' quarterly *Laboratory*.

ELF values per person per discipline (without animal, greenhouse, and pilot areas):

Organic chemistry	24–28
Physical chemistry	24–33
Instrumental analytical chemistry	33–41
Microbiological and immunological	20–31

Net lab square footage per person according to the preceding ELF values (based on a 10 ft 6 in. wide module):

Organic chemistry	126–147
Physical chemistry	126–173

▼ *Floor plan, Jahwa Shanghai Lab, Shanghai, China. Perkins & Will, architect.*

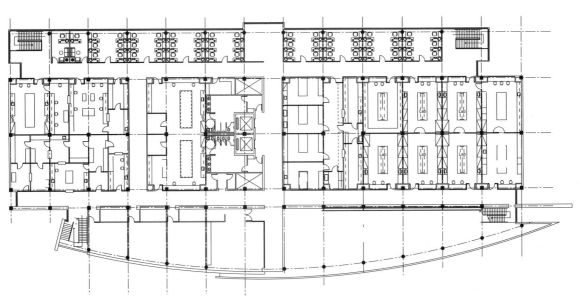

Instrumental analytical
chemistry   173–215

Microbiological and
immunological   103–163

The numbers are typical for the kind of research being conducted but may vary considerably depending on individual research efforts.

Case Studies

Jahwa-Shanghai Lab

Shanghai, China

Architect: Perkins & Will
97,000 GSF
(9,000 gross square meters)
Construction cost: To be determined

The new Jahwa-Shanghai research facility is part of a master plan at the firm's manufacturing campus in Shanghai. The 97,000 GSF facility contains pharmaceutical, cosmetic, fine chemistry, and basic research laboratories, combined with an administrative and creative development and exhibition component. The building is intended to provide closure and definition to the campus front lawn, creating a sense of place by reinforcing the southern edge of the site. The architectural expression of the building reinforces the programmatic dichotomy of the creative and the scientific. Public and administrative functions make up the southern bar of

▼ Model, night view, Jahwa-Shanghai Lab.

▶ *Twelve ft fume hood. DuPont Medicinal Chemistry Building, Wilmington, Delaware. The Hillier Group, architect.*

the project, the most striking feature being the three-story-high glass exhibition space, or "creative idea salon." The south bar acts as a screen or filter, making a transition from the more open and public functions to the highly technological lab and research spaces in the northern block.

The laboratories are based on the latest ideas and technology developed in the United States: open labs, equipment zones, modular design of architectural and engineering systems, zoning of the building between lab and non-lab spaces, and team-based research and computer applications. The fume hoods, other key types of lab equipment, and the main mechanical systems serving the building will be built in the United States or Europe, then installed in the facility in China.

DuPont Medicinal Chemistry Building

Wilmington, Delaware

Architect: The Hillier Group
Occupied: 1996
Size: 132,000 GSF
Construction cost: $42,000,000 (1995)

The DuPont Medicinal Chemistry Building (MCB) received special mention in *R&D* magazine's 1997 Lab of the Year awards. It is an excellent example of a private-sector laboratory.

The participation of a user group throughout the design process was key to the overall success of the design. DuPont gathered scientists together to develop a wish list, which included three-person labs with three 12 ft hoods. (Each scientist received a 12 ft hood.) The bench space was increased to 7 linear ft

▼ *Second floor plan, Building E-500. DuPont Medicinal Chemistry Building.*

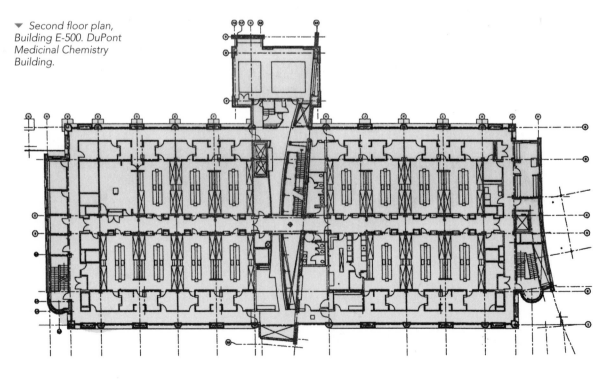

per occupant to take advantage of the latest instrumentation technology. The chemical handling areas are immediately adjacent to the labs and can be accessed from the service corridor, which is separated from public areas of the building. Offices are on the opposite side of the labs, directly adjacent to them, and can be accessed from the public corridor. More ventilated chemical storage space was provided to reduce the risk of personnel exposure, and more ventilated bench space for chemical transfer operations was constructed. A creative, interactive environment improved the ability to recruit and retain top scientists.

The building design is based on a 21 ft x 27 ft module that allows plenty of space for a principal investigator and two scientists. The 12 ft fume hoods have four independently operating vertical sashes for maximum flexibility. Depending on the work area required, two sashes can be fully raised or all four sashes can be raised to half height, providing a total operating face opening of 50 percent.

Flexibility was created with a service corridor, which has all the engineering systems exposed in an open ceiling. The systems connect to the rear of each lab, allowing maintenance workers to make changes without entering the lab areas. Glassware and chemical storage can also be accessed from the service corridor without lab entry.

The offices are located around the outside wall, affording views to the exterior. The scientists can write up their research while overseeing their lab spaces.

Key design features include the selective placement of glass in the walls separating

corridors, offices, and labs to create a transparency that allows one to see through the building from the public corridors to the outside (if the blinds are not down). Suspended indirect lighting

▲ Service corridor. DuPont Medicinal Chemistry Building.

LABORATORY TYPES

▶ *Central atrium space as "core" of building. DuPont Medicinal Chemistry Building.*

▶ *Suspended indirect lighting. DuPont Medicinal Chemistry Building.*

◢ *Wood and metal casework. DuPont Medicinal Chemistry Building.*

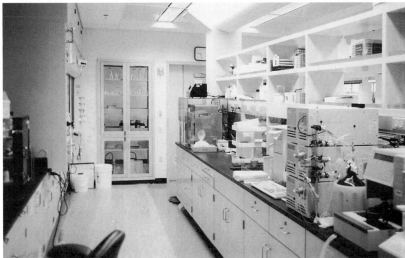

fixtures hang in vaulted ceiling areas over the reagent shelving. The combination of wood and metal casework is visually appealing. Transparent glassware cabinets are accessible from the labs and service corridors.

The central atrium space, where all common amenities are located, also allows people to meet throughout their daily routines and offers opportunities to "cross-pollinate" ideas. Marker boards are located throughout the building. The use of different materials and colors ensures that the entire building is detailed at the same level of quality as the atrium. During design, a mock-up synthetic chemistry lab and offices were constructed (at a cost of $30,000) so that researchers could tour it and provide feedback.

Chiron Life Sciences Building (Building 4)

Emeryville, California

Architect: Flad & Associates, Inc.
Occupied: 1998
Size: 285,000 GSF (building)
Construction cost: Confidential
(The central utility plant, 10,000 sq ft, houses the main electrical switch gear, HVAC systems, chillers, boiler systems, and cooling towers.)

When Chiron made the commitment to redevelop its site in Emeryville, California, Flad & Associates was selected as architect of record for Phase One (Building 4) of the 11-phase, 30-year development plan. Flad worked with a team of nationally and internationally known consultants, including Mexican architect Ricardo Legorreta, who developed the master plan for the 2.2 million sq ft build-out of the campus. From the beginning, Chiron made it clear that this project was fundamental to meeting its goal of creating a productive and stimulating work environment for science. Chiron wanted to create a new type of lab building.

The concept of Legorreta Architectos' master plan was inspired by the plan of traditional Mexican cloisters. A series of atriums, patios, plazas, and open spaces are organized around working spaces. The spaces, each unique, interconnect with one another to create a large, multilevel campus of research villages that encourages communication and interaction among employees.

The laboratory incorporates a philosophy of business integration that stresses teamwork and the sharing of ideas. The first level of high bay space includes building mechanicals, specialized

◀ *Courtyard, inspired by the plan of traditional Mexican courtyards. Chiron Life Sciences Building 4, Emeryville, California. Flad & Associates, Inc., architect. Photograph copyright Lourdes Legorreta, courtesy Flad & Associates, Inc. Other photographs, pages 48–50, copyright John Sutton Photography, courtesy Flad & Associates, Inc.*

◥ *Exterior view. Chiron Life Sciences Building 4.*

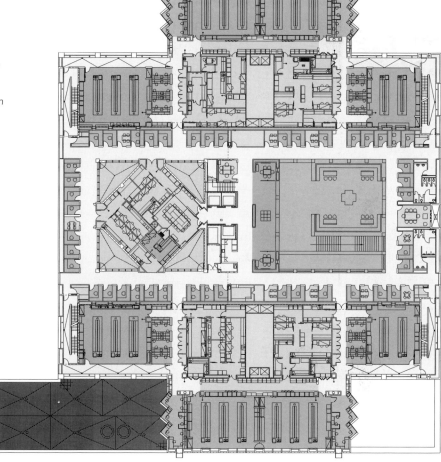

- ▢ Lab
- ▢ Lab Support
- ▢ Office
- ▢ Office Support
- ▢ Fellows Area
- ▢ Corridor
- ▢ Mechanical
- ▢ Courtyard
- ▢ Water Feature
- ▢ Roof Terrace

▲ *Floor plan. Chiron Life Sciences Building 4.*

lab spaces, and offices, allowing business groups to support the efforts of their researchers. The next three levels include labs designed to maximize availability of daylight as well as to be flexible enough to adapt to the needs of diverse business groups. These labs are located around interior courtyards and atriums to facilitate interaction, demonstrating the owner's commitment to the social as well as the technical aspects of science.

The lab planning goals remained a keen focus throughout project planning and design. The labs are inviting, functional, and flexible. Each has three 24 ft long island benches, with 7 ft of bench space per person and a sink at the end of each benchtop. The perimeters of the labs have no fixed casework, reserving space for large equipment such as refrigerators, freezers, and mobile workstations used for stacking electronic equipment and moving it where needed as experiments change.

The lab offices are directly next to the lab interiors but separated from them by dividing walls. Office windows look into the labs for convenient viewing of ongoing experiments. The result is a pleasant and functional lab environment, with natural daylight and views to the surrounding hills of Berkeley. This design gives priority to the human side of science. This facility received "Laboratory of the Year" distinction by *R&D* magazine in 1999.

▼ *View of exterior courtyard from lab. Chiron Life Sciences Building 4, Emeryville, California. Flad & Associates, Inc., architect.*

▲ *Atrium, adding visual connectivity between all levels. Chiron Life Sciences Building 4.*

Glaxo Group Research, Ltd.

Stevenage, United Kingdom

Architect: Kling Lindquist
Occupied: Spring 1995
Size: 1,800,000 GSF
Construction cost: $571,000,000

This new research campus, about 30 miles north of London, accommodates approximately 1,400 employees. The campus houses chemistry, microbiology, pharmacology, and biochemistry research and drug evaluation; pilot plants for chemical and microbiology development; and administrative support. The campus is organized around a courtyard. Approaching the site, you are stopped at the security gate. After permission to enter is obtained, you drive up to the parking area that is north of a man-made water feature. You proceed by walking over a bridge, then into the administrative building, which is located to the north. Employee parking is to the left and right of the administrative building. The administrative building houses a 200-seat lecture hall, a cafeteria, an executive dining area, and offices for more than 200 employees, including research executives, administrative staff, and internal scientific affairs personnel.

To the east is the chemistry wing and chemistry pilot plant, supporting more than 500 scientists. The building rises

▼ Aerial view. Glaxo Wellcome Medicines Research Center, Stevenage, United Kingdom. Kling Lindquist, architect. All photographs, pages 51–53, courtesy Glaxo Wellcome.

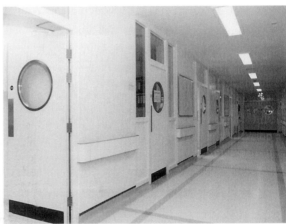

▲ *Research lab. Glaxo Wellcome Medicines Research Center, Stevenage, United Kingdom. Kling Lindquist, architect.*

◥ *Microbiology lab corridor. Glaxo Wellcome Medicines Research Center.*

▶ *Gateway to research facility. Glaxo Wellcome Medicines Research Center.*

four stories above the courtyard; a lower level houses building support services. A central node provides space for administration and support functions on each floor. The research building connects directly to the pilot plant. It is organized around a dedicated three-corridor system: the central corridor for services to the labs, and two perimeter corridors for personnel circulation outside the labs.

The labs are generic, with the write-up areas immediately adjacent. There is plenty of interior glazing to allow people to see one another, the research labs, and the exterior views.

The microbiology complex is at the southwest corner of the campus. The vivarium and microbiology buildings are the only two buildings constructed with an interstitial space. The generic microbiology lab is similar to the chemistry labs, with the write-up stations immediately adjacent to the labs and plenty of interior glass. The corridor system uses only a single-corridor scheme because the services are handled above, in the interstitial space.

The biology building is to the west and houses approximately 250 researchers. The first three floors are for pharmacology, the upper floor for biochemistry and cell biology.

The entire complex of buildings is linked with a "tour route" on the first floor that wraps around the entire courtyard. The building services, including loading docks, are located at the lower level with a common corridor. There is a central plant that services the entire complex.

The exterior facades are constructed of precast concrete fabricated in the United States. The windows all have light shelves to minimize glare into the labs. The exterior facades of all the buildings are of similar design and detail. Most of the buildings were planned for future expansion, and, in fact, the microbiology building has already been expanded.

GOVERNMENT LABS

Though federal funding for research and new construction had for a time declined, that trend appeared to be changing by the late 1990s. The National Institutes of Health (NIH), for example, has increased grant money for research to several academic research institutions. In February 1999, the National Science Foundation documented that the differential growth of federal research dollars for various agencies had resulted in increased shares for the life sciences and for mathematical and computer sciences; fairly constant shares for the environmental sciences and psychology; and declining shares for the social sciences and engineering.

The life sciences should see continued research growth. Much of the funding for the life sciences involves NIH. In a 1996 research and development symposium, NIH representatives explained what they believe some of the future trends will be:

- More human(e) environments
- Continued team concept
- Continued focus on safety
- Reduction in fume hood requirements
- Increase in support labs
- Modular basic labs
- Decrease in the size of instrumentation, but more of it
- Increase in repetitive tasks

Government research facilities are similar to those of the private sector in that they focus solely on research; they usually have few or no teaching labs. Government labs usually follow the private sector in developing new and innovative facilities. Several government labs test the research findings of many private-sector companies. For example, the primary focus of the Food and Drug

Bridge links entire complex. Glaxo Wellcome Medicines Research Center.

Another view of bridge. Glaxo Wellcome Medicines Research Center.

Administration (FDA) is to review and approve the findings presented by private corporations before products can be marketed.

Image

In the past, laboratories and public areas in government research facilities tended to be more conservatively designed than in private-sector facilities. The main reason for the conservative approach was that government agencies are funded with tax dollars, and decision makers were concerned about taxpayers' perceptions of how their money was being invested. In the past few years, however, the federal government has developed programs for major new laboratories that, like those in the private sector, focus on team-based labs.

The typical government laboratory building (including state-funded as well as federal facilities) has a clearly defined entry and, usually, a gracious lobby. Most lobbies have information boards, computer kiosks, and display areas that show examples of the research that has been conducted there in the past (some such display areas are aimed at the general public). The lobby is monitored by security personnel, cameras, and, typically, a card access system. It is very difficult for a visitor to get beyond the entry lobby unescorted.

The following list of program objectives for the National Neuroscience Research Center (on the NIH's Bethesda, Maryland, campus) is representative of many government laboratory facilities:

- Create a complex that promotes world-class biomedical research through communication and collaboration as a means to facilitate innovation and creativity.

- Serve the government's needs for functional research and support space that is efficient, reliable, flexible, adaptable, safe, secure, readily maintained, cost-effective, energy efficient, and supported by state-of-the-art infrastructure systems.

- Provide biomedical research laboratories, vivarium facilities, and shared support spaces that foster interaction among scientists and promote a collaborative work environment.

- Enhance security and access control.

- Develop a functional and congenial research environment to ensure a high quality of life for staff that will help attract and retain world-class researchers.

- Complete the project at the most reasonable cost to the government.

- Complete the project on schedule in the most efficient and expeditious manner.

- Minimize disruption to ongoing NIH functions/building programs.

- Provide a visual testimony to scientific integrity and public accountability in the conduct of science.

- Facilitate NIH's neuroscience research mission with a structure that serves as a worldwide research icon and an asset to both the NIH campus and the neighboring community.

Replacement Facilities/Strategic and Master Planning

Many government laboratory facilities have been in use since the late 1940s or early 1950s. Over five or six decades, they have been renovated, repaired, and adapted. Now, some federal and state government funding is available to build new laboratory facilities that incorporate the latest technology and that are flexible enough to be changed quickly and cost-effectively.

Another key objective for government research campuses is to provide strategic and master planning evaluations before new buildings are constructed. Many government research campuses do not have a resolved strategic plan with clear phasing or smart, cost-effective programmatic uses for renovated facilities.

Strategic planning is also beneficial in identifying the level of quality for the facilities and in creating basic design standards. The U.S. economy and research environments are very strong today, providing the country a unique opportunity to provide truly state-of-the-art facilities. All too often, government research buildings have been constructed

with labs and offices that are smaller than desired because of budget considerations or because of the number of people they will house. An alternative strategy is to

▲ Partial Interstitial space. NIH Building 40, Bethesda, Maryland. HLM, architect.

◀ Open lab under construction (with interstutial space above). NIH Building 40, Bethesda, Maryland. HLM, architect. Courtesy NIH.

design optimal-sized labs and offices, and then move only as many staff into the new building as it will comfortably accommodate. When the next funding package for an addition or new building becomes available, the remaining researchers can move into that facility. If decision makers simply try to maximize the program, placing as many people in the spaces as possible, then for the next several decades government research buildings will have to be adapted, renovated, and retrofitted just to make ends meet.

Scheduling

Typically, a publicly funded project can take two to three times longer to construct than a private-sector laboratory facility. The funding is appropriated each year. If Congress or a state legislature does not include the project in a particular year's budget, the work stops.

Many state and federal laboratory projects have experienced significant delays during design and construction. Money is usually appropriated for programming, which is often contracted to an architectural firm that has an indefinite delivery contract with the ruling agency. Once programming is completed and funding for the project has been made available, the government publicly announces a request for proposal (RFP). The interview process can take three to four months to resolve before the architectural and engineering design and documentation can occur. After the design is started, there can be months of review by various federal agencies after each submittal. And most projects are competitively bid.

There has been some progress, however. On some recent projects, the federal government has hired a construction manager to accelerate the construction process. The construction of Building 40 at NIH has been a fast-tracked project. "Fast-tracked" simply means that the contractor starts to clear the site and begin construction of the foundation while the contract documents (drawings and specifications) are being completed on other areas of the project.

▶ Building 40 was constructed on an accelerated schedule. NIH Building 40, Bethesda, Maryland. HLM, architect.

Case Studies

Rodman Materials Research Laboratory

Aberdeen, Maryland

Architect: The Benham Group
Occupied: 1999
Size: 292,000 GSF
Construction cost: $73,300,000

The purpose of this project is to provide a national center of excellence for materials research and development, including processing and manufacturing research, in support of future U.S. Army acquisition systems and cost reduction of current systems. The design promotes interaction between scientists and engineers outside the laboratories, while providing a state-of-the-art research environment in 149 separate laboratories.

The research laboratory is located on the crest of a hill along a major approach route to Aberdeen Proving Ground. The facility, consisting of more than 290,000 sq ft of research laboratories and support spaces, is tucked into an existing tree line, with the utility-intensive laboratories backing up to an existing forest. The laboratories are screened from public view by the offices, library, and atrium areas across the front of the property.

The interior layout emphasizes the visibility of people's movement within the building. A secure exterior courtyard between the administrative and research spaces allows personnel to discuss classified work outdoors while remaining in a secure environment. Numerous "nodes" encourage scientists and engineers to interact regularly. Moreover, the lab's four-story atrium makes

▼ *Building exterior. Rodman Materials Research Laboratory, Aberdeen, Maryland. The Benham Group, architect. All photographs, pages 57–60, courtesy Alan Karchmer.*

movements visible and links offices with lab spaces, creating closeness and community despite the large size of the total structure.

The building, a highly energy-efficient facility, was designed to integrate certain mechanical and electrical systems into the overall building aesthetics. Bright yellow outside air intakes make a bold statement, signaling that this is a laboratory facility. Energy consumption is reduced through extensive use of natural lighting, accomplished through an integrated architectural and engineering approach to the building's design. Atriums, clerestories, and skylights allow daylight into the interior of the building,

▷ *Main entrance lobby. Rodman Materials Research Laboratory, Aberdeen, Maryland. The Benham Group, architect.*

▼ *Secure exterior courtyard. Rodman Materials Research Laboratory.*

where photo-sensors automatically dim the installed lighting in response to ambient light levels. Light shelves on the building exterior provide a shading effect during mid- to late afternoon and reflect light into the building at other times of day. The interior office layout features a circulation corridor adjacent to the exterior windows, thereby introducing natural light into the open office areas.

The new lab provides significant life-cycle cost savings through its sustainable design and energy-efficiency features. Building finishes, selected with durability and environmental soundness in mind, include drywall and ceiling tile made from recyclable material, nontoxic paints, carpet with low volatile organic emissions, chlorofluorocarbon-free insulation, and chemically nonreactive countertops.

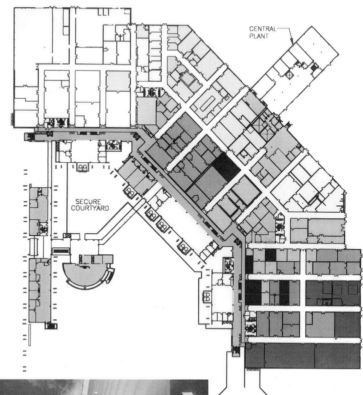

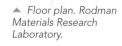

▲ Floor plan. Rodman Materials Research Laboratory.

◀ Mechanical systems integrated into overall building aesthetics. Rodman Materials Research Laboratory.

▲ NEC accelerator laboratory. Rodman Materials Research Laboratory, Aberdeen, Maryland. The Benham Group, architect.

◥ Robotics accelerated Aging laboratory. Rodman Materials Research Laboratory.

▶ Exposed mechanical systems in the interior. Rodman Materials Research Laboratory.

Walter Reed Army Institute of Research (WRAIR)

Forest Glen, Maryland

Architect: HLW International
Occupied: Fall 1999
Size: 474,000 GSF
Construction cost $147,300,000

This Department of Defense laboratory, housing 1,000 scientists, is a state-of-the-art research facility focusing on infectious disease, combat casualty care, operational health hazards, and medical defense against biological and chemical weapons. The exterior of the building is predominantly red brick with precast concrete trim. One architectural feature is the inclusion of a passive sun-screening system to reduce glare and heat gain through the perimeter windows. The roof penthouse contains much of the mechanical equipment. The exhaust stacks march along the penthouse, based on the lab module. The mechanical exhaust system is primarily a manifolded system, requiring fewer exhaust stacks at the building exterior. There are some dedicated exhaust stacks located within the rectangular stack enclosures. The use of glass along the main entry corridor admits light into the building, frames views of the site, and complements the

▲ Building exterior.
Walter Reed Army Institute of Research, Forest Glen, Maryland. HLW International, architect. All photographs, pages 61–63, courtesy HLW International.

61

▶ Atrium stair. Walter Reed Army Institute of Research, Forest Glen, Maryland. HLW International, architect.

artworks located along the interior solid walls.

Shared amenities include a 300-seat auditorium, classrooms, conference rooms, a cafeteria, a library, a central atrium space, and an exterior terrace. The auditorium has a level floor and removable seating that allows for multiple uses by WRAIR personnel and the local community. State-of-the-art telecommunications capabilities are provided in the auditorium and adjoining conference room and classrooms. The library houses the institute's collection of rare books as well as materials from the former Gorgas Hospital in Panama. The central stair is constructed of wood, concrete, and metal, providing a visually pleasing centerpiece in the volume of space. People can easily see each other at multiple floor levels. The atrium occurs at the intersection of the two wings of the building and is a logical place for people to meet. At the main level, wood-crafted display cabinets are located within the various departments, providing researchers with an opportunity to present information about their work. There are wood tables and chairs for informal meeting and work sessions, as well as lounge chairs for relaxing. "If scientists rub shoulders they will create a different science," said planning chief Colonel Henry Fein, M.D.

The desire to create a collegial research environment inspired the use of wood finishes throughout. It was agreed that it was extremely important to have a quality facility that people would want to work in and that could be used to draw other researchers.

The organization of the laboratories and research offices is modular, with the mechanical systems located in an interstitial space above each lab. The interstitial space should provide the needed flexibility to accommodate current and future military medical research and development as program

evolution and consolidation continue. The clear area in the interstitial is 6' 11", since if the space had 7' clear it would count as an additional floor and would affect building code compliance.

Instead of customizing the labs, designers planned five generic types of

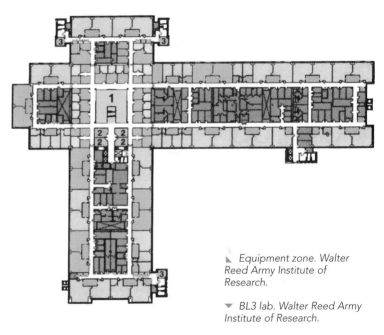

▼ Floor plan. Walter Reed Army Institute of Research, Forest Glen, Maryland. HLW International, architect.

◤ Equipment zone. Walter Reed Army Institute of Research.

▼ BL3 lab. Walter Reed Army Institute of Research.

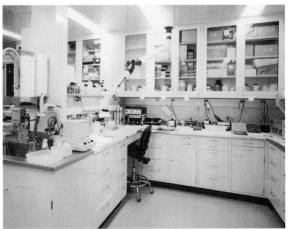

labs to serve most research functions. Each researcher is then placed in a lab, where minor alterations can be made. The labs are located along the perimeter of the building, with support spaces at the interior. In addition to the generic Biosafety Level 2 (BL-2) labs, there are seven BL-3 labs, three of which are stacked above each other and share an exhaust fan system. All seven labs have shower-out facilities.

The building is run off a central plant, with a separate mechanical system for the vivarium. The vivarium is located in the basement and also has a full interstitial space for engineering services. The corridor of the vivarium is painted in multiple colors to add interest to what in most facilities is a boring space.

The design process for the new building involved the end users in programming and design. A particular group was responsible for policy for the overall building. Design decisions were based on tried-and-true, economical, and state-of-the-art ideas. At the beginning of the project, the decision makers toured other relevant laboratory facilities. The Lewis Thomas Laboratories in Princeton encouraged the WRAIR team to develop the building as a collegial environment. The WRAIR facility places senior scientists directly across the corridor from their laboratories. Technicians' and junior scientists' offices are directly adjacent to the laboratories, separated only by large windows and sliding glass doors. The interstitial design was mandated by Army guide plates for hospital construction. The general and mechanical contractors visited the Hutchinson Cancer Center in Seattle to understand the high-quality interstitial space and returned to conduct extensive coordination meetings to ensure that the space was easily traversable for modification and service work.

The researchers were asked to provide input on their laboratory space. A full-size lab mock-up was constructed at the end of design development. Each researcher was encouraged to visit the mock-up and "kick the tires." Involving the researchers and other key decision makers throughout the entire design process minimized changes during construction and made for happier clients when the building was occupied. Each scientist was assigned one lab module to work in, and all were treated equally to minimize the creation of fiefdoms. A 30 ft x 30 ft lab (two lab modules) is assigned to two scientists.

Georgia Public Health Laboratory

Atlanta, Georgia

Architect: Lord, Aeck & Sargent, Inc.
Occupied: 1998
Size: 66,027 GSF
Construction cost: $10,501,943

The Georgia Public Health Laboratory—named Laboratory of the Year by *R&D* magazine in 1988—is functional, pleasant, and well lit with natural indirect sunlight. The key idea guiding the facility's creation was the open lab. *R&D* magazine quoted Richard Rietz, one of the competition's jurors, as saying, "That's quite a departure for a public building, but especially for a building full of technicians. These people generally get the short end of the stick when it comes to accommodations. Here finally they have a nice work space."

The building is organized with a two-story entry lobby that has painted aluminum sunscreens allowing soft, indirect light into the space. The research

offices are located along the outside wall, administrative workstations in a large open area, large open labs in the center, and lab and building support along the back wall. The large open labs are located on the second floors, with the teaching labs at the ground level.

The clinical testing laboratory will conduct about 2.5 million tests on more than 1.5 million clinical specimens each year. The open lab concept evolved from a decision to separate the accessioning and testing functions. The open BL-2 lab creates a collaborative environment. The open labs have write-up areas along the main corridor adjacent to the bench space and near the administrative workstations. Clerestory windows below the curved ceiling allow light into the

main labs and permit views to the exterior. Elizabeth Franko, lab director, explained, "A bright, open work area was the number one request from my staff. Everybody wanted to have some sense of light and the outside. So care was taken to create an environment that is pleasant to work in, promotes interaction, and inspires pride." The interior glazing allows light in and creates a safer environment: if an accident occurs, it can be seen and managed more easily.

The client desired to change the way its lab employees work in two fundamental ways: through the utilization of a central accessioning facility and the development of an open laboratory concept.

A more streamlined method of getting specimens to the labs was developed

▲ Building exterior. Georgia Public Health Laboratory, Atlanta. Lord, Aeck, & Sargent, Inc., architect. All photographs, pages 65–67, copyright Jonathan Hillyer.

▲ Two-story entry lobby. Georgia Public Health Laboratory, Atlanta. Lord, Aeck, & Sargent, Inc., architect.

The open lab concept was a key feature in achieving project goals. Previously, the various laboratory groups worked in smaller, separate laboratories, with limited daylight and limited contact with others outside the group. To make the new idea of an open lab work for people who were accustomed to small, subdivided spaces, the project team provided all disciplines ample equipment and instrumentation in a bright and spacious laboratory environment. All benches are the same, with common infrastructure elements that accommodate individual research requirements. Gas, vacuum, and emergency power, deionized water capability, first aid, spill control, a burn kit, and fire extinguishers are available at each bench. Slightly wider than normal bench-to-bench spacing (10' 8") is provided to accommodate different scientific operations conducted side by side.

Program requirements dictated that the open lab should be located in the middle of the building, between the service corridor and the open clerical area, creating a "building within a building." Therefore, to get natural light to the lab space, the ceiling plane was given a gentle curve upward to the west, with clerestory windows added beneath. Windows between the lab and the clerical area further open the space and provide visual communication between the two areas. Windows are placed between the clerical area and the west offices, allowing laboratory staff to see through the offices to the landscaping outside. The view through the clerestory reveals the tops of trees and the sky.

A sunscreen consisting of curved aluminum tubes surrounds the glazed curtain wall in the lobby area. To the

with central accessing, utilizing a single location for opening containers and distributing specimens. Specimens and materials flow from receiving to the central accessioning area, where they are opened, numbered, and recorded. This procedure allows more reliable tracking, with information electronically recorded. The specimens are then sent to the large open lab, which accommodates the BL-2 lab groups, or to the separate BL-3 lab area.

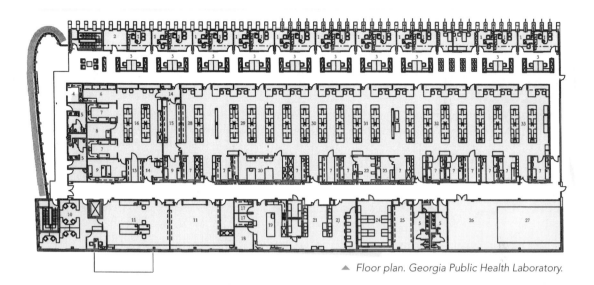

▲ Floor plan. Georgia Public Health Laboratory.

west, granite piers are configured to act as vertical sunscreens, which help to shade the office areas from late-day sun. Insulating low-emissivity coated glass is utilized on all exterior applications to reduce energy costs. The roof is configured as a single uninterrupted slope for easier construction and low-cost maintenance. The six fume hood exhaust fans interrupt the roof surface like a sculpture.

Georgia granite recovered from tombstone scrap was used to provide an inexpensive, durable, and long-lasting ground-level connection with the site. It is particularly effective around the loading dock, where durable, low-maintenance materials are required. The beautiful, low-maintenance copper-shingle siding used in this building was fabricated from recycled material at about the same initial price as a brick wall and will be even more cost-effective over the life of the building.

▼ Clerestory glazing allows light in. Georgia Public Health Laboratory.

▲ Different colors and tile patterns add to the visual appearance of a space. Georgia Public Health Laboratory.

ACADEMIC LABS

Academic laboratories include both research and teaching labs. Academic research labs can be very similar to those of the private and government sectors; teaching labs are unique to the academic sector.

Undergraduate Teaching Labs

Teaching laboratories differ from research labs in a number of ways. Because instruction occurs in them, a specific bench or lectern for the lecturer may be required. Benches are oriented toward the professor and the marker boards. Computer equipment, such as electronic cameras, computer boards, and Elmos (overhead projectors tied into a computer), enhances the learning environment. Casework is usually fixed around the perimeter, though many teaching labs have mobile casework in the middle to allow lectures and research to occur in the same space. To increase utilization, casework is installed in a way that allows for different teaching environments and for multiple classes to be taught in the same space. Storage for student microscopes, book bags, and coats is necessary for most teaching labs. Casework is commonly equipped with locks. There is less instrumentation in teaching labs than in research labs. For undergraduate courses, write-up areas are usually provided inside the lab. (Write-up areas for graduate students are generally located outside the lab, in offices.) A teaching lab must accommodate more people (i.e., students) and stools than does a typical research lab. Prep rooms, which allow faculty to set up supplies before classes, may be located between two teaching labs.

The number of students typically enrolled in a course usually determines the size of the teaching lab used for that course. A typical lab module of 10' 6" x 30' (320 net square feet [NSF]) may support four to six students. An organic chemistry lab for 24 students would be approximately 1,600 NSF. Usually there is very little, if any, overhead shelving in the center of a lab. Overhead storage is at the perimeter walls, and the center of the lab has only base cabinets so as to maintain better sight lines for teaching and learning.

Lab courses are commonly taught Monday through Friday from 9 A.M. to 5 P.M. Most faculty and students prefer not to have classes in the evening or on Saturday. As budgets tighten and

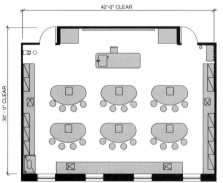
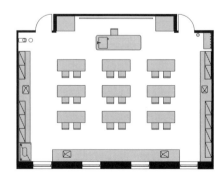

▶ Casework designed for teams of four compared to the typical table with two students.

continuing education and distance learning continue to grow in popularity, however, evening and Saturday classes may become more common in many colleges and universities. Moreover, some teaching labs being designed today will also be used for research. Because of these reasons, mechanical systems should be designed to be able to run at full capacity 24 hours a day, seven days a week.

Depending on the discipline and number of students, shared bench space can range from 15 to 30 linear ft per teaching laboratory, is usually configured as perimeter wall bench or center island bench, and is used for benchtop instruments, exhibiting displays, or distributing glass materials. Ten to 20 linear ft of wall space per lab should be left available for storage cabinets, as well as for built-in and movable equipment

such as refrigerators and incubators. A typical student workstation is 3–4 ft wide with a file cabinet and data and electrical hookups for computers.

Some teaching labs use casework that a student can easily change in height to accommodate sit-down (30 in.) or stand-up (36 in.) work. The flexibility of the furniture encourages a variety of teaching and learning scenarios. The additional cost of flexible furniture is offset by the amount of space saved by eliminating the requirement for separate sit-down and stand-up workstations. Fume hoods shared by two students should be at least 6 ft wide. The distance between student workbenches and fume hoods should be minimized to lessen the possibility of chemical spills.

A flexible design is recommended to accommodate enrollment fluctuations.

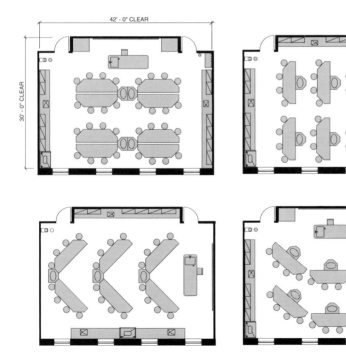

◀ Consider casework that can be organized in many different ways in the same space.

▼ Team station with computer and sink to be used during lecture and research.

▼ Another example of a team-oriented workstation.

A separate discussion room shared by several teaching labs may be an alternative to accommodating lectures in the lab. Teaching labs may be located adjacent to research labs in order to share resources. For example, advanced organic and inorganic chemistry labs and introductory chemistry labs can share some equipment.

The illustrations opposite and on page 72 represent a range of teaching labs.

Integrating Teaching and Research Labs

As the need for flexibility has grown and as science instruction, even at the undergraduate level, more and more focuses on hands-on experience, the traditional distinction between teaching and research labs becomes less important. An increasing number of institutions are integrating these areas to enhance undergraduate curricula and to facilitate communication between faculty and students at all levels. The greatest variances between teaching and research labs are space allocation and equipment needs. To compensate for those differences, some new facilities are designed with greater flexibility to allow lab space to be more adaptable and productive. There are several reasons for creating homogenous lab facilities:

- Students at all levels are introduced to current techniques.

- Such facilities encourage interaction between faculty, graduate students, and undergraduates.

- A standard laboratory module with basic services accommodates change quickly and economically.

- Common and specialized equipment may be shared.

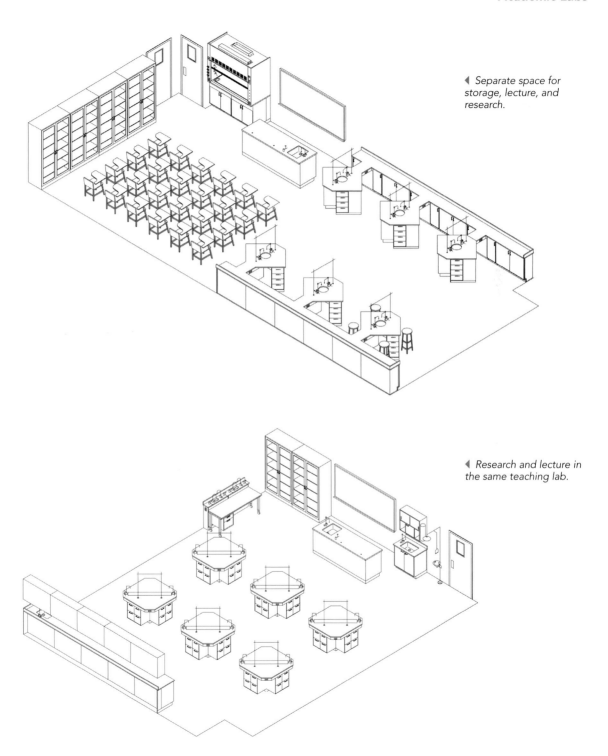

◀ Separate space for storage, lecture, and research.

◀ Research and lecture in the same teaching lab.

LABORATORY TYPES

▶ *Another example of
research and lecture in the
same teaching lab.*

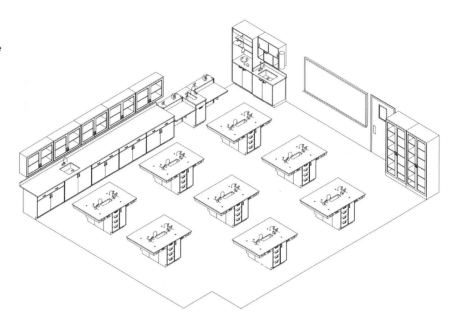

▶ *Sinks as docking stations
organize this teaching lab.*

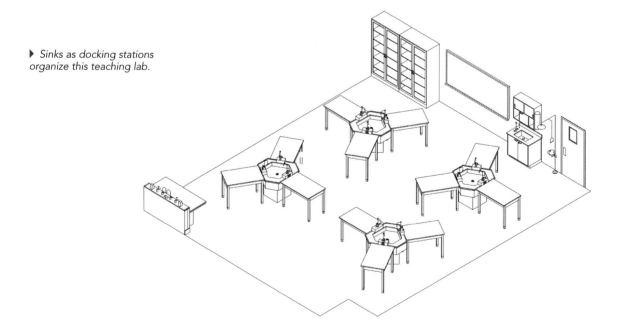

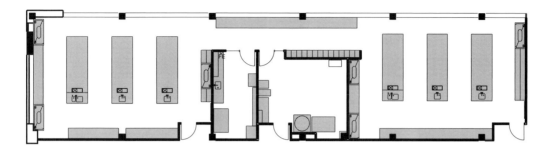

▲ Research and lecture
in the center of the lab with
the fume hoods around
the perimeter.

- Common facilities can share support spaces, such as instrument rooms, prep rooms, and specialty rooms.
- Greater utilization of space and equipment enhances project cost justification.
- Teaching labs can be used for faculty research during semester breaks.

Academic Lab Design Requirements

Requirements differ widely according to the kind of lab being designed. Academic labs include the following categories:

Biology labs

Physics labs

Chemistry labs

Engineering labs

Geology labs

Computer science labs

In general, biology labs require the most services to the benches and chemistry labs the most fume hoods. Physics labs have minimal requirements for services.

Biology labs

Biology Labs are wet labs requiring the following:

- Layout and equipment to serve a variety of teaching models
- Fume hoods and biosafety cabinets

- Space for incubators, refrigerators, and freezers of various sizes
- Bench and storage space for equipment and student materials
- High-quality water at the sink
- Cabinets for chemical and flammables storage
- Adjacent prep, storage, and equipment supply to support efficient use of the teaching lab

Biology labs should be flexible enough to accommodate anatomy, biochemistry, general biology, microbiology, cellular biology, and molecular genetics.

Support spaces for biology labs include vivarium facilities, greenhouses, tissue culture areas, environmental rooms, incubators, growth chambers, glass washing areas, darkroom areas, instrument rooms, storage, and shops. Plant and animal specimen storage and display rooms should be located in close proximity to the biology teaching labs.

Physics labs

Physics labs require significant computer and telecommunications support. The key design issues for physics labs include the following:

- Layout and equipment to serve a variety of teaching models

LABORATORY TYPES

▶ *Some examples of biology labs. Fixed casework around the perimeter with moveable casework in the center.*

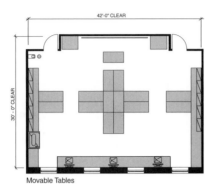
Movable Tables

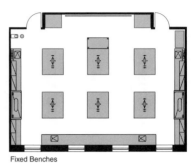
Fixed Benches

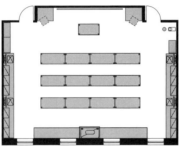
Movable Tables

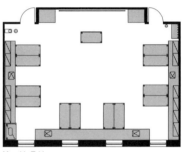
Movable Tables

- Noise and vibration control for accurate measurements
- Magnetic shielding
- Extensive electrical power requirements
- Durable and mobile casework
- Extensive computer networking
- Flexible workspace
- Storage on shelves or in cabinets for experiment "kits" in small containers

Some physics labs are dry labs that do not require 100 percent outside air. There is minimal need for fume hoods. Labs with specialized requirements include workshops for optics, metalworking and electronics, high bay pilot and equipment areas, isotope labs, and equipment storage. Physics labs require storage

rooms for large equipment. Mobile carts may be used to move equipment between labs and storage. Floor loads may be higher than in most other labs.

Chemistry labs

Areas to focus on in designing teaching labs for chemistry include the following:

- Layout and equipment to serve a variety of teaching models
- Adequate bench space for equipment and instrumentation
- Under-hood or under-bench storage for student experiments
- Large number of fume hoods along perimeter walls
- Write-up areas for documenting research experiences

Synthetic chemistry (organic and

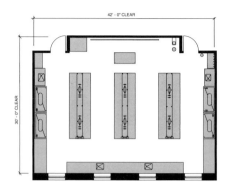
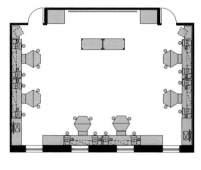

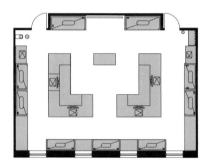
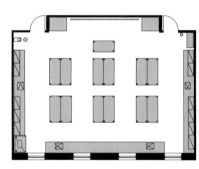

◀ *A variety of physics labs.*

inorganic) labs generally require 3 linear ft of fume hood for each student. Adjacent prep, storage, equipment, and chemical and glassware supply areas help to support efficient use of the teaching lab. Instrument labs often have split benches and flexible utility service carriers for unique equipment needs.

Chemistry labs are wet labs requiring piped gases, heavy electrical and data infrastructure for instruments, and 100 percent outside air ventilation. Chemistry support and research areas include gas chromatography labs, mass spectroscopy, NMR apparatus, and imaging.

Engineering labs
Engineering labs are typically like large workshops, often requiring custom-made setups or provisions for equipment that may be too tall for a standard lab ceiling.

The labs are usually open, with little fixed casework; utility services are located along the wall and overhead. The following are key characteristics of engineering labs:

- Flexible open space for large equipment
- A greater volume of space for tall apparatus
- Overhead cranes to move large and/or heavy equipment
- Heavy floor loads (may require locating such labs on the lowest level of the building)
- Wide and tall doorways to allow forklifts to haul in equipment

Engineering labs may be wet labs, requiring fume hoods and 100 percent outside air. There are also many dry labs for engineering research.

LABORATORY TYPES

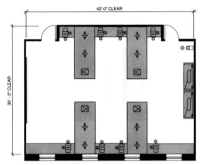

General Chemistry
Fixed Pennisula Benches

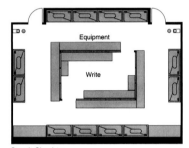

Organic Chemistry

▲ *Chemistry labs with fume hoods along the outside walls.*

▼ *Organic and inorganic chemistry labs with prep and equipment support in the middle.*

▼ *Engineering labs are designed in a variety of sizes depending on the equipment and amount of bench space necessary.*

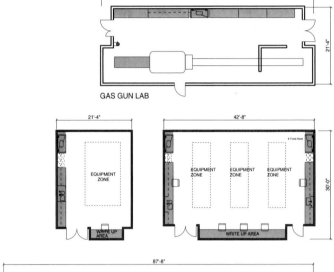

GAS GUN LAB

WRITE UP AREA

WRITE UP AREA

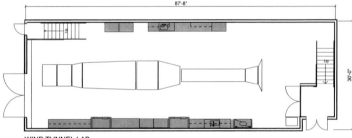

WIND TUNNEL LAB

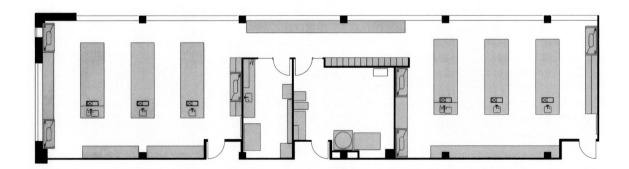

Geology labs

General geology labs are usually dry labs that require a significant amount of space for the hanging of maps and for rock storage and display. The casework is unique to these types of labs. Large flat files (4 ft wide and 3 ft deep) are necessary to hold maps. Cabinets for rock storage need to have sturdy drawers of various sizes. It is important to reserve wall area above the casework for hanging maps. Some geology labs may require hoods and sinks that may need water service and drains to support large experiments with custom apparatus. Small hydraulic lifts are often provided to assist in moving large, heavy rocks.

Computer science labs

The computer science lab is a fairly new type of space. Most are dry labs that need extensive wire management. Electrical and data wiring must be readily accessible at the floor, walls, and ceiling to accommodate the teaching and research needs. An individual lab needs to be flexible enough for both lectures and hands-on learning. Glare from natural light always is a concern. A variety of lighting options should be provided to accommodate research at the computer and the team work environment. Curtains may be necessary to control lighting in an area of the lab.

Many computer science labs require magnetic-field shielding and an extensive lightning protection system. Clean power, separate from the ordinary electrical outlets, is necessary in each room. The length of wire runs should be minimized for efficiency of operation. Raised flooring may be helpful for wire management and for underfloor delivery of cool supply air. Because of the heavy

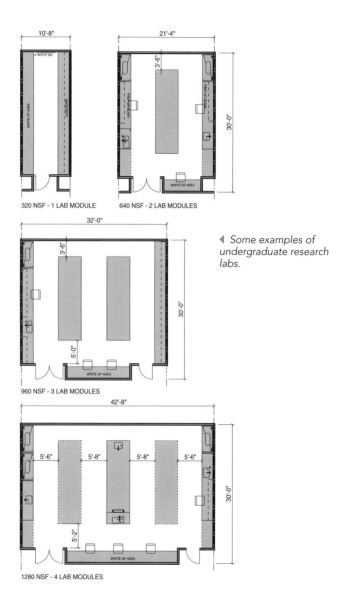

◄ *Some examples of undergraduate research labs.*

use of computers and other equipment the need to cool the space is of high importance. The raised floor can also help protect the room from electro-magnetic fields.

Computer science labs also require a vacuum system and compressed air. Lab doors should be wide enough to allow large equipment and racks of computers to be moved in and out. Some doors and rooms for chip design and circuitry will require special shielding to minimize the penetration of radio frequencies.

Research Labs for Faculty/Students

The faculty's primary responsibility is teaching first, then research, at most undergraduate facilities. Faculty research and advanced-study student research is often performed in shared faculty/student research labs. Shared research labs for faculty and upper-level students are typically two lab modules in size (640 NSF). Such labs often require multiple research and write-up stations within the lab. Overhead service carriers are often used to bring utilities to the bench or equipment, while allowing for the most flexible use of floor/bench space.

Space Guidelines

Today's teaching labs are designed to provide experimental experiences that are open-ended and hands-on. Undergraduate lab work is no longer limited to textbook experiments that are begun and completed in one class period. To accommodate these changes in curriculum and teaching styles, the following guidelines should be consulted in designing space in teaching labs:

- Space requirements depend heavily on the discipline, course level, equipment used, lab type, and the amount of flexibility needed.

- Standard NSF per student for various disciplines:

General biology	50–60
General chemistry	50–80
General geology	40–60
General physics	40–60
Psychology	30–40
Biochemistry	50–70

The table opposite compares several universities across the country and the NSF per full-time faculty for various departments.

The square footage for each student in a class laboratory can vary greatly because of the differing space requirements of different kinds of laboratories. Moreover, graduate-level laboratories usually require more space per station than undergraduate labs. The University of North Carolina has developed assignable square footage (ASF) per station for different discipline categories of space:

- Highly intensive (engineering labs): 108 ASF

- Intensive (biological and physical sciences): 70 ASF

- Moderately intensive (computer/ information technologies, psychology): 50 ASF

Total student stations can be estimated for certain disciplines by dividing the number of teaching labs into the number of students in a class. The following table, drawn from Susan Braybrooke's *Design for Research* (1993), shows typical sizes for some disciplines:

Lab	Students/lab
General biology/ microbiology	32–40
Other biology	20–24
Chemistry	16–24
General physics and geology	24–32
Other physics	16–20
Planetarium	20–50

SPACE REQUIREMENTS PER FULL-TIME FACULTY, TEACHING UNIVERSITIES

Institution	State	Space Requirements by Discipline (NSF)			
		Biology	Chemistry	Psychology	Physics
Institution A	NC	1,461	2,043	2,075	2,030
Institution B	GA	1,378	1,142	356	1,664
Institution C	IL	2,489	2,178		1,380
Institution D	WI	2,375	2,102		3,800
Institution E	AL	2,200	2,270	2,050	1,983
Institution F	ME	3,043	3,683	2,400	3,275
Institution G	MN	3,976	2,917	2,604	2,783
Institution H	ME	2,400	3,029		1,117
Institution I	NC			1,167	
Institution J	PA		2,613		1,436
Institution K	IA	2,551	3,038		3,198
Institution L	MI	2,012	1,793	646	
Institution M	WI	3,804	3,109		2,925
Institution N	MN	2,699	2,561	1,314	3,029
Institution O	GA	1,067	1,223		1,812
Institution P	GA	1,451	1,292		1,570
Institution Q	NJ	2,505	2,052		1,302
Institution R	GA	1,267	1,221		1,142
Institution S	MN	2,117	1,858		2,222
Institution T	GA		1,618		
Institution V	MA	2,168		1,393	
Total NSF		**40,963**	**41,742**	**14,005**	**36,668**
Number of Universities		**18**	**19**	**9**	**17**
Average		**2,276**	**2,197**	**1,556**	**2,157**

Standard classrooms

The number of students that a classroom can accommodate is an important factor in determining how efficiently classroom space can be used. This can be measured in terms of net square feet per seat and the average number of seats per classroom. The table below is used by the state of North Carolina and others to program classrooms.

Typical classroom prototypes are illustrated on the oppposite page. The prototypes should be used as a guide, especially during the programming and design phases.

In the State University System of Georgia's 34 colleges and universities, the following were the average square footages assigned campus-wide for each full-time student in 1995:

- 10.8 for classroom space. This figure was calculated by dividing the total assignable square feet of classrooms campus-wide by the equivalent full-time enrollment. The classrooms include general classrooms and large lecture halls used primarily for instruction.

- 6.7 for teaching laboratories. Teaching laboratories include physics and chemistry labs and other types of specialized classrooms used primarily for instruction. This figure was calculated by dividing the total assignable square feet of teaching laboratories campus-wide by the equivalent full-time enrollment.

The State of North Carolina in 1997 completed a study of public and private facilities that inventories space utilization of colleges and universities. The purposes of the study include providing facilities data to federal and state authorities, making data on North Carolina facilities available to other commissions for comparative purposes, and providing participating institutions with data that may be helpful in the management of their facilities. The table at right is from this study of 112 institutions in the State of North Carolina.

Classroom utilization rates

To determine the number of classrooms required, one must look at class scheduling to determine classroom utilization rates.

To maximize efficiency, classroom scheduling should be done campus-wide, not by department. Some schools have policies requiring higher or lower utilization rates than those given in the preceding. Utilization rates may also take into account evenings and Saturdays.

CLASSROOM SPACE REQUIREMENTS			
Number of Seats	Area per Seat (NSF)		
	Tables & Chairs	Armchair Desks (small)	Tablet Armchair Desks (large)
10–29	20–30	18	22
30–39	20–24	16	18
40–49	18–22	15	16
50–59	18–22	14	16
60–99	18–22	13	15
100–149	16–20	11	14
150–299	16–20	10	14
300+	16–18	9	12

CLASSROOM UTILIZATION RATES		
	Hours Used per Week	Seats Occupied (%)
Classrooms	25–30	60
Lower-level labs	15–20	80
Upper-level labs	8–12	80

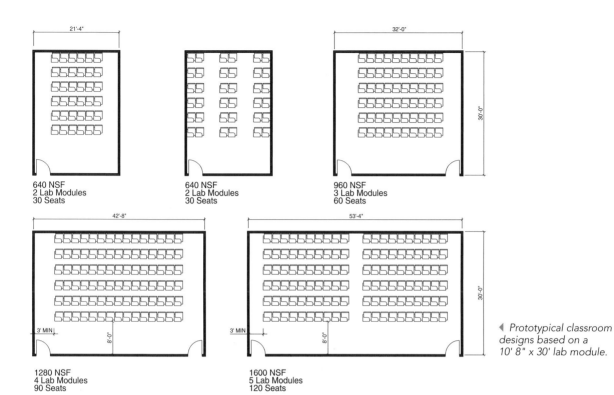

640 NSF
2 Lab Modules
30 Seats

640 NSF
2 Lab Modules
30 Seats

960 NSF
3 Lab Modules
60 Seats

1280 NSF
4 Lab Modules
90 Seats

1600 NSF
5 Lab Modules
120 Seats

◀ *Prototypical classroom designs based on a 10' 8" x 30' lab module.*

SPACE UTILIZATION, COLLEGES AND UNIVERSITIES*

	1997	1996	1995	1994	1993
Academic Facility Area Per Full-Time Student (sq ft)					
Research universities	170	169	164	137	139
Master's universities & colleges	92	92	89	96	93
Baccalaureate universities & colleges	142	143	134	127	122
Average Weekly Hours of Instruction in Classrooms					
Research universities	30.0	28.5	28.2	29.4	28.3
Master's universities & colleges	25.1	24.2	24.4	25.2	25.7
Baccalaureate universities & colleges	22.1	20.5	21.4	20.4	19.0

The University of North Carolina standard is 35 hours of instruction in classrooms per week.

	1997	1996	1995	1994	1993
Average Weekly Hours of Instruction in Laboratories					
Research universities	18.4	11.3	11.3	13.0	12.2
Master's universities & colleges	15.4	14.1	14.7	14.1	14.2
Baccalaureate universities & colleges	11.6	11.2	11.1	11.0	9.1

The University of North Carolina standard is 20 hours of instruction in laboratories per week.

* Based on a State of North Carolina Study, 1997.

High-Technology Instructional Environments

Interactive learning

Most educators today agree that problem-solving and reasoning skills should be fostered and that learning should be an active process. The challenge of preparing for a lifetime of learning, growing, and changing requires abilities far different from those that helped people learn and thrive in more predictable times. Learning in a diverse, multidisciplinary team environment is increasingly emphasized, with the intent that students will be better prepared to address the changing demands in their research. Teaching is much more cooperative and collaborative, with departmental groupings replaced by interdisciplinary groupings and a curriculum that connects learning with the real world.

Two fundamental concepts are important for team-oriented learning and research environments: flexibility and visibility. The engineering systems, as well as the furniture, must be flexible, encouraging the users to change their environment. The spaces should be highly visible, with minimal walls and overhead shelving and some interior glazing.

▶ *Teamwork area provided in the lab encourages several people to work together. Stevenson Center Complex Chemistry Building, Vanderbilt University, Nashville, Tennessee. Payette Associates, Inc., architect.*

A number of schools have begun decreasing the time students spend in lectures and have introduced more opportunities for smaller-group learning activities. Computer-assisted instructional programs are being used to supplement teaching on specific topics. Teaching labs and classrooms are often combined into one space.

Teachers are promoting interactive learning, requiring students to communicate more with one another. Computer boards, electronic kiosks, and other multimedia systems are being incorporated throughout lab buildings. Corridors, meeting rooms, lounges, mail rooms, and conventional and electronic libraries are necessary extensions of the laboratory. The entire building should be utilized for research opportunities.

Distance learning

According to Michael D. Kull, "Distance learning technology is driving the trend toward 'virtual universities'" (Kull 1999). In designing distance-learning environments, it is important to distinguish between synchronous and asynchronous learning environments. The synchronous delivery mode for distance learning requires the learner to be available at the same time the course is being delivered. The asynchronous mode of delivery allows the learner to participate off-site; questions and group discussions take place via e-mail or other types of remote correspondence and collaboration that does not require everyone to be present at the same time.

Synchronous distance learning

Synchronous learning is popular because many educators (and students) believe that classroom collaboration is an important part of the learning and educational process. The challenge of emulating a classroom environment is inherent in designing space for synchronous distance learning. This objective may be accomplished by the following:

- Placing monitor(s) toward the back of the room so that instructors can "see" the remote classroom as a virtual extension of the existing environment without having to turn their backs on the people in the class. Conversely, a wall-mounted monitor placed in the front of the room or a screen splitter (a device that allows a display to be divided into distinct view ports) will allow those present to "see" remote students displayed in a small window on the main screen.

- Screen splitters will also allow instructors to display inputs from multiple sources (e.g., Elmo, VCR, computer-based images, etc.).

- Audio classroom participation is achieved by the use of microphones. Microphones may be either voice activated or push-button activated. Cameras can be programmed to automatically pan to "active" microphone locations.

The instructor should feel free to move about during his or her lecture without being concerned about camera placement or audio pickup. Effective use of wireless microphones and infrared tracking devices on cameras are one way to accomplish this. The instructor should also be able to easily control what will and what will not be displayed on the classroom monitors or what information (audio or video) is broadcast to the remote sites.

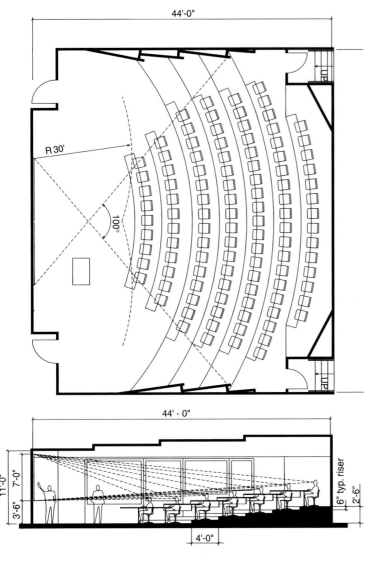

44'-0"

R 30'

100°

44' - 0"

11'-0"
7'-0"
3'-6"

6" typ. riser
2'-6"

4'-0"

▲ Lecture hall.

Asynchronous distance learning

Asynchronous distance-learning systems include correspondence courses, electronic bulletin boards, and Web-based courses. The objective is to create a learning environment that allows students to see the visual presentation and hear oral presentations or comments easily and to be comfortable with both the delivery medium and their physical surroundings.

Asynchronous learning environments allow instructors to record the audio portion of their programs through the use of instructor and student microphones. A determination must be made as to the level and type of asynchronous distance-learning program desired. For example, it is possible to record the audio portion of the classroom but not the visual (video). Thus, handouts and classroom presentation materials, along with the recorded classroom session, can be posted for download and review at a later date or time.

Computer labs facilitating both synchronous and asynchronous learning need proper integration of information technology into the building and each classroom, as well as appropriate furniture that is wired for computers, ergonomically correct, and flexible to operate. Realistic funding for equipment, design, maintenance, and technical support is also necessary. The cost of wiring, computer equipment, and furniture designed for the computer can easily be as much as 15 percent of the construction cost.

Attention to detail

The World Wide Web and e-mail now provide easy access for scientists and students to collaborate with colleagues around the world. This requires attention to detail, including the amount of desk space (personal area) that should be allocated to accommodate computers, notebooks, and other accessories in the classrooms and large lecture halls. Lecture halls should be configured to allow instructors to control the classroom environment from a teaching podium with a touch-screen computer interface. The interface should allow the user to control light levels, acoustic levels, peripheral display equipment (VCR, visual display devices, compact disc player, etc.), electronic screen, and cameras.

The lectern for computer controls should be small and placed on the right or left front edge of the room, facing the students. This arrangement is similar to that needed for slide presentations. Faculty will find it desirable to face students when using a computer in a classroom. Massive desk/console barriers between faculty and students should be avoided. For comfortable viewing, television sets should be 52 in. above the floor. The center of the screen will be approximately 66 in. from the floor, and the student's sight line to the TV screen will be the same as the sight line to the teacher's head in the classroom. At this height the controls are easily accessible. For fixed monitor (or TV) locations (e.g. wall mounted), it is important to keep in mind the uniform federal accessibility standards and guidelines of the Americans with Disabilities Act (ADA), which state that "objects protruding from walls more than 4" shall have 80" minimum clear head room."

▼ Each room should be designed to accommodate multiple layouts.

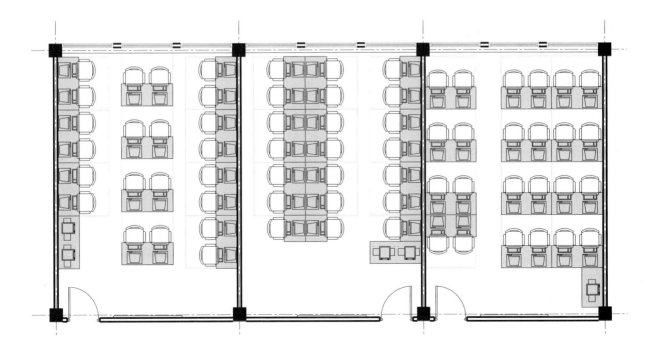

▲ *Mobile computer boards can be very cost effective and flexible for the students and faculty.*

▶ *Motorized tables can be raised or lowered during class. Marist High School, Atlanta, Georgia. P&W, architect.*

Proper room lighting can go a long way toward preventing screen flicker and glare. One way to minimize glare from ceiling lights is to tilt the display slightly toward the floor. Generally, a 2 in. high wood strip under the back of the display should provide enough tilt to prevent glare. As a rule of thumb, one monitor can serve a classroom of 35 students; two are required for 35–60 students. Students should sit no closer to the monitor than four times the diagonal measurement of the display device and no farther than seven times the diagonal measurement of the display device. The best viewing for a 27 in. display device is between 9 and 16 ft; for a 31 in. display, between 10 and 19 ft.

Equipping computer labs and classrooms with movable furniture allows experimentation with a variety of teaching and learning modalities (e.g., a typical lecture arrangement with all desks facing forward or a grouping arrangement that encourages break-out sessions

or team collaboration). At the State University of West Georgia's Technology Enhanced Learning Center, the computer labs were designed with data and electrical outlets along the walls and in the floor. There is one standard 4 ft wide workstation for each student. The workstations can easily be moved by the students and faculty to create different teaching and learning environments in the same space.

Specially outfitted classrooms are augmented with gear that includes one or more electronic white boards, as well as audio and video equipment. Slides and other images projected on white boards are recorded along with the voice of the lecturer—and even extra notes written in the margins of slides as the class progresses.

Facilitating hands-on learning was the main focus of a recent science department renovation at Marist High School in Atlanta. The students and faculty were provided new adjustable research tables, which could be raised or lowered electronically. The instructor controls the switch, and a student simply turns a key at an individual table until it is at the appropriate height. Each table accommodates four students, two computers, a chemically resistant top, and a sink. The table can be adjusted to seating height (approximately 30 in.) for lectures. When active research begins, the height of the table can be increased to stand-up height (approximately 36 in.) within two minutes. The tables can be set at the height that is most comfortable for the students. The computers are networked together, and students can download information during class time. The advantage here is that much less time is spent on the traditional note taking

and more time is spent on hands-on learning activities.

Computer boards in teaching labs

The computer boards being used in many learning environments today are designed to interface directly to a PC or data network. At this time, there are three types of computer boards:

- Copy-boards are stand-alone white boards that come with their own printers and can be mobile. The cost can range from $1,000 to $5,000.
- PC-peripheral boards connect to the computer, allowing sessions to be saved as files for printing or electronic distribution. The cost can range from $600 up to $3,000.
- Interactive boards can be used with projectors or laptops to transform a computer board into an interactive computer screen. Prices range from $1,000 to $25,000.

At the State University of West Georgia, students in the chemistry teaching studios use sit-down stations during lectures and hands-on research activities (see illustrations on pages 88–89). By simply turning around, students can work in their own 36 in. high wet bench research area. During research time the professor can easily walk around to each station and talk with the students. Large computer boards are located on the front and side walls to assist in the educational process during both the lecture and research time.

The laptop environment

In most labs the PC is more common than the laptop, primarily because of the difference in cost. A PC takes up more space than a laptop, but as the development of the latter continues and the price becomes more competitive, laptop use is expected to increase. Laptops will become personalized notebooks that can be used anywhere by their owners, allowing them to maximize both their workday and their leisure time. This dynamic creates the need for ubiquitous computing environments that allow people to access these campus networks anywhere, anytime, and on demand. Many campuses are becoming laptop institutions, requiring students to bring their laptops to class.

Security issues

Security becomes a more important issue when computers are being used. The main problem with laptops and PCs is that they are relatively easy to steal (a common problem in both private industry and academia). Many academic facilities have had problems with people, usually students, stealing PCs, laptops

and audio video equipment. For this reason, security systems are being used that extend from main entrances, along each departmental zone, and into specific rooms. To prevent thieves from moving from one room to another (by removing the ceiling tiles), wall construction may go all the way to the underside of the floor system above. Closed-circuit TV can monitor main corridors, entryways, exit points, and doors into high-security labs. It is good practice to provide a means of locking portable computers when they are not in use.

Budget issues

Inadequate budgeting for presentation systems has been a recurring problem. Historical cost data for such technologies are limited. Furthermore, these technologies are advancing at such a pace that the historical data that do exist are potentially misleading.

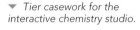
Tier casework for the interactive chemistry studio.

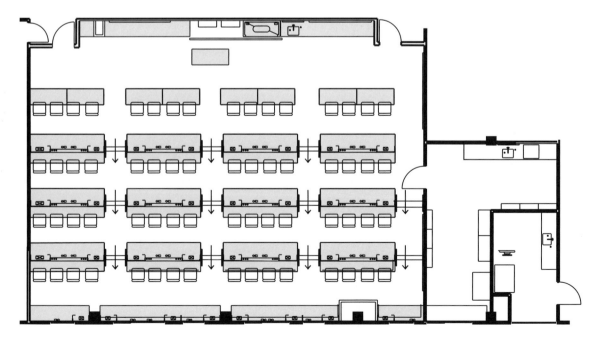

Data do indicate, however, that adding instructional presentation systems can increase the overall cost of a new building project by 8–15 percent. This budgetary impact results from the installed cost of the cable plant, equipment, and design. Provisions for specialized lighting or acoustical treatments should also be considered. In addition, the computer furniture discussed above costs more than the traditional furniture used in the past.

Furthermore, presentation systems require routine maintenance and may need to be upgraded over time. Costs for adding trained technical staff familiar with the systems and their individual components should be considered, although they will typically be borne in administrative budgets rather than project construction budgets. Many school systems are allocating 3 percent of the operating budget for computer technologies expenses, including (but not limited to) advanced local- and wide-area networks, high-speed cable plants (e.g., fiber-optic and Category 5e+ UTP copper infrastructures), computers, servers, storage devices, video devices, and communication equipment. Marketing courses and student support services are additional costs.

Case Studies

Charles E. Schmidt Biomedical Science Center, Florida Atlantic University

Boca Raton, Florida

Architect: Perkins & Will
Completion: Winter 2002
Size: 90,000 GSF
Construction budget: $15,100,000

Florida Atlantic University has created a new concept that combines both open and closed labs to accommodate core research teams. Many researchers still prefer to have some research space of their own. Consequently, 640 NSF are provided for each researcher, primarily for his or her own use and specific equipment. Another 640 NSF have been programmed for each researcher, located in a large open lab. This lab has fume hoods, laminar flow hoods, equipment, and casework to be shared by the entire research team. There can be a variety of research core areas (82 ft x 82 ft) on the second and third floors.

Another idea implemented in this facility is a two-directional grid that allows the casework to be organized in either the north/south or east/west orientation. This provides for maximum

▲ Both sit-down and standup casework is provided in this chemistry studio.

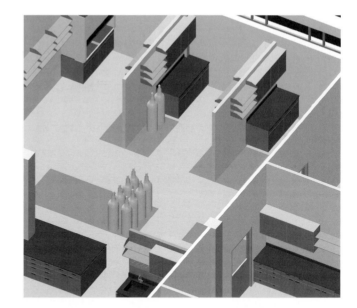

▶ *Research core area. Charles E. Schmidt Biomedical Center, Florida Atlantic University, Boca Raton. Perkins & Will, architect.*

▼ *View of atrium. Charles E. Schmidt Biomedical Center.*

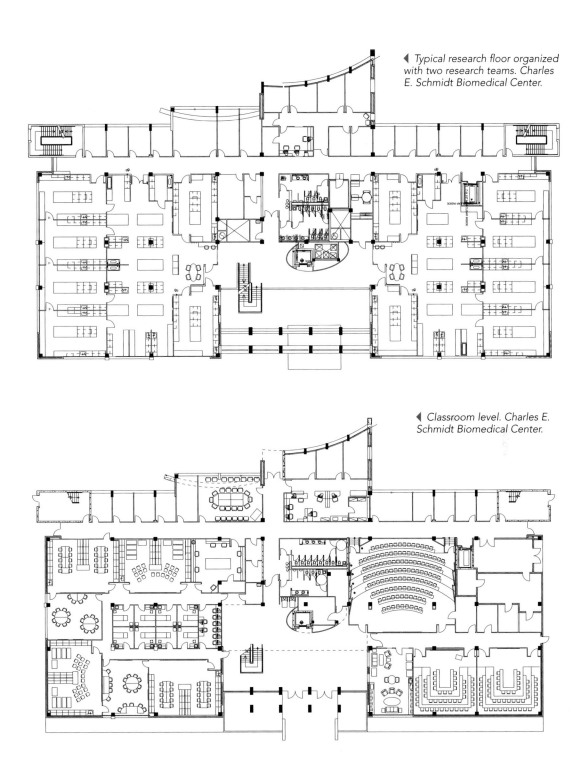

◀ *Typical research floor organized with two research teams. Charles E. Schmidt Biomedical Center.*

◀ *Classroom level. Charles E. Schmidt Biomedical Center.*

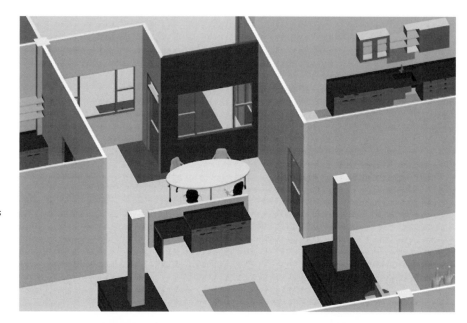

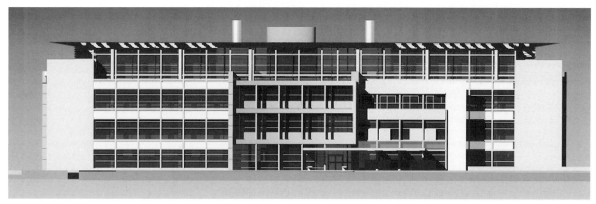

▶ Team area as you enter the main open labs. Charles E. Schmidt Biomedical Center, Florida Atlantic University, Boca Raton. Perkins & Will, architect.

▼ North elevation. Charles E. Schmidt Biomedical Center.

flexibility and allows the researchers to create labs that meet their needs.

The labs are arranged with 50 percent casework and 50 percent equipment zones. The equipment zones allow the research team to locate equipment, mobile casework, or fixed casework in their lab when they move in. The equipment and future casework will be funded with other budgets or grants. This concept is very important for this project for two reasons.

First, the university has not yet hired the faculty, so the specific research requirements are still unknown. Second, this concept reduces the casework cost in the initial construction budget by at least 40 percent ($600,000). The cost will be added to the furniture budget when the mobile casework is purchased.

The interior design is being developed with the use of the three-dimensional (3-D) modeling. The computer modeling

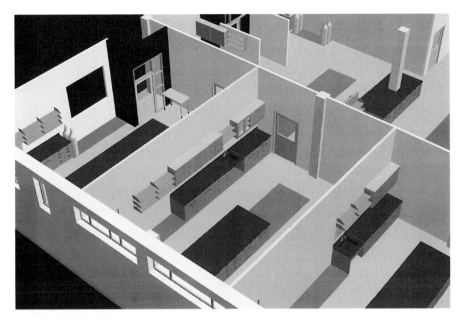

◀ *Lab interior. Charles E. Schmidt Biomedical Center.*

▼ *South elevation. Charles E. Schmidt Biomedical Center.*

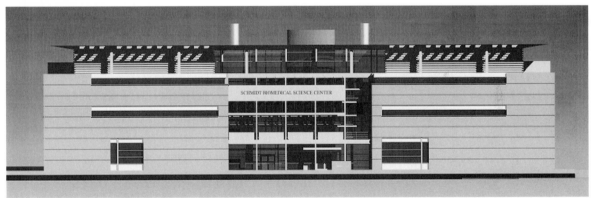

gives the design team and, most important, the client an opportunity to study all aspects of the interior spaces as they will exist when the project is completed. The 3-D modeling also ensures that all design decisions are thoughtfully resolved by the end of the design development process.

Concept diagrams for all the engineering systems are fully coordinated at the end of schematic design. Creating these diagrams gets the engineers involved in the design, ensures that the design team has fully coordinated all systems in the building (not just architectural), and should simplify coordination for the rest of the project. The intent here is to be proactive early in the design process, so as to reduce the number of change orders during construction. The building is zoned with lab and non-lab spaces to decrease overall construction costs.

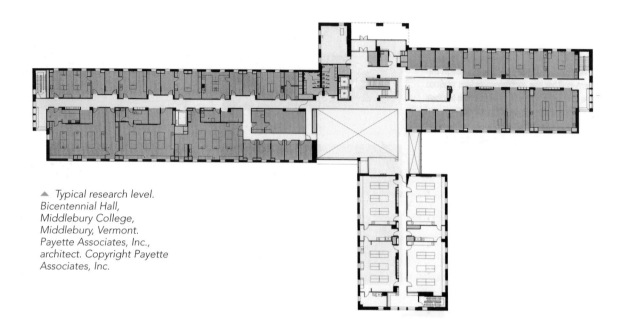

▲ *Typical research level.*
Bicentennial Hall,
Middlebury College,
Middlebury, Vermont.
Payette Associates, Inc.,
architect. Copyright Payette
Associates, Inc.

Bicentennial Hall, Middlebury College

Middlebury, Vermont

Architect: Payette Associates, Inc.
Occupied: 1999
Size: 215,000 GSF
Building cost: $38,574,308

The goal of this project was to create a multidisciplinary science teaching and research building, designed to encourage cross-pollination between the six departments: Biology, Chemistry and Biochemistry, Geography, Geology, Physics, and Psychology.

Planning began with a rigorous assessment of growing enrollment needs. Fostering discovery while keeping pace with the rapidly changing science landscape and a more student-centered experience with student research spaces, even for undergraduates, has become a signature of science at Middlebury. The college has adopted a more collaborative pedagogy, whereby students thrive in an inquiry or problem-based setting that includes design experiments, working on multidisciplinary teams, independent investigations, learning to make connections between disciplines, and communicating ideas effectively.

Because all the science departments are housed in this building, the size and scale posed several challenges, such as integrating the building into the campus fabric and life. This objective was achieved by:

- Designating the building for true multipurpose academic uses

- Creating shared teaching, research, and social spaces

- Locating a two-story science library on the main entry floors

The distinctive topography of the site and the building's cruciform shape define four distinct outdoor spaces that link the internal program with the exterior

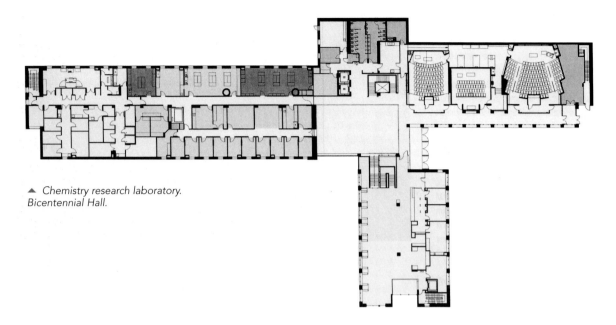

▲ Chemistry research laboratory.
Bicentennial Hall.

environment at multiple levels. The Great Hall, a four-story atrium space, forms the pivot, connecting the separate functions in each wing of the building as well as allowing vertical visual and spatial connection. The hall—the central space at the heart of the building—functions as a village square, heavily used for study, meeting, and informal learning. Bridges leading from each wing to the soaring Great Hall are accented by informal "learning lounges." The ends of each wing also have lounges that allow independent work or collaboration in a quieter setting. The hall affords dramatic views of the Adirondack Mountains, drawing the lush green countryside into the life of the campus.

In fact, the intense use of this space and the building by students to study, collaborate, interact, and gather throughout the semester has caused the college to rethink its future plan for a central library and student center. The

center of gravity of the entire campus has shifted to Bicentennial Hall.

The exterior image is reminiscent of New England mill buildings, composed of quarried and cut Adair limestone, with significant sections of curtain wall filtering in natural daylight.

Another success of this project is its approach to sustainability, striking a healthy balance between sustainable technologies, costs, and benefits. This academic structure contains "green certified" timber harvested and processed by ecologically sensitive means. Other environmental features include linoleum flooring made from wood flour and linseed oil, super-insulated walls and roof, an energy-responsive HVAC system for a 100-year design mandate, and recycled plastic decking on walking portions of the roof. The drywall is composed of 65 percent recyclables; recycled steel is used in the soundproofing system; and mortar netting used for masonry work is from

recycled plastic. Sustainable aspects of mechanical, electrical, and plumbing (MEP) systems include:

- An energy-efficient building envelope and low-impact effluent discharge
- Absorption refrigeration to enhance campus cogeneration performance
- Air side heat recovery and process cooling loop
- Exhaust plume mitigation and vibration control to accommodate the needs of the observatory

The innovative generic lab concept used in this project was developed for a number of reasons:

- To reduce the quantity of space required by dedicated introductory labs by creating shared space for all departments except Chemistry
- To encourage the exchange of ideas between departments that share the spaces
- To allow other disciplines and programs to utilize the space outside the academic schedule

The generic lab consists of a 36 ft x 28 ft lab plus a 12 ft x 28 ft support room. Electrified epoxy-topped tables can be arranged in a square, a horseshoe, back-to-back rows, front-facing rows, or other desired layouts to accommodate various teaching styles.

In the two main laboratory wings, teaching labs run down the west side of a central corridor, with associated research labs and faculty offices across from them on the east side. Unlike some academic buildings where researchers' offices are sharply segregated from student labs, Bicentennial Hall was designed to put students in proximity to serious research, grouped in clusters according to speciality.

Specialized lab setups include the following components:

- A 600 sq ft chemistry/biochemistry lab with a laminar flow hood and an incubator station on the biochemistry side, and a fume hood, refrigerator, bench space, and desks on the chemistry side
- A theoretical chemistry research lab designed to accommodate intensive computer work
- A field geology lab that can handle long cores taken from Lake Champlain
- A physics lab containing a large atomic beam apparatus, mounted on track rails in the center of the room, plus a laser
- A 300 sq ft cell culture facility
- A 1,000 sq ft advanced microscopy laboratory

Bicentennial Hall won a Laboratory of the Year (2000) award from *R&D* magazine and the Scientific Equipment and Furniture Association.

McDonnell Research Building, Washington University School of Medicine

St. Louis, Missouri
Architect: Perkins & Will
Occupied: 1999
Size: 230,000 GSF
Building cost: $55,000,000

The Washington University School of Medicine required additional space for its renowned pediatric, biomedical, and cancer research programs. The new 11-story facility includes generic laboratories, support space, and offices for biomedical research. A repetitive laboratory plan allows for maximum flexibility among

◀ Atrium at the heart of the building, used for study, meeting, and informal learning. Bicentennial Hall, Middlebury College, Middlebury, Vermont. Payette Associates, Inc., architect. Photograph copyright Jeff Goldberg/Esto.

diverse tenants and future research practices. The project construction was fast-tracked to accommodate the earliest move-in date for researchers.

The laboratory facility is located in the midst of a dense medical school campus, which includes Washington University School of Medicine and four prominent hospitals affiliated with the school. The new biomedical facility connects to adjacent facilities, providing direct circulation patterns between research areas, animal facilities, and clinical services located in St. Louis Children's Hospital.

The floor plan allows for a courtyard at the north side of the building for pedestrian access and laboratory support space and provides direct natural light into the laboratories and offices throughout. A unique plan was developed that incorporated a linear equipment space to provide the most flexible and

adaptable research environment possible. Offices were clustered on the building's exterior, separate from the interior lab spaces, permitting both spaces to take advantage of the building's perimeter and allowing natural light to flow through the spaces.

The most important aspect of the new building has been Washington University's clear direction that it be a state-of-the-future research facility. As a research institution consistently ranked within the top five in the country, Washington University wanted to project a strong image with this new facility. The idea of the traditional research lab as a tight rectilinear building was challenged by the design team working directly with the lead principal investigator. A curvilinear, sculptural building mass was developed, incorporating a highly efficient laboratory plan.

◀ *Exterior. McDonnell Research Building, School of Medicine, Washington University, St. Louis, Missouri. Perkins & Will, architect.*

◀ *Typical laboratory. McDonnell Research Building, School of Medicine, Washington University, St. Louis, Missouri. Perkins & Will, architect.*

CHAPTER 3
ARCHITECTURAL DESIGN ISSUES

Over the past 30 years, architects, engineers, facility managers, and researchers have refined the design of typical wet and dry laboratories to a very high level. This chapter focuses on many of the lessons learned and identifies the best solutions in designing a typical lab. (At the end of the chapter, design considerations for specialized labs are discussed.)

Much of the information gathered here comes from researchers, administrators, and facility managers of more than 150 laboratory facilities in the United States and Europe. Design guidelines promulgated by the National Institutes of Health (NIH), the Association for Assessment and Accreditation of Laboratory Animal Care (AAALAC), the Veterans Administration (VA), Glaxo Wellcome, and several state agencies have also been reviewed, studied, and incorporated.

The chapter is organized as follows:

1. The programming, design, and construction process
2. General architectural design issues
3. The lab module
4. Site planning
5. Exterior image
6. Massing
7. Interior spaces
8. Adjacencies
9. Interior finishes
10. Acoustical issues
11. Casework
12. Ergonomics
13. Fume hoods
14. Safety, security, and regulatory considerations
15. Wayfinding, signage, and graphics
16. Specialized lab areas
17. Specialized equipment and equipment spaces
18. Vivarium facilities

THE PROGRAMMING, DESIGN, AND CONSTRUCTION PROCESS

The programming, design, and construction process is complex. For a new laboratory building, it usually takes several years to complete. The various phases, along with the key architectural responsibilities, are discussed in the following paragraphs.

Programming

Very early in the programming phase, designers should determine the project's overall goals and objectives. Often, programmers employ a questionnaire, circulated among laboratory managers and other staff, to define problems and possible solutions. The following are among the questions such a questionnaire might ask:

1. What are the overall objectives of this new research facility or renovation?
2. What type of research culture do you want to create?
3. What image would you like the building exterior to convey?
4. Where should offices be located in relation to labs?
5. How important is it that labs have views to the exterior and natural daylighting?

6. How often do customers visit this laboratory?

7. What do you like best about your current laboratory workspace?

8. What do you like least about your current laboratory workspace?

9. What can be shared within a project team, and between teams?

10. What are the main traffic flow patterns in the laboratory?

11. List spaces (existing and required).

12. List major items of equipment requiring floor space and special services.

13. Do you need any special casework?

14. What types of hoods are necessary?

15. What waste-management plan will you require?

16. How flexible do you want the labs and building to be?

The following matters should be determined during the programming phase:

- All budgets for the project
- Probable construction cost as compared with project budget (based on unit cost per gross sq ft [GSF] of the building)
- Flexibility requirements
- Size of typical lab module
- Number and types of individual rooms required
- Architectural and engineering criteria for each room
- Desired relationships between rooms and large groups of researchers
- Preferred location of the labs in relation to offices and lab support
- Number and types of fume hoods

Programmers should also obtain data on any special pieces of equipment that will go into the lab and develop a preliminary floor plan illustrating the casework, fume hood, and equipment layout. By the end of the programming phase, the overall project schedule should also be determined.

The sample room criteria sheet at right illustrates many of the architectural and engineering issues that must be resolved during programming.

During either the programming or the schematic design phase, it may be beneficial to tour other, similar laboratories to benefit from lessons learned by peer institutions.

Schematic Design

During schematic design, designers focus on the following:

1. Development of the exterior image

2. Building configuration, coordinated with the laboratory module

3. Blocking and stacking: where rooms are located on each floor and how the floors relate to one another

4. Conceptual diagrams of the individual engineering systems, based on the lab module

5. Update of statement of probable cost

Code reviews must also be performed during this stage. The local building agencies may have to review the initial floor plans.

Design Development

During design development, the schematic design is developed three-dimensionally and all design decisions regarding the site development, exterior image, and casework layouts for each lab

TYPICAL LAB CRITERIA SHEET

DEPARTMENT	**Chemical and Materials Engineering**
SPACE NAME	**Typical Research Lab**
FUNCTION	
NUMBER OF SPACES	
SIZE	
STUDENTS/STAFF	

Architectural
Floor

VCT (Chemical Resistant)
VCT
Welded Seam Mipolean

Carpet
Sealed Concrete
Partitions
Gyp Board, Paint
Gyp Board, Epoxy Paint
Concrete Block
Shielding
Base
4" Vinyl
Integral w/ Floor
Ceiling
Exposed Structure

Acoustic Tile
(2x4), (2x2)
Gyp Board
Height

Doors
Width

Height
Vision Panel (Glazing)
Lighting

Natural Daylight - Preferred
Natural Daylight - Indifferent
No Natural Daylight

Special Considerations
Glass at the entry alcoves only
Offices on outside wall
Write up areas along the corridor

Security
Level of Security

Locks Only
Card Access
Other
Card Access for Building only

Mechanical
Temperature

72 degrees + 2 degrees
68-75 degrees + 2 degrees
Humidity

General or Individual Stacks
50% + 20%
Uncontrolled
Hoods
Chemical Fume Hood
Radioisotope Hood
Laminar Flow Hood
Bio Safety Cab (30-100%)
Snorkel
Canopy Hood
Low Slotted Exhaust
Other

Air Changes

Electrical
110V / 20A, Phase 1

208V / 30A, Phase 1
208V / 30A, Phase 3
400V / 100A, Phase 3
Isolated Ground Power Outlet
Emergency Power

UPS (OFO)

Phone
Data

Cable TV
In Use Light
Task Lighting
100fc at Bench / Desk
75fc at Bench / Desk

Safe Light
Special Lighting

Darkenable
Zoned Lighting
Dimming System
Other

Plumbing
Laboratory Natural Gas(LG)

Laboratory Vacuum (LV)
Laboratory Air (LA)
Compressed Air, 100psi

Industrial Hot Water (IHW)
Industrial Cold Water (ICW)
Potable(Drinking) Hot Water
Potable(Drinking) Cold Water
High Purity Water (DE)
Processed Chilled Water
Steam Condensed Return
Carbon Dioxide (CO_2)
Nitrogen Gas (N_2)
Cylinder Gases
Inert
Flammable
Toxic
Floor Drain (FD)
Floor Sink (FS)
Safety Shower / Eyewash (SS)

Drench Hose (DH)
Temp Require. Process Piping

Structural
Vibration Criteria
125-150 psf for live loads

Equipment

Adjacency Requirements / Special Considerations

Remarks

---

are finalized. By the end of this phase, all engineering systems should be fully coordinated with the architectural plans. As part of the design development work, sessions should be held with the end users to coordinate room adjacencies, color schemes and finishes, and final casework selections.

103

Design development should finalize:

1. Detail layouts for each laboratory, including service requirements for raceways, panel boxes, and piping for mechanical and plumbing

2. Specifications for systems and materials

3. Strategy for add alternates or deductive alternates if there is to be a bid process

In addition, the statement of probable cost should be updated.

Construction Documents

During the construction document phase, all working drawings and specifications necessary to build the project are completed. The architects and engineers spend most of their time during this phase coordinating and finalizing all issues related to the building construction. The end users need to be available only to answer any questions that may come up or to review the documents to make sure the drawings and specifications meet their requirements.

Construction documents include:

1. Drawings and specifications for bidding and construction

2. Final cost estimate

Bid Phase

The project is bid and the construction price is finalized before the actual construction begins. (There are some instances in which a contractor or construction management team gets involved earlier in the project to determine the construction cost.)
During the bid phase:

1. Drawings and specifications are issued for bidding.

2. Construction bids are received and reviewed.

3. The contract is awarded.

Some projects involve a negotiated price. Contractors are asked to on bid the project, and then the owner negotiates the final cost with the preferred contractor. During this process, there may be a value engineering session with the architects and engineers. The contractor proposes options to reduce cost, and the owner and design team decide whether to accept these choices. With this approach there is usually less risk for both the owner and the contractor, because the scope and costs are discussed, then agreed upon. The hard bid process, which does not allow for negotiation, is used for almost all publicly funded projects. If the design-build process is used, a guaranteed maximum price (GMP) is usually agreed upon at the end of the design phase or during the construction documentation phase. The design-build process does not require a bid phase, which saves some time and money.

Construction Administration

Construction of a typical laboratory building can range from 15 to 36 months—the larger and more complex the project, the more time necessary. This phase involves the review, coordination, and approval of shop drawings. The architect makes regular site visits to make sure that construction is proceeding in accordance with the contract documents.

GENERAL ARCHITECTURAL DESIGN ISSUES

Ceiling Height

The standard 9'6" ceiling height is recommended for most labs. With this height, there is enough space for the use of indirect light fixtures. (Indirect lighting grows in importance as computers are increasingly used in the lab environment.) Large labs may require more height and volume for better proportions. Some labs may need to be two stories high to accommodate large equipment or specific research processes. There are some research setups over 10' high that can fit between the ductwork; where these will be used, the lab should be designed with an exposed rather than a lay-in ceiling, to allow the researcher to use more of the volume of the space. No lab should have a ceiling height below 8'.

Lab Doors

The recommended minimum door width for a lab is 38", but a 42" door is preferred. Large equipment, such as fume hoods, may have to be dismantled to be moved in and out of the lab if the doorway is less than 38" wide. Double doors or doors with active and passive panels may be useful. Double doors eliminate equipment bottlenecks and enhance traffic flow but are more expensive than 42" wide single doors. Glazing in the doors should be considered for most labs. There should always be two means of egress from a laboratory area where hazardous chemicals are present.

Aisles

Aisles between workstations should measure at least 5' to permit a person to pass behind another person who is working. A 5' aisle also conforms to the guidelines of the Americans with Disabilities Act (ADA). Aisles wider than 6' are not recommended for most labs, because users tend to clutter the space with carts and equipment. Workstations should be staggered back-to-back to allow people to work more easily.

Basic Furniture Considerations

Base cabinets

Select 30" high units for seated work and 36" high units for standing work. Flexible casework is an option that allows the height to be varied, from 28–38", either manually or electronically.

Wall cases

Place the bottom of a wall case 4'6" from the floor, whether the case is to go with a sitting- or standing-height cabinet. A 4'6" height above the floor is usually acceptable to most people.

Tables

When a high level of flexibility is desired or cost is a major concern, tables may be preferable to base cabinets. In the future, lab tables will be used more extensively because of teams working in open labs, space allocated in equipment zones, and the economical and practical need to address churn quickly.

Shell Space

During initial construction, shell space includes exterior walls and main building systems such as the restrooms, mechanical equipment, and elevators. The interior finishes for the walls are completed later, when funds are available.

Expansion can occur more easily when shell space is provided in the initial construction. Following the master plan, the building is designed to accommodate growth. Some new and remodeled facilities are now incorporating some shell space to accommodate affordable and quick expansion, as well as to have space available to draw new researchers to their campuses. The construction cost of shell space is initially similar to the cost of office construction. The cost savings for the construction of shell space are really created in the time saved when expansion occurs.

The shell space provides more space for laboratories (either additional labs or expansion of existing labs) and requires no renovation. During the fit-out of the shell space, daily operations in the building can be maintained. Many institutions are building some shell space that is fitted out at the end of construction. The researchers acquire grant money that funds some or all of the fit-out of their labs. This approach usually allows for more laboratory space to be constructed initially.

THE LAB MODULE—BASIS FOR LABORATORY DESIGN

The laboratory module is the key unit in any lab facility. When designed correctly, a lab module will fully coordinate all the architectural and engineering systems. (Coordination of engineering systems is presented in detail in the next chapter.) A well-designed modular plan will provide the following benefits:

- *Flexibility.* The lab module should encourage change within the building. Research is changing all the time, and buildings must allow for reasonable change. Many private research companies make physical changes to an average of 25 percent of their labs

each year. Most academic institutions annually change the layout of 5 to 10 percent of their labs.

- *Expansion.* The use of lab planning modules allows the building to adapt easily to needed expansions or contractions without sacrificing facility functionality.

Basic Lab Module

A common laboratory module has a width of approximately 10'6" but will vary in depth from 20' to 33'. The depth is based on the size necessary for the lab and the cost-effectiveness of the structural system. The 10'6" dimension is based on two rows of casework and equipment (each row 2'6" deep) on each wall, a 5' aisle, and 6" for the wall thickness that separates one lab from another. The 5' aisle width should be considered a minimum because of the requirements of the Americans with Disabilities Act (ADA) and to allow one researcher to pass another without interference. The 6" wall thickness should also be maintained for all walls between labs, whether the walls are built during initial construction or may be added later during renovation.

If the lab module is not well thought out, two things can happen. If the lab module is too wide, the building's net-to-gross ratio will not be as efficient or cost-effective as it could be, and the building will be bigger and more expensive than it needs to be. If the lab module is too narrow, then either the aisle will be too narrow, creating an unsafe research environment, or there will be room for casework on one wall only. If the design of the laboratory building is not based on a lab module, then the initial and long-term operational costs will be higher because of less efficient construction.

The different types of laboratory spaces, such as labs, lab support spaces, and offices, are expressed as multiples of the basic module. Should a new laboratory building be designed using masonry units, the module dimensions should be adjusted to 10' 4" or 10' 8" to incorporate the brick module, which is typically based on an 8" increment. The 10' 4" module should be fine for a building with labs that comprise at least two lab modules. The 10' 8" module should be considered if there are several small labs that will require only one lab module.

Two-Directional Module

Another level of flexibility can be achieved by designing a lab module that works in both directions. Employing the common width of 10' 6" and a depth of either 21' (2 modules at 10' 6") or 31' 6" (3 modules at 10' 6") allows the casework to be organized in either direction. This concept is more user-friendly than the basic lab module concept but may require more space.

The use of a two-directional grid is beneficial to accommodate different lengths of run for casework. The casework may have to be moved to create a different type or size of workstation. Many times it is helpful to have movable casework, which lets researchers rearrange the casework to accommodate the particular research their team is doing. Utility drops, if necessary, should occur at the intersection of the 10' 6" modules.

Three-Dimensional Lab Module

The three-dimensional lab module planning concept combines the basic lab module or a two-directional lab module

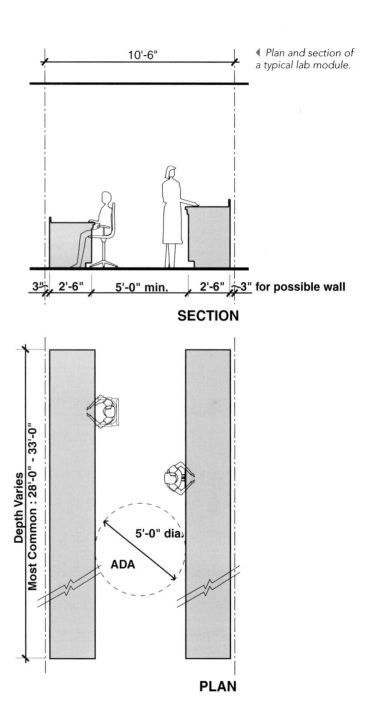

◄ *Plan and section of a typical lab module.*

SECTION

PLAN

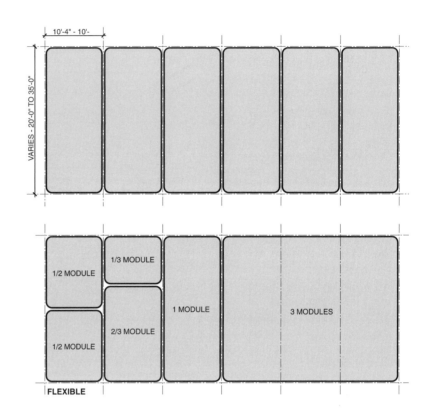

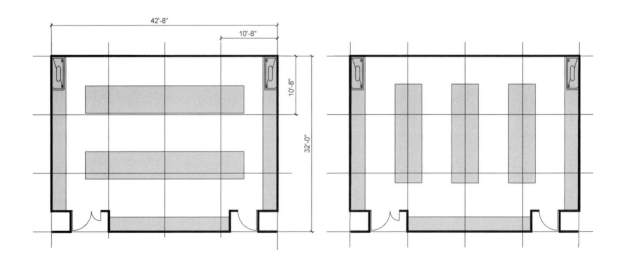

▶ Typical lab module and its inherent flexibility based on a brick masonry exterior.

▼ Two-directional grid.

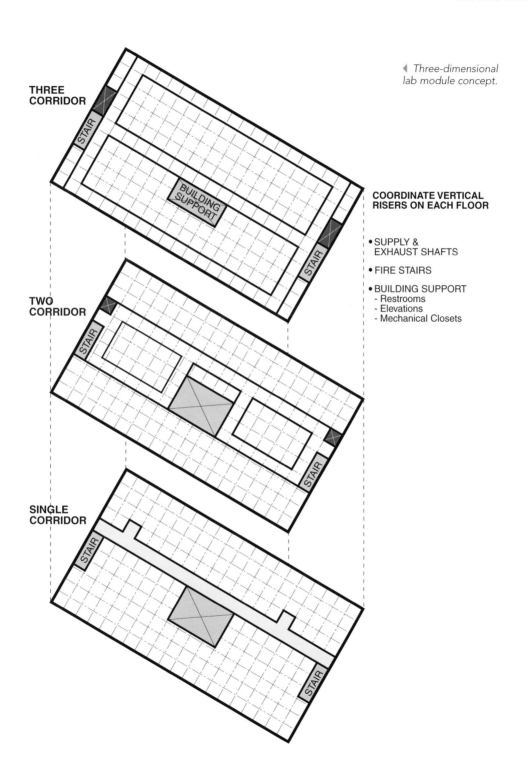

THREE CORRIDOR

TWO CORRIDOR

SINGLE CORRIDOR

STAIR

BUILDING SUPPORT

◀ *Three-dimensional lab module concept.*

COORDINATE VERTICAL RISERS ON EACH FLOOR

- SUPPLY & EXHAUST SHAFTS

- FIRE STAIRS

- BUILDING SUPPORT
  - Restrooms
  - Elevations
  - Mechanical Closets

109

with any lab corridor arrangement for each floor of a building. This means that a three-dimensional lab module can have a single-corridor arrangement on one floor, a two-corridor layout on another, and so on. To create a three-dimensional lab module:

1. A basic or two-directional lab module must be defined.

2. All vertical risers must be fully coordinated (vertical risers include fire stairs, elevators, restrooms, and shafts for utilities).

3. The mechanical, electrical, and plumbing systems must be coordinated in the ceiling to work with the multiple-corridor arrangements.

Focusing on a building three-dimensionally allows the designer to be more responsive to the program needs of the researchers and faculty on each floor. A three-dimensional design permits the corridor arrangement on any floor to be easily changed, facilitating renovations. This approach is highly recommended for most facilities, but it requires much more thought and coordination in the initial design.

SITE PLANNING

Several issues must be considered in planning the site for a new laboratory building. The view of the building and its entrance that a person has on arriving at the site is important for wayfinding and security. Visitor parking should be near the front door for convenience and security. There may be need for a security gate as a control point for access to the building.

Parking for employees is always an issue. Surface parking requires more land than structured parking but costs approximately one-tenth the price. Parking under

laboratory buildings is not very common, because the typical lab module does not easily correspond to the typical parking module, and owners pay a premium for incorporating structured parking into a laboratory building.

Loading docks should be accessible for delivery and service but remote from pedestrian and automobile circulation. Remote loading docks (and the trucks using them) can be unsightly, requiring thoughtful location and screening. Mechanical equipment and dumpsters, usually located near loading docks, should be screened with a fence, wall, or landscaping.

Another key site-planning issue involves the location of the air supply grilles and exhaust stacks. A wind wake analysis will help designers understand how the exhaust will be dispersed and whether it is likely to create any problems for nearby buildings.

All site-planning solutions must be compliant with the Americans with Disabilities Act (ADA). (ADA compliance issues are treated at greater length under "Safety, Security, and Regulatory Considerations," pages 169–171.)

EXTERIOR IMAGE

Several issues influence the exterior image of any building:

1. Site context

2. Architectural and cultural context

3. The client's objectives

Additionally, there are two exterior design issues specific to most lab buildings:

1. The physical organization and design of offices, laboratories, and major mechanical spaces (the program)

2. The size, number, and architectural expression of exhaust stacks

General Exterior Image Issues

Site context

Site context issues differ depending on whether a building is being constructed on an open greenfield site or is being added to an existing campus and must relate to the buildings surrounding it.

Architectural and cultural context

Architectural style is a function of the client's desires, the architect's tastes, prevailing contemporary styles, climate, program, and context. Two projects designed by Venturi Scott Brown Associates (VSBA) are shown on page 114. Most of VSBA's designs for exteriors are characterized by facades, brick patterns, and details that represent the past in an abstract, contemporary architecture.

Client's Objectives

The client's objectives have a significant impact on the final image of a project.

Client objectives may include designing the building within certain cost criteria, defining the overall image and message the company wants to convey, constructing spaces that encourage communication among teams, and providing a research environment that results in higher-quality research.

Lab-Specific Exterior Image Issues

Physical organization and design

The proper physical organization and three-dimensional massing of offices, laboratories, and supporting mechanical spaces are critical to defining the image of a laboratory building. Office construction is simpler and less costly than lab construction. When they are clustered in a sufficiently large area (usually at least 25–50 percent of the building), offices can incorporate more sculptural details and massing. The office design does not have to be based on the lab module. There can be more glass on the exterior;

◀ Spelman College's new science building relates to the college's historic quadrangle. Atlanta, Georgia. Perkins & Will, architect.

▶ *The new Northwestern University biomedical facility relates to its Gothic setting with deep window reveals and lacy window mullions. Chicago, Illinois. Perkins & Will, architect.*

▲ The site of the Smith Kline Beecham facility north of London was previously farmland. There are no other structures near the largely glass structure that houses 1 million sq ft of research space. Stevenage, United Kingdom. The Hillier Group, architect.

◀ The addition to the Joslin Diabetes Center, Harvard University, was necessarily vertical, because of land-use restrictions. The four-story addition was constructed without interruption of research on the floors below. Cambridge, Massachusetts. Ellenzweig & Associates, architect.

Thomas Laboratories, Princeton University, Princeton, New Jersey. Venturi Scott Brown with Payette & Associates, Inc., architect.

Clinical Research Building, University of Pennsylvania, designed and constructed more than 10 years after Thomas Laboratories at Princeton. Venturi Scott Brown with Payette & Associates, Inc., architect.

the walls can be of a variety of shapes and angles; and the mechanical systems can be simpler and more cost-effective than those required for lab construction.

Most researchers prefer their offices to be located along the exterior wall to allow for natural light and views. The labs usually are organized in a rectangular massing to permit the cost effectiveness and efficiency of designing with a lab module. The more efficient lab buildings have floor plans of at least 20,000 sq ft. A laboratory building with 30,000 GSF per floor is usually the most efficient, since it will not require additional fire stairs, elevators, restrooms, or mechanical space.

Another key aspect of the visual image of a laboratory building involves the amount of glass. Decisions on the incorporation of glazing are based on the amount of light desired for interior spaces, the preferred exterior image, and the cost of the glass. Most labs do not require much glass. Typically, casework is located 3' high along the entire outside wall or a significant portion of it. The recommended ceiling height is usually 9' 6" to 10'. This allows for some indirect lighting (if desired), the appropriate volume of air to circulate through the lab, and the appropriate volume of the lab from a psychological point of view. For most labs, exterior as well as interior glazing should be located between 3' and 9' 6" above the finished floor, for three main reasons:

- A glass wall can cost 50–100 percent more than a masonry wall.

- Glass can have an impact on the heating and cooling bills each year. Code officials require an energy analysis of every new building to determine the quality and quantity of the glass and its effect on the energy efficiency of the entire building.

- Researchers need a certain amount of wall space for office furniture, casework, and equipment.

▲ For their main headquarters, Glaxo Wellcome wanted a facility that would provide all amenities for their researchers and aid in the recruitment of new talent. Stevenage, United Kingdom. Kling Lindquist, architect.

Mechanical equipment can be located in any of several different places:

At the roof. At the new chemistry and biology building at the University of California, Los Angeles, the curved roof and expression of the stacks are part of the overall sculptural massing and image of the campus.

In the basement. The sloping site at the State University of West Georgia's Technology Enhanced Learning Center allows mechanical equipment to be located in the basement, reducing the scale of the building. The building will be more than 50 percent larger than any other on campus, even with the mechanical equipment located in the basement. The university focused on keeping the building massing as small as possible, while providing easy access for the facility engineers to the mechanical equipment in the basement.

In a structure immediately adjacent, The Iowa Advanced Technology Labs Building has a large mechanical room located at the ground level, east of the lab block. The mechanical room is constructed with a curved roof, and its walls are clad in copper. The location of the mechanical equipment provides easy access to the equipment and labs. This option is not much used because it requires prime real estate at ground level and the space above the mechanical room is not developed.

Mechanical rooms on each floor. The Hutchinson Cancer Center in Seattle is designed with the air handlers located on each floor to eliminate the need for a basement, penthouse, or interstitial space. Because of the high water table on the site, a basement was not possible, and a penthouse or interstitial space would have increased the building height significantly.

Interstitial space. Interstitial space is an option that should be discussed at the beginning of each project. In the early

▲ The Georgia Public Health Laboratory is designed so that lobby and research offices are visible from street. The mechanical equipment is located on the much less visible service side of the building. Atlanta, Georgia. Lord Aeck Sargent, Inc., architect.

▼ At Yale, the Bass Center has the offices located along this exterior, with the mechanical equipment in an attic-like penthouse. The exhaust stacks are expressed as chimneys. New Haven, Connecticut. Kallmann McKinnell & Wood, architect.

◀ The Hutchison Cancer Research Center has articulated bay windows that, in effect, provide each researcher with a corner office. Seattle, Washington. Zimmer Gunsul Frasca Partnership, architect.

▶ Exhaust stacks on the outside. Molecular Sciences Center, University of California at Los Angeles. Anshen & Allen, architect.

▼ Mechanical equipment located in basement. Technology Enhanced Learning Center, State University of West Georgia, Carrolton. Perkins & Will, architect.

1960s, Jonas Salk worked with Louis I. Kahn and Earl Walls to develop the Salk Institute. That building, which pioneered the use of interstitial space, has exemplified the flexible laboratory facility for more than 30 years. Salk set out to create a research environment for open-minded people who could learn from each other. The building can be changed and modified within a basic framework, and change is the norm at the Salk Institute. Many of Salk's ideas remain valid and important today, even though technology has changed.

Interstitial space is located above the ceiling of each lab floor; it is basically another floor containing all the engineering services for the floor below. Typical floor-to-floor height (including the interstitial space) can range from 17 to 19 ft, creating a more massive structure. The interstitial concept—generated to enable quick, cost-effective modifications of laboratories without any interruptions—does work well, but it is not considered on many projects because of the additional initial construction costs. There may be some savings in construction time and cost, however, if the contractor is knowledgeable about this concept.

Screen walls. Screen walls, which hide the mechanical systems, are constructed on the roof, separate from the building enclosure. The walls can vary in height and design, depending on aesthetic intent. Screen walls provide an affordable option if the short-term budget is more critical than the long-term operational costs. They do, however, allow mechanical equipment to be exposed to the weather, which reduces its life expectancy. In bad weather, it will be difficult for the facility engineers to

maintain the equipment properly. At North Carolina State's Centennial Campus, the lab building is constructed with screen walls that create four boxes along the skyline. The use of screen walls can have a major impact on the massing, image, and cost of the building.

The mechanical space generally takes up 6–14 percent of the total gross square footage of a lab building. (The high end of this range—as much as 14 percent—applies when mechanical equipment is located in the building.) If the building is run off a central plant, then the actual building size can be reduced by approximately 5 percent. Moreover, larger buildings usually have higher design efficiencies.

Expression of exhaust stacks

The design of the exhaust stacks also helps create a lab building's distinctive image. The top of the stacks should be at least 10 ft above the highest point of any other part of the roof to ensure that the exhausted air is pushed high enough and far enough away from any air intake on the building or nearby buildings. The exhaust stacks can be expressed as individual stacks or bundled.

Individual stacks. Several individual stacks can be provided, one for each fume hood in the building. At Massachusetts Institute of Technology Building 68, individual stacks are randomly located, distinguishing the top of the building as it meets the sky. Dedicated fume hood exhaust is also expressed on the exterior of the Pickle Center at the University of Texas in Austin. The stacks are colorfully painted and visible from the highway. The stacks are tall enough that when the air is exhausted it is not pulled back into the air supply system. Individual stacks

▲ *Engineering Graduate Research Center, Centennial Campus, North Carolina State University, Raleigh. Odell & Associates, architect.*

▶ *Individual stacks on the roof distinguish the elevation. MRDC II, Georgia Institute of Technology, Atlanta. Perkins & Will, architect.*

may be required because of the research being conducted and the fume hoods being used. For example, perchloric and radioactive hoods should always have separate, dedicated exhaust stacks. This approach is very safe because it eliminates any chance of cross-contamination between exhausts.

Bundled stacks. Duke University's Levine Center has bundled individual stacks that create a more massive and organized statement compared to the individual stacks at MIT Building 68. A manifolded exhaust system is another common option that is visually expressed as a few large stacks. Vanderbilt University's Chemistry Building has a manifolded exhaust system; the exhausts at the roof are wrapped in curved metal and detailed

◀ *Dedicated stacks bundled together. School of Medicine, Northwestern University, Evanston, Illinois. Perkins & Will, architect.*

as a key exterior design feature. The stacks create a unique identity and landmark for those who use or visit the campus.

A laboratory building's exhaust stacks are often used as a design opportunity to articulate the massing and visually enhance the skyline of the campus. At the University of Illinois Chemical and Life Sciences Building, the exhaust stacks help define the entry to the campus.

Some lab buildings do not have fume hoods or the requirement for exhaust stacks. For example, the Sam Yang Research Facility in Seoul, South Korea, is an electronics lab facility that does not require fume hood exhaust stacks. Some computer lab facilities also do not require exhaust stacks. Yet, as for most lab buildings, the mechanical systems for these facilities are extensive, since spaces filled with computers and other electronic equipment have high heat loads and, therefore, substantial cooling requirements.

▶ Manifold exhaust system creates a landmark. Stevenson Center Complex Chemistry building, Vanderbilt University, Nashville, Tennessee. Payette & Associates, Inc., architect.

▶▶ Exhaust stacks help to define entry to campus. Chemical and Life Sciences Building, University of Illinois, Urbana-Champaign. Perkins & Will, architect.

▼ Computer labs. Sam Yang Research Center, Seoul, South Korea. Perkins & Will, architect.

▲ *Image at night. Glaxo Wellcome headquarters, Stevenage, United Kingdom. Kling Lindquist, architect.*

Image at Night

The image a lab building projects after dark can be very dramatic. Both interior and exterior lighting can play a role in creating the drama. Many researchers work late into the evening, and they and the interior finishes, equipment, and casework can be seen in the labs if the lights are on. If the mechanical piping is exposed in the ceilings, it can also be seen.

BUILDING MASSING

Most lab buildings are massive because of floor-to-floor height, mechanical space, and the exhaust stacks. Most clients try to minimize the massing of a building to relate to the scale of other, nonlaboratory buildings on a campus and to reduce the cost of construction. As a general rule of thumb, an additional foot of floor-to-floor height will increase the total construction cost by approximately 1 percent.

The floor-to-floor height is determined during the schematic design phase because the volume of the building will have cost implications. Most labs range from 14 to 16 ft in floor-to-floor height (at least 2 ft more than a typical office building). If a building has interstitial spaces, the floor-to-floor height can range from 17 to 19 ft. To calculate the floor-to-floor height, the following factors must be estimated and designed:

Ceiling height	9–10 ft
Mechanical systems	3–4 ft
Structural system	±2 ft
Total	14–16 ft

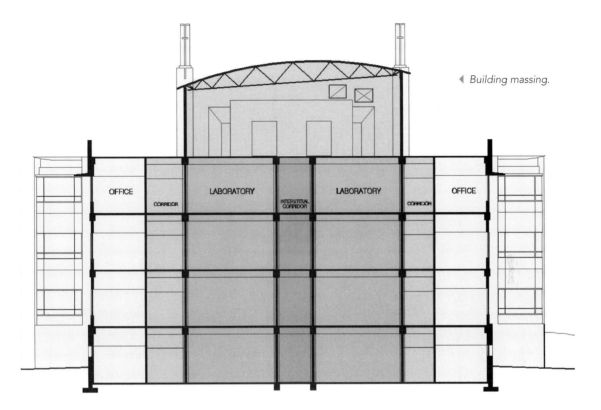

◀ *Building massing.*

It is important to leave some room between the ceiling and the structural beams for head clearance during construction as well as during routine maintenance or renovation. When the supply and exhaust ductwork is being designed, it is important to minimize or, ideally, eliminate the crossing of the supply and exhaust ducts. If the ducts cross one another, the floor-to-floor height may have to be increased or the ceiling height lowered in the labs.

INTERIOR IMAGE

The key interior areas to focus on include the reception and lobby, lounges and break rooms, corridors, elevators and stairs, labs, offices, and office support spaces.

Reception and Lobby

The reception and lobby areas make a statement about the culture of an organization and provide opportunities to welcome workers, visitors, and service staff into the building. The lobby may be a central atrium space that allows people to be seen at multiple floors and gives the building a friendly and open feel. This can become the heart of the building: not just a place where people enter and exit, but a place for meeting and carrying on spontaneous conversations during the day. It may be somewhat informal, with tack boards, display areas, wood wainscot, and built-in window seats.

The photo on page 127 shows the two-story lobby/reception space at Tuft University's Science and Technology Center. This atrium is located in the

▲ *This formal lobby sets a tone and also serves as a security control point. Argon, Chicago, Illinois.*

▶ *The lobby can express the culture of an organization. Physics Building, University of Washington, Seattle.*

◀ *Lobby design that exploits color and variety in materials. Science and Technology Center, Tufts University, Medford, Massachusetts. Cannon (Boston, Massachusetts), architect.*

▶ *Two-story atrium of the Chemical and Life Sciences Building, University of Illinois, Urbana-Champaign. Perkins & Will, architect.*

center of the building; a bridge carries people moving from one side of the building to the other through this space. The use of multiple materials and colors adds visual interest to the space.

Corporate atrium spaces, such as that at the 3M facility in Austin, Texas, shown on page 38, provide opportunities for many people to gather at special events and make an impressive statement about the company. The conference rooms, offices, laboratories, and corridors are adjacent to the atrium. Individuals in the atrium are able to see people at multiple levels of the facility.

An atrium can become the main showpiece for a facility—an inviting entry, a main circulation hub, and a great space for large gatherings. Data ports should be provided to allow for the use of computers in this area.

Lounges and Break Rooms

Lounges and break rooms are also important common amenities. It must be decided early in the design of a new facility whether to have a lounge or break room on each floor or a single such amenity, in one central location, for the entire building. Either approach may work, depending on the culture of the researchers and how the entire building is designed.

In a large facility, it may be desirable to provide small break rooms—suitable for local copying, office supplies, and coffee-makers—in the office areas themselves. The size of such rooms generally ranges from 80 to 100 net sq ft (NSF).

Corridors

Corridors are key elements in the organization of a laboratory facility. In the ceilings of a corridor are the ducts,

piping, and wires for the mechanical, electrical, and plumbing systems. The ceiling should allow easy access, without having to disturb laboratory activities, to the facility staff who maintain and operate the building.

A lay-in ceiling costs about the same as an exposed ceiling with painted piping. The choice between a lay-in ceiling or no ceiling comes down to two issues: What is the desired look of the corridor? Will the building be easier to maintain without the ceiling?

Corridors also offer opportunities for people to see one another and exchange ideas. Some corridors provide a "tour route," allowing guests to view the labs safely without interrupting the activities within. The tour route generally is along the outside wall of the first floor, with views to some interior labs and the exterior campus, or at one end of the building on all floors. At the 3M facility in Austin, there are display areas along the tour route showing the history of the company and the products it has developed. Boards and displays with information about the company, the campus, or the type of research being conducted are usually part of a tour route. A variety of boards and graphics can enhance communication and interaction and add to the image of the facility.

Public corridors should be well lit to allow people to read the information located along the walls. Different colors and patterns can the used on the floor and walls. Marker boards and tack boards can provide additional opportunities for people to share information and work with one another. The doors from the labs should be recessed to prevent their swinging into the path of a passerby.

▲ Tour route. 3M. Austin, Texas. HOK, architect.

▶ A variety of boards are located along the public corridors. Levine Center, Duke University, Durham, North Carolina. Payette & Associates, Inc., architect.

Seating areas can be created adjacent to or at the end of a corridor to provide opportunities for people to talk with one another outside the lab area. Seating along the corridor is very important in most academic buildings, as it provides a place for students to wait between classes.

The office corridors also allow people to walk by, stop in, and talk. Studies have shown that the probability of once-a-week communication between researchers drops to less than 5 percent when their offices are located more than 100 ft apart.

Service corridors usually provide all the engineering services to the labs. Equipment and gas cylinders can also be located in a service corridor. If the service corridor is at least 10 ft wide, both walls can be used for storage of equipment and supplies. Some institutions use this space as an "equipment corridor" to help improve the efficiency of their buildings, to keep noisy equipment out of the labs, and to take advantage of the wall space in the corridor.

See the examples of lab corridors opposite and above. The most successful lab corridors have interior glazing, provide places to sit, are well lit, include information boards, and are finished with a variety of colors and materials.

The corridors, stairs, and elevators, which together make up the public circulation system in a building, should all be easy to find and should allow for convenient, pleasant, circulation.

▲ Public corridors with views to the exterior and a place to sit. Stevenson Center Complex Chemistry Building, Vanderbilt University, Nashville, Tennessee. Payette Associates, Inc., architect.

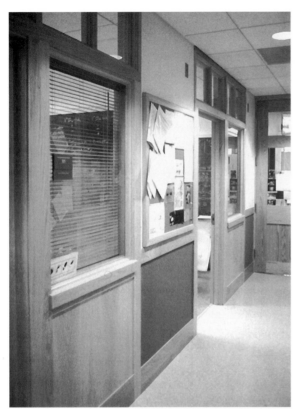

▲ Office corridor with multiple colors and materials is visually appealing. Lewis Thomas Laboratories, Princeton University, Princeton, New Jersey. Venturi Scott Brown with Payette & Associates, Inc., architect.

◤ Service corridor with direct access to utilities. Manufacturing Related Disciplines Complex, Phase II, Georgia Institute of Technology, Atlanta. Perkins & Will, architect.

▶ Interior glazing allows views through to the outside. Technology Enhanced Learning Center, State University of West Georgia, Carrolton. Perkins & Will, architect.

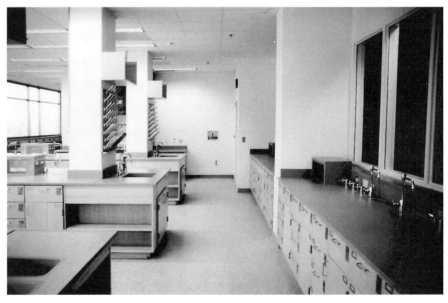

◀ *Stairs next to the elevator encourage more people to use them. 3M, Austin, Texas. HOK, architect.*

Elevators and Stairs

The elevators should be located in highly visible areas and along the main corridors for easy wayfinding. Some buildings may have one elevator that is used to carry both materials and people. Most laboratory buildings, however, need at least one

▼ Fire shutter to cover the glass is required by fire codes. Boyer Center for Molecular Medicine, Yale University, New Haven, Connecticut. Cesar Pelli & Associates, architect.

passenger elevator and one freight elevator. The passenger elevator should be located near the main entrance and reception area. It is a good idea to have an architectural stair near the elevator in case the elevator is broken, and to encourage people to use the stair. The freight elevator is typically located adjacent to the other elevator(s) for cost and efficiency, or separately, near the loading dock. Keeping the freight elevator separate can help ensure that a building is secure and safe. The freight elevator can be controlled by a security access card and used only for transporting materials, supplies, or equipment. A separate freight elevator is usually located in an area away from the main pedestrian traffic in the building.

Stairs offer another great opportunity for people to meet one another serendipitously. Wide stairways make it easy to get from one floor to another. There should be a communicating stair that leads a person from the main lobby to the upper floors of the building. These stairs are usually detailed and well finished to enhance the entire lobby space. Stairs also allow people to see others on different floors.

Fire stairs must be located within a certain distance from each other, usually less than 300 ft if the building is fully equipped with sprinklers. The stairs should be highly visible, for wayfinding and for security, and should be located along the outside wall to allow for exterior glazing. The glass will allow people to see one another, which should make for a safer building and campus, especially at night. Fire stairs should be wider than the minimum standards required by the building codes, allowing two people to walk up and down the stairs at the same time.

The design team for Yale University's Boyer Center made a utilitarian fire stair a design feature of the building—with wood, metal, and tile finishes; a window seat; natural daylight; and views to the exterior. With interior glazing, the fire stair is also visible and inviting from the main corridor. A fire shutter automatically drops from the ceiling to cover the glass in case of a fire. Although the shutters cost about $5,000 per floor, their use allowed the fire stair to become one of the building's most successful design elements.

Labs

The image and quality of the lab are among the most important issues to the end users. The use of materials, type of casework, color scheme, natural lighting, interior glazing, light fixtures, space for equipment, and efficiency are the key issues to study.

Beyond accommodating the specific needs of the current research team, casework should be flexible for future researchers. How much casework to buy initially is an important question. The ratio of fixed to mobile casework must be evaluated. Some casework should be capable of being adjusted vertically. The researchers should be given an opportunity to review the layout and specific design of each type of casework to ensure that money is being well spent. As discussed in chapter 1, mobile casework is becoming very popular for many types of labs today, reducing the need for fixed casework.

Lab layouts can be organized with modular casework. Color—in floor tile patterns and along the wall—is a very affordable design element that can have a dramatic impact on the visual image of

each lab and of the entire building. The color and finish of the casework is also an important part of the visual imagery. Casework and countertop colors should complement those of the walls, floor, and ceiling.

▼ Casework that can be adjusted vertically. Chemistry addition, University of Virginia, Charlottesville. Ellenzweig & Associates, architects.

▶ *Tables move easily. Engineering Graduate Research Center, North Carolina State University, Raleigh. Odell & Associates, architect.*

▼ *Three ft modular works well, especially with knee spaces.*

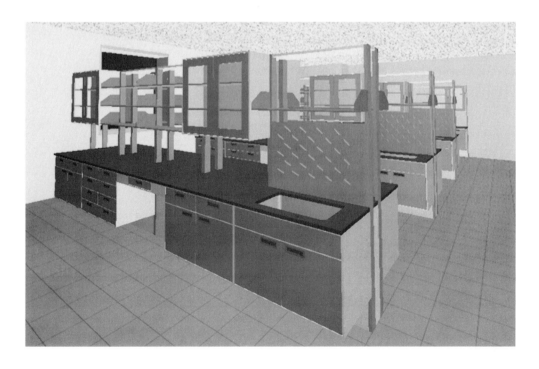

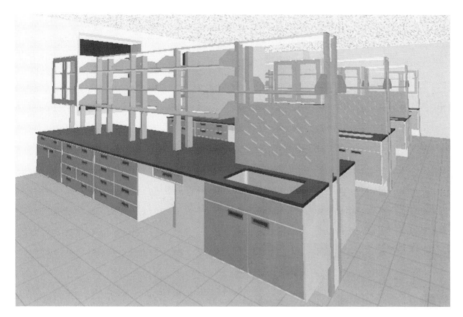

◀ Casework and knee space can easily change.

▼ Different materials in a lab. Courtesy Fisher Hamilton.

▼ This lab has an excellent view of its environs. Storm Eye Institute. Medical University of South Carolina, Charleston. LS3P Associates, Ltd., architect.

Regarding materials used in the lab, the most important issue is the choice of material for the casework (metal, wood, plastic, or a combination of wood and metal). Chemical-resistant tops and stainless-steel counters can present very strong images.

Whenever possible, allowing natural daylight into the labs will improve the image and quality of each space. Where there are panoramic views to the exterior, designers should take full advantage of them by locating appropriate labs and offices along the outside walls. Interior glazing allows people to see other people. And light will be filtered through the building, making a more pleasant research environment. The design and location of light fixtures can add to the overall quality of the space so long as glare is controlled and there are clear brightness-contrast ratios and accurate color rendition.

Space for equipment must be coordinated with the design of the entire lab and the location of the case-work. Some equipment is tall and will block views. When the equipment is located along one wall or in separate rooms, the labs can be left more open and visible. It is extremely important to create efficient bench space, casework, and places for storage throughout each lab. Efficiency is the basic idea behind the concept of the lab module; modules are meant to create as much space for research as needed and an appropriate amount of space for cir-culation. Today and in the future, labs will be designed and used to take advantage of the volume of space. Storage is critical in most labs. Shelving and cabinets above the benches must be fully coordinated to use the volume of the space as efficiently as possible. In locating storage high above the benches, the requirement for sprin-klers must be taken into account. Using the wall space efficiently is another option. Many researchers would rather have wall space for storage or the placement of equipment, instead of glazing, to better use the full volume of space in their labs.

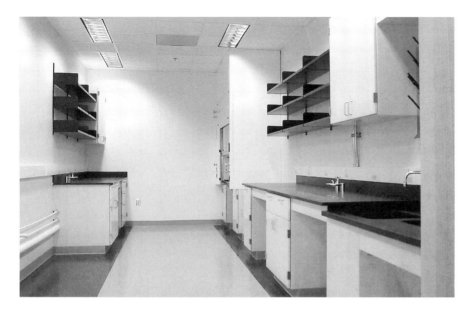

◀ Equipment space. Manufacturing Related Disciplines Complex, Phase II, Georgia Institute of Technology, Atlanta. Perkins & Will, architect.

▼ The size and image of an office is very important. Biochemistry Building, University of Wisconsin, Madison. Flad & Associates, Inc., architect. Photo by Christopher Barrett, Hedrich Blessing.

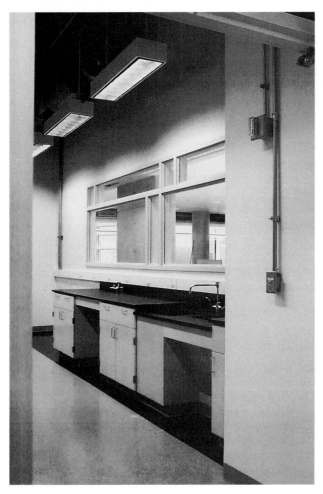

▲ Location of light fixtures in relation to casework. Manufacturing Related Disciplines Complex, Phase II, Georgia Institute of Technology, Atlanta. Perkins & Will, architect.

▶ Office prototypes.

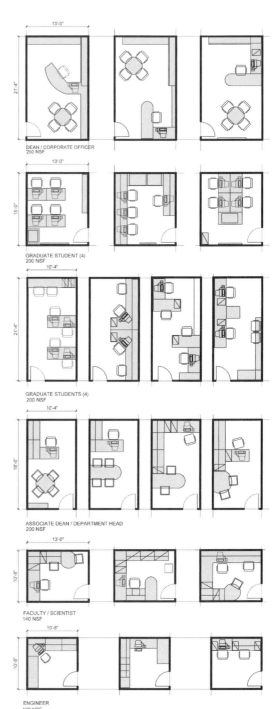

DEAN / CORPORATE OFFICER
250 NSF

GRADUATE STUDENT (4)
200 NSF

GRADUATE STUDENTS (4)
200 NSF

ASSOCIATE DEAN / DEPARTMENT HEAD
200 NSF

FACULTY / SCIENTIST
140 NSF

ENGINEER
100 NSF

Offices

Researchers spend approximately half of their time in the lab and the other half in their offices. Offices can get cluttered very quickly, and designing a visually successful office therefore not only involves the quality and quantity of furniture and the amount of glazing, but also space-related issues such as the ability to work on a computer and to meet with other people comfortably, and the amount of shelving and other storage.

Several organizations publish office size standards. Most offices fall in the range of 100–200 NSF. In the future, offices may have to be larger to allow space for computers and support equipment. But there is also a trend toward smaller offices. A *USA Today* article of December 7, 1998, reported, "The International Facility Management Association reports that the average office space middle managers got was 151 sq ft in 1994. Today, they have 142 sq ft. Senior professionals today get 114 sq ft, about the size of a walk-in closet."

Space Allocations for Office Support

For conference and seminar rooms, allow 150 NSF for 6 or fewer people, 20 NSF per person for capacities of 6–20, and 18 NSF per person for capacities of 20–30. Room sizes may have to be increased if rooms are used for extensive audiovisual presentations.

For a mail room allow 100 NSF per mail room supervisor. Increase the space if the mail-room will house the central copier and duplicating equipment.

ADJACENCIES

The relationship of the labs, offices, and corridor will have a significant impact on the image and operations of the building. The first question must be: Do the end users want a view from their labs to the exterior, or will the labs be located on the interior, with wall space used for casework and equipment? Some researchers do not want or cannot have natural light in their research spaces. Special instruments and equipment, such as nuclear magnetic resonance (NMR) apparatus, electron microscopes, and lasers (to name a few), cannot function properly in natural light. Natural daylight is not desired in vivarium facilities or in some support spaces, so these are located in the interior of the building.

Corridors

There are three basic ways to organize adjacencies with corridors:

- Single corridor
- Two-corridor arrangement
- Three-corridor arrangement

Each has advantages and disadvantages, and there are a number of options to explore with each. Note that there are many possible variations on the options given on the following pages.

Single corridors

Most single corridors are located in the middle of the building, with little or no daylight coming into the space. Whenever possible, interior walls should be glazed or lounges created along the outside wall to allow natural light into the corridor. It is usually preferable to have a view open to the exterior from the corridor—either at the end or somewhere along it—where an open, shared space is created. A view helps to orient people as they walk along a corridor.

▲ *Daylight is not desirable for some support spaces. Chemistry Building, Stevenson Center Complex, Vanderbilt University. Payette & Associates, Inc., architect.*

Advantages

With a single corridor, the building net-to-gross ratio is usually 60 percent or greater. One corridor provides better opportunities for communication by creating a "main street."

Disadvantages

A single-corridor approach may not meet program needs for the labs and offices or building operations. Usually, a single corridor limits the width of the building, in turn limiting floor-plan design. Some labs may need to be interior, without any natural light, which may be difficult to achieve with the single-corridor design.

Options

Labs and offices adjacent to each other. The researcher has access from his or her office directly into the lab. The office is also directly off the corridor to allow easy exiting in case of emergency. The offices will not have direct views to the exterior unless the walls between the lab and office have glazing. To get into the main lab, it will be necessary to enter through the office or lab support area (Option 1A, opposite).

Labs on one wing with offices at the end or in the middle. The office-cluster arrangement creates a sense of neighborhood, encouraging researchers to talk with one another on a daily basis. The offices are located within a short

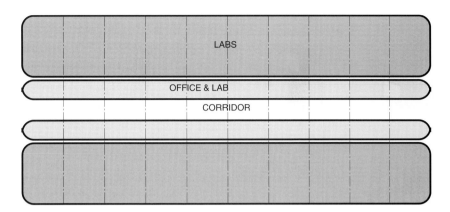

▶ *Option 1A.*

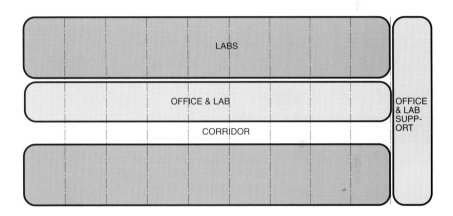

▶ *Option 1B.*

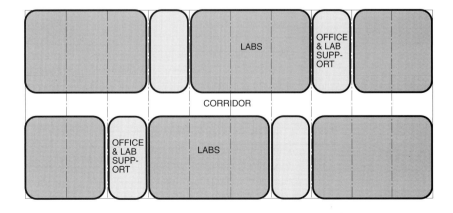

▶ *Option 1C.*

walk of the generic labs, which have internal doors connecting each to adjacent labs. The easy accessibility from one lab to another provides another opportunity for researchers to talk and work together. This is a typical single-corridor scheme (Option 1B).

Office clusters access main labs directly. Teams of researchers are organized in office clusters that can open directly into labs and exit corridors. Interior glazing allows researchers to oversee their lab spaces from their offices. Locating offices directly next to and immediately accessible to the labs is preferred by most researchers but is more costly than locating the offices in a central area (Option 1C).

Two-corridor arrangements

Two-corridor ("racetrack") arrangements are usually developed to create larger, wider floor plans than are possible with the single-corridor approach. More lab buildings are constructed with a two-corridor layout than with either a single- or three-corridor arrangement.

Advantages

The building has a wider floor plan. Two corridors allow for labs to be designed back-to-back. There are many layout options. Labs can be located on the interior or exterior. The building can also allow for "ghost corridors," which permit a person to walk from one lab to another without having to go out into a separate corridor. (The ghost corridor is walkway area through each lab that connects with a door allowing movement from one lab to another. Ghost corridors, which are used as a second means of egress, are more common in large open labs or in labs where security is not so much of a

concern because the researchers know one another. Ghost corridors improve a building's efficiency and cost-effectiveness, and a ghost corridor usually means that a second, separate public corridor will not be necessary.)

Disadvantages

The two-corridor plan separates people by creating a building with "two sides." This concept is approximately 5 percent less efficient (more costly) than a single-corridor arrangement.

Some open labs have a ghost corridor design that allows a person to walk through the lab to get to another part of the building. This can be a very efficient and cost-effective concept if the end users can work with others coming through their lab spaces. Security may, however, be a concern to some researchers.

Options

Offices on the outside and labs at the interior. Researchers can be located in office clusters across from their labs and have views to the exterior. The labs are internal, with wall space that can be used for storage or interior glazing. The corridor along the outside wall provides views and natural light for everyone. With this concept, the main labs and support labs can easily be reconfigured as one large lab area (Option 2A, page 146).

Labs and offices on the outside, lab support on the interior. The main labs and offices have views to the exterior, but the offices are separated somewhat from the main labs by the centrally located support labs. The lab support area will work well for research that cannot have natural light coming into the space (Option 2B).

Office clusters adjacent to main labs along

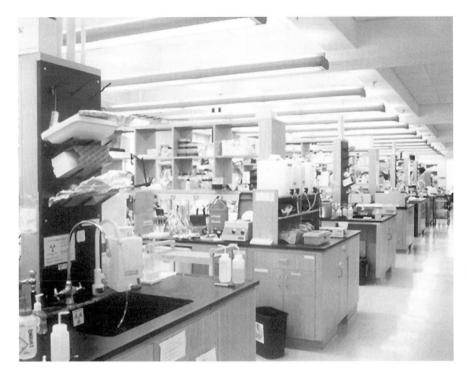

◀ An example of a ghost corridor design. Lewis Thomas Laboratories, Princeton University, Princeton, New Jersey. Venturi Scott Brown with Payette & Associates Inc., architect.

the outside walls, with the lab support located on the interior. This concept is very functional and is desired by many researchers, but cost may be a problem. The operations of most research teams should work well with this design. The entire building will have to be designed for laboratory construction, which is the most costly approach (Option 2C).

Office clusters along one outside wall, main labs along the other outside wall, and some main labs with lab support located in the interior. This approach is similar to Option 2B, except that the building is wider to allow for the typical main labs to be in the center and to locate the offices in clusters. A wider building is more efficient because there is more net usable space with the same corridor arrangement. This option is more cost-effective than 2C, because all the offices are located on one side of the

building. The mechanical systems can be designed for lab and office construction, which is more cost-effective (Option 2D).

Offices at one end of the building, with labs located in a "lab wing." This arrangement is similar to Option 2D. In both cases, the separation of office and lab space allows the office space to be constructed as office construction, saving money on the project. Despite its cost-effectiveness, however, this approach has two disadvantages: (1) some researchers may not be satisfied if labs and offices are not adjacent, and (2) the office space will be expensive to renovate as wet lab space if desired in the future (Option 2E).

Three-corridor arrangements

The three-corridor concept provides a public racetrack corridor around the outside and a central service corridor.

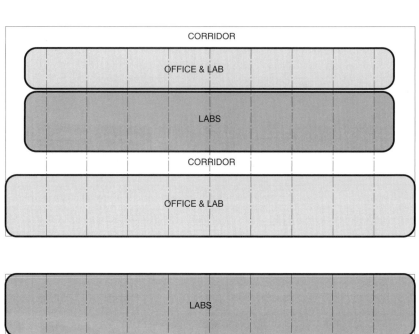

▶ *Option 2A.*

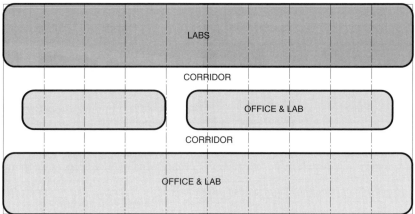

▶ *Option 2B.*

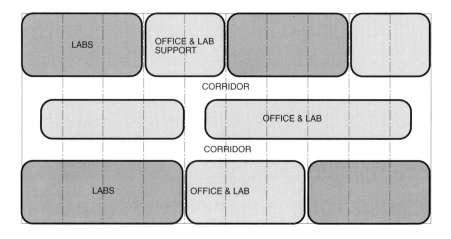

▶ *Option 2C.*

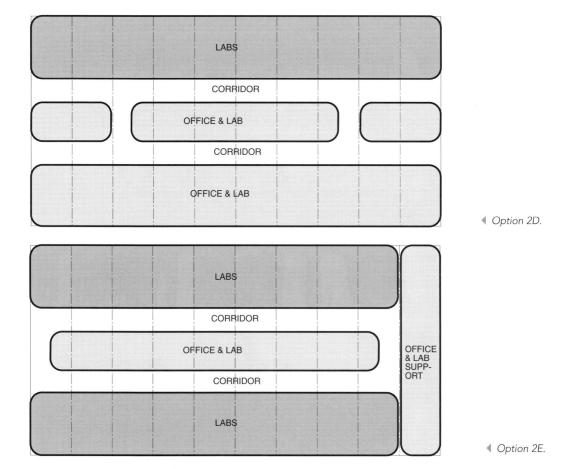

◀ Option 2D.

◀ Option 2E.

Advantages

The three-corridor plan includes a central service area that can be accessible only to maintenance people or can allow researchers to have access to most of the engineering services. The central service corridor can be used as a shared "equipment corridor." The three-corridor plan can be used to create a "clean and dirty" arrangement.

Disadvantages

This is the least efficient and most expensive corridor arrangement. The three-corridor layout is approximately 10 percent less efficient than a single-corridor design and 5 percent less efficient than the two-corridor scheme.

Options

Offices on the outside walls, the people corridor on both sides of the building, and a service corridor in the middle. Offices at the end can be used for shared administrative purposes. Clustered offices for the research teams are adjacent to their labs. All labs are internal; the main labs and lab support spaces are interchangeable and have direct access to the service corridor (Option 3A).

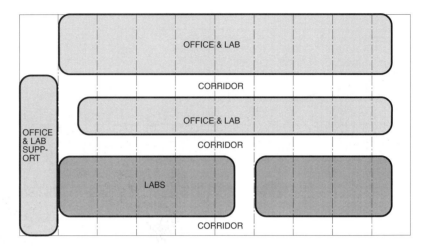

▶ *Option 3A.*

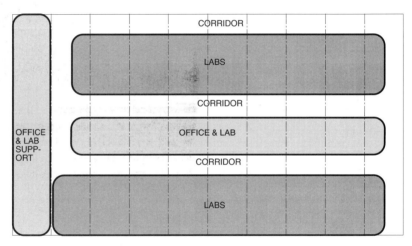

▶ *Option 3B.*

People corridor located on both sides of the building, labs and offices on the interior, with the service corridor in the middle between labs. The service corridor can be accessed from two-thirds of the labs. This scheme provides a choice by locating a third of the labs with direct views to the exterior (Option 3B).

Open versus Closed Plans

For laboratory space planning there are two basic options: the open plan and the closed plan. The open plan reduces construction costs because it requires

fewer walls and doors, improves square-footage efficiency, and accommodates more casework and equipment in the lab. The open lab and its usefulness for team-based research are discussed in more detail in chapter 1.

The closed plan allows for tighter security; allows for private, individual research; and addresses containment issues better than an open lab.

The image of the lab building differs significantly depending on whether an open or closed lab plan is used. The open lab is more visible, and the size of the room is much larger. The individual closed plan can be similar to an open lab plan if much of the interior wall space incorporates interior glazing, but in many cases this is not possible because the walls are needed for casework, shelving, and equipment. (Interior glazing also adds to construction costs.) When closed labs have solid walls, then the spaces are smaller and it is more difficult for people to see one another and, possibly, harder for them to meet for informal exchanges of information.

Write-up Areas

In addition to researchers' offices, most facilities have write-up areas within or immediately adjacent to the lab. The decision regarding where to locate write-up areas is based on four key design issues:

1. Should the write-up area be in the lab?

2. Should the write-up area be on the outside wall to allow people to enjoy the views to the exterior?

3. Should the most dangerous elements (fume hoods) be located on the outside wall and the least dangerous elements (write-up areas) be located near the entry to the lab?

4. Should the write-up area be adjacent to the lab for safety reasons, with direct access to the labs?

For safety reasons, always avoid placing a write-up station behind or near a fume hood. Options for the location of write-up areas include the following:

Along the outside wall. Desks are located perpendicular to the exterior wall, are near windows, and are directly adjacent to the laboratory bench. Researchers sit back-to-back in a low-traffic area, have direct access to natural light and a view, and claim the adjacent fixed laboratory bench

as their own. Fume hoods should be located in alcoves along the corridor wall.

At the end of the bench. Desks are located at the far end of a peninsula lab bench, away from the exterior wall with windows. If write-up areas are at the end of the bench, fume hoods should be located in a separate room or in an alcove along the corridor wall. The peninsula will create dead ends and will not allow people to circulate around the casework.

Interior remote clustered desks. Desks can be clustered in an area exterior to the

▼ *Write-up area separate from casework along outside wall.*

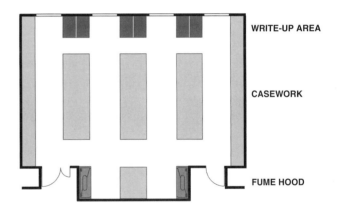

WRITE-UP AREA

CASEWORK

FUME HOOD

▼ *Write-up area at end of casework along outside wall.*

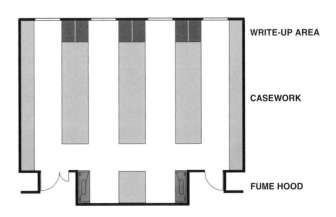

WRITE-UP AREA

CASEWORK

FUME HOOD

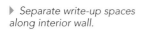

▶ *Separate write-up spaces along interior wall.*

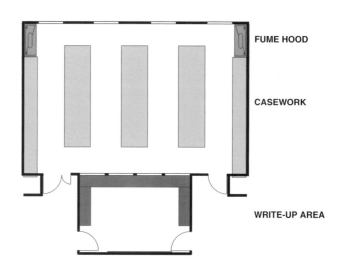

FUME HOOD

CASEWORK

WRITE-UP AREA

▶ *Separate write-up area along outside wall and adjacent to lab.*

WRITE-UP AREA

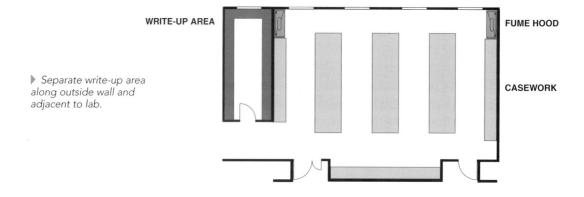

FUME HOOD

CASEWORK

▶ *Write-up area along corridor wall.*

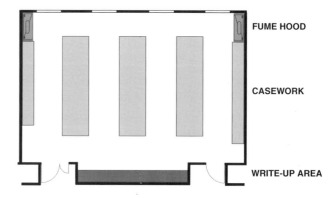

FUME HOOD

CASEWORK

WRITE-UP AREA

laboratory. This scheme can provide the maximum degree of safety, because the desks are not located within the laboratory. Fume hoods are located along the outside wall, as far as possible from the write-up areas.

Perimeter remote clustered desks. This option provides alternating laboratory and office zones along the perimeter of the building. Researchers are afforded natural light and a view to the exterior. This is a very safe arrangement because the desks are not located within the laboratory.

Along the corridor. Locating the write-up area near the entry alcove and along the corridor wall is a common approach in laboratory design. The greatest hazards are farthest from the door (fume hoods), and the safest areas (write-up spaces) are closest to the door. Above the desk can be a solid wall with shelving or interior glazing to allow people to see into the lab.

INTERIOR FINISHES

Floors
There are a variety of floor finishes for labs. To find the most appropriate floor finish, various finishes should be compared for durability, chemical resistance, cost, and aesthetics.

Exposed concrete
Exposed concrete is a very durable, inexpensive floor finish and reasonably easy to clean. Its disadvantages include poor chemical resistance and the fact that it is uncomfortable to walk on and not very attractive.

Resilient tile (vinyl composite tile)
Vinyl composite tile (VCT) is cost-effective, durable, reasonably easy to clean, easy to replace, pleasing to look at, and somewhat comfortable to walk on. Its

disadvantages include the fact that its chemical resistance is only fair, and a VCT floor has many joints where bacteria can collect.

Resilient sheet vinyl
This flooring is durable, easy to clean, comfortable to walk on, and aesthetically pleasing. Chemical resistance is good, and there are fewer joints than with tile flooring. Its chief disadvantages are its high cost (160–180 percent more than resilient tile) and the fact that it is difficult to repair.

Troweled epoxy
Troweled epoxy provides excellent resistance against chemicals, is durable, and is easy to clean. Disadvantages include cost (more than 4 times the cost of resilient tile and 2.5 times more than sheet vinyl), limited color options, and difficulty of repair.

Carpet
Carpeting is an excellent floor finish for offices, large lecture halls, and common areas, but it is inappropriate for wet laboratories because of chemical spills and because bacteria may grow in the carpet.

Walls
Lab walls are typically constructed of gypsum wallboard and usually painted with an epoxy finish. Corners may need wood or metal corner guards to protect them from scrapes when carts and equipment are being moved. A wall along a corridor may also require a chair rail or bumper guard.

Ceilings
Ceilings either have lay-in ceiling tile or are open to the structure and mechanical systems. If the mechanical systems are exposed, acoustical liners should be used

to minimize the noise from the air flowing through the ductwork, and the pipes should be painted. With a sufficient number of air changes flowing through the room, little or no dust is likely to collect on the pipes.

ACOUSTICAL ISSUES

Acoustical issues are fairly common in most labs. Noise problems typically occur because the mechanical supply and exhaust ducts are too loud, the equipment generates a significant amount of noise, or the room surfaces are very hard and bounce the noise around the space. Noise problems with ductwork are usually the result of too much air being moved through the ducts or the lack of sound attenuators in the ductwork. When the equipment is too loud, the noise can be minimized by locating the equipment in a separate room.

Finishes for the lab floor and walls are typically hard surfaces for ease of maintenance, and there really is not anything that can be done with these surfaces to mitigate noise. Insulation can be provided in the walls and above the ceiling to reduce the amount of noise transmitted from one room to another. There are a few acoustical design options for ceilings. A ceiling can be constructed of acoustical tile. If there is no lay-in ceiling and the piping and structure are exposed, acoustical baffles can be placed up in the space. However, there are two problems with acoustical baffles: additional cost and a surface that can be easily contaminated.

The following are the recommended noise criteria (NC) for laboratory spaces:

Space	NC Level
Auditorium	20–25
Conference room	25–30
Classroom	30–35
Open plan offices	35–45
Office	40
Lobby	40
Research laboratories	40–45
Corridors	45

CASEWORK

The casework plays a large role in creating a lab's image. A lab that has just been completed—before researchers move in—has a completely different image than a lab that is in full use.

Types of Casework

There are four basic types of casework:

- Fixed casework
- Hung casework
- Cantilevered casework
- Mobile casework

Fixed casework

Fixed casework is a conventional arrangement in which base cabinets support countertops and the base cabinets are mounted on the wall. Base cabinets are typically 22 in. deep, countertops 30 in. deep. The countertop has a 1 in. overhang along the front and a 7 in. space along the back to run all the utility services.

Advantages

This is the most affordable casework based on initial costs, because the system is the easiest to build and has the fewest parts.

Disadvantages

The system is not very flexible, because the casework is attached to the wall,

◀ New, unoccupied lab with ample space. Hollins Cancer Center, Medical University of South Carolina, Charleston.

▼ The same space as a working lab, with every inch of space used. Hollins Cancer Center, Medical University of South Carolina, Charleston.

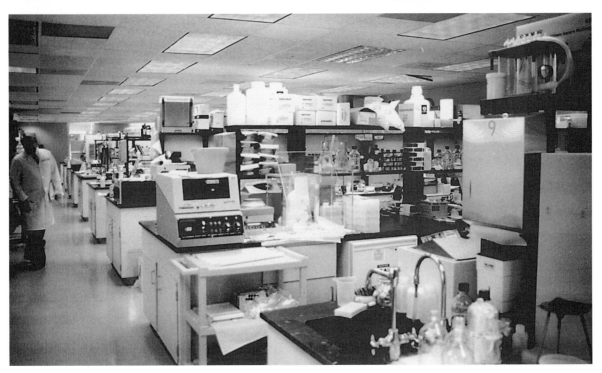

*Fixed casework.
Glaxo Wellcome
Headquarters,
Stevenage, United
Kingdom. Kling
Lindquist, architect.*

▶ *Hung casework.*

utilities, and countertop. To renovate such a casework system, the lab must be shut down. Renovation costs include lost research time as well as contractors' costs.

Hung casework

In a hung casework system the cabinets and countertops are hung from a rail that is attached to the wall. Because the countertop is supported by the rail instead of the base cabinets, individual cabinets can be relocated without affecting the rest of the casework system.

Advantages

This system is flexible, because the countertops and cabinets are independent of the utilities and can be easily detached from the structural rail system. Base cabinets on wheels or with leveling feet can be easily moved.

Disadvantages

Hung casework can cost 5–10 percent more than fixed casework. Because this type of system is mounted on a wall, there may be some concern if it holds instruments sensitive to vibration.

Cantilevered casework

Cantilevered casework is designed as a self-supporting system separate from the wall system and utilities.

Advantages

The casework can easily be moved, and in some cases researchers can relocate it by themselves. With the use of this type of casework, floors are easier to maintain and bacteria is not likely to collect under the casework.

Disadvantages

This casework can cost up to 20 percent more than fixed casework and may have 20 percent less storage capacity.

Mobile casework

Mobile casework includes tables, carts, and casework on wheels. The mobile casework should conform to the same module (usually 3 ft to coordinate with knee space) as the fixed casework.

Advantages

This type of casework provides some flexibility for the end users to create and change their own lab spaces. The inventory of mobile casework can easily be moved from one place to another. Many tables, carts, and casework items can be adjusted vertically to be more ergonomically correct. Long-term operational costs can be reduced.

Disadvantages

The initial cost of mobile casework is higher than fixed casework. Mobile casework may create some management problems, especially if it is placed in front of doors or aisles, jeopardizing safety.

Many labs combine fixed casework with movable casework such as carts, write-up stations, tables, and storage cabinets. This approach allows the researcher some flexibility with more affordable casework. Such a combined system allows a lab to be designed to meet researchers' exact needs and even reconfigured in the future with very little cost or effort. Flexible furniture systems work well alone; they can also be paired with fixed base cabinets to increase lab capacity.

Casework Material Selection

Wood is the most popular casework material for academic environments, primarily because of its appearance. Wood performs well with moderate chemical usage and is easy to repair. Wood construction is available with flush or standard pulls and a wide array of

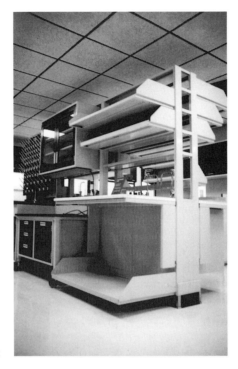

◀ *Cantilevered casework.*

▼ *Tables that can easily be moved and shelves that can be adjusted. Technology Enhanced Learning Center, State University of West Georgia, Carrolton. Perkins & Will, architect.*

finishes to provide just the right look for a unique laboratory setting. Wood is quieter than metal cabinetry and is usually easy to repair. There are some drawbacks to wood casework: it is flammable and may warp

▲ Fixed and mobile casework. Technology Enhanced Learning Center, State University of West Georgia,.Carrolton. Perkins & Will, architect.

because of water or chemical absorption.

Highly resistant to chemicals and abuse, steel casework has long been the material of choice in laboratory environments where spills, corrosive agents, and heavy use are common. One concern with metal is that it will corrode. Metal casework is easy to dent, noisier in use than other materials, and usually more difficult to repair than wood.

The costs of metal and wood cabinets are quite similar and vary slightly depending on the manufacturer and the demand.

Plastic laminate should not be used in most labs because water and chemicals can easily damage it. The short-term cost of plastic laminate is a little less than that of metal or wood, but because it will have to be replaced much sooner, it will eventually cost more. In specifying casework, it is important to make sure that the base cabinets have removable back panels to allow access to the utility services. Security panels between drawers—which prevent someone from gaining access by removing the drawer above—may be advisable.

The selection of sink material depends

on the work surface selected. For example, epoxy resin sinks can be used only with epoxy resin work surfaces and stainless-steel drop-in style sinks can be used only with plastic laminate or Chemsurf work surfaces. Drain and trap materials must also be chosen carefully; they must be suitable to the application and comply with the applicable codes. One-piece cast epoxy resin sinks are highly resistant to acids, solvents, and salts. Single- and double-compartment stainless-steel sinks feature polished, sound-deadened interiors and include an integral back ledge to accommodate deck-mounted fixtures. One-piece polyolefin sinks, molded from specifically selected resins, offer physical strength (making them long-lasting) and resiliency (reducing glassware breakage). The casework should include, at the sinks, a paper towel dispenser and a pegboard that allows glassware to dry.

ERGONOMICS

To ensure workers' comfort it is important to keep in mind that people are of different shapes and sizes, vary in age, and are likely to have a range of physical requirements. Ergonomic designs take these facts into consideration, allowing employees to be comfortable while using equipment, tools, and materials. When offices and laboratories are more comfortable, they are usually more productive.

The *work zone* is defined as the work surface area available when the user's forearms are resting on the countertop. A large, effective work zone allows the user to access and manipulate more laboratory material in the cabinet. The ability to rest forearms minimizes reaching and reduces strain on the arms, shoulders, and neck.

Cool white fluorescent lighting reduces glare in the work zone, creating less eye fatigue during long work periods.

A fixed work-surface height of 30 in. can reasonably accommodate a person who is less than 6 ft 2 in. in height, sitting in a laboratory chair at a biological safety cabinet.

An ergonomically designed laboratory chair should have a star-based platform, five casters that lock when the chair is occupied, an adjustable back support, and an adjustable lumbar support; and it should be adjustable to move to different height requirements. A built-in adjustable footrest is also recommended. A properly designed chair should minimize muscle activity to maintain posture and reduce pressure on the spine, which could lead to disc injuries. Chairs must allow for changes in body position. The user should be able to adjust the chair's height to varying work surfaces.

Classroom chairs, too, should be ergonomically designed and possess the following attributes:

- Adjustable height (preferably pneumatic). Ease of adjustment ensures that students can assume and retain proper posture.

- Back tilt. This useful feature enables students to adjust eye-to-monitor distance.

- A broad seat and back design, providing adequate comfort with minimal sculpting. This design meets the needs of a large number of users. Although lumbar support and forward-tilt functions may be a necessity in the office, in the classroom it is more important to make users comfortable for the duration of the class.

Electrically adjustable workstations offer pushbutton up-down height adjustment, enabling researchers to sit or stand comfortably while working, as well as wheelchair accessibility and support for heavy monitors and large digitizing pads.

FUME HOODS

A fume hood, the prime protection device in a laboratory, should be used when a researcher is:

- Working with chemicals known or suspected to be hazardous

- Working with unknown substances

- Pouring, mixing, weighing, or dispensing chemicals

On the simplest level, a fume hood can be understood as a box and a blower. Fumes generated in the box are pulled away by the blower and safely dispersed into the atmosphere, thus protecting the worker.

▼ Air flow through fume hood. Courtesy Fisher Hamilton.

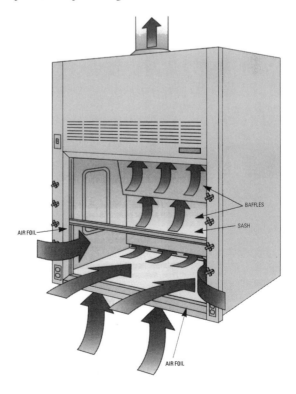

157

To minimize risk in the event of an explosion, hoods should be located on outside walls whenever possible. Standard sizes are 4 ft, 5 ft, 6 ft, and 8 ft for hoods that are 2 ft 6 in. deep. If fume hoods are located on an outside wall, the write-up stations should be along the inside corridor wall, preferably with interior glazing. If it is preferred to have write-up stations along the outside walls, for views to the campus, then the fume hoods should be located along the interior wall in alcoves. If the labs are located internally rather than along the outside wall, then the fume hoods should be situated in a remote location farthest from the door. The write-up stations should be adjacent to the entry, along the corridor wall, preferably with interior glazing.

Special Types of Hoods

Perchloric acid hoods

A perchloric hood is similar to a standard fume hood but is designed specifically for perchloric acid, with a stainless steel interior. The acid can be explosive if it is combined with organic chemicals and condenses in the exhaust system. To prevent such problems, the hood is designed with a wash-down mechanism for the exhaust system, which should be employed after each use. A shutoff valve and trough allow for the wash-down. The hood should be prominently labeled with a sign that states, "Perchloric Acid Work Only." The exhaust will require a dedicated duct and fan constructed of stainless steel. The duct should have no horizontal runs and should go from the hood directly to the fan and exhaust stack at the roof. The duct

sections should be heliarc welded to prevent leakage of the perchloric acid. The hood should be built with an integral liner of a single piece of stainless steel, such as 316 stainless. The liner should have coved corners (continuous, without joints) and as few joints as possible. Lights inside the hood must be explosion-proof.

Radioisotope hoods

Radioisotope fume hoods are designed to minimize risk to the researcher. The liner is a single piece of stainless steel, which must be seamless for purging radioisotopes. There are a variety of exhaust filters to choose from. When there are very high levels of radioactive materials being used at a hood, a HEPA filter may be necessary. The filter should be located at the portal of the hood, and a device to monitor the air velocity through the face of the hood should be installed. Because it must support lead shielding, the base cabinet of a radioisotope fume hood may have to be stronger than is typical for other hoods.

Glove boxes

Glove boxes are airtight, sealed on all sides, and operated through gloves. A glove box is not a chemical fume hood.

Biological safety cabinets

Biological safety cabinets are intended to protect the researcher from harmful agents inside the cabinet, to protect the research, and to protect the environment from contaminants. All biological safety cabinets have a HEPA filter to remove particles and aerosols from the air. There are three levels of cabinets:

1. *Class I cabinets* are primarily for low or moderate risk, protecting the researcher but not the research from dirty room air.

2. *Class II cabinets* protect the researcher, the environment, and the research. This class of cabinet is often used in laboratories where particle-free work is necessary. Within Class II are cabinets of Type A, Type B, and Type B2 designs. A Type A cabinet recirculates 65 percent of the air, and 35 percent is exhausted through a duct or exhausted back into the lab through a HEPA filter. With Type B, 35 percent of the air is recirculated and 65 percent exhausted. Type B2 cabinets require bag-in and bag-out filter housing. Type B2 cabinets exhaust 100 percent of the air, with none recirculated.

3. *Class III cabinets* are 100 percent exhausted; no air is recirculated. Class III cabinets are sealed enclosures and are used for the highest-risk biological agents.

Canopy hoods

Canopy hoods are placed over work areas or equipment to capture heat or steam. The recommended design flow rate is 75 cubic ft per minute (CFM) per linear foot of open perimeter.

Snorkels

Snorkels (also called "elephant trunks") are small capturing cones attached to an adjustable exhaust arm, suspended from the wall or ceiling, to capture heat or fumes from equipment or processes. Typical flow rates are 100 to 200 CFM. Both canopy hoods and snorkels can be fastened directly to equipment if necessary.

For engineering-related issues in fume hood design, see chapter 4.

BIOLOGICAL SAFETY CABINETS				
Type	Face Velocity (ft per min)	Airflow Pattern	Radionuclides/Toxic Chemicals	Biosafety
Class I	75	In at front; rear and top through HEPA filter	No	2, 3
Class II Type A	75	70% recirculated through HEPA filter, exhaust through HEPA filter	No	2, 3
Class II	100	30% recirculated through HEPA; exhaust via HEPA and hard ducted	Yes (low levels/volatility)	2, 3
Class II Type B1	100	No recirculation; total exhaust via HEPA and hard ducted	Yes	2, 3
Class II Type B2	100	Same as IIA, but plenum under negative pressure to room and exhaust air is ducted	Yes	2, 3
Class III Type B3	N/A	Supply air inlets and exhaust through two filters, HEPA		3, 4

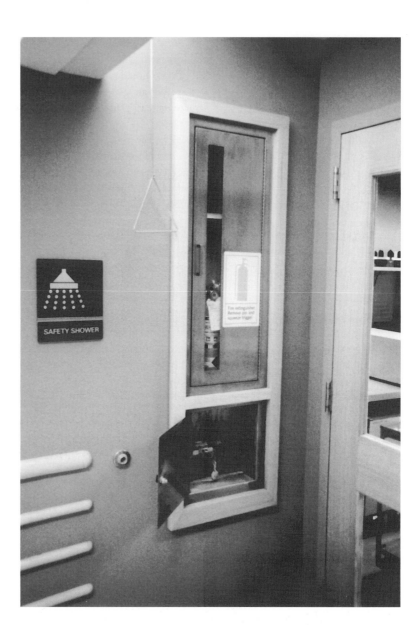

▶ *Locate safety devices at the entry alcove to each lab. Joslin Diabetes Center, Harvard University, Cambridge, Massachusetts. Ellenzweig & Associates, Inc., architect.*

SAFETY, SECURITY, AND REGULATORY CONSIDERATIONS

Protecting human health and life is paramount, and safety must always be the first concern in laboratory building design. Security—protecting a facility from unauthorized access—is also of critical importance. Today, research-facility designers work within a dense regulatory environment. This section addresses all these related concerns.

Safety

General safety principles

For safety and ease of maintenance, it usually makes sense to locate a safety shower, fire extinguisher, and shutoff valves at the entry alcove of each lab. Interior glazing permits easy surveillance of the laboratory. Warning signs with the appropriate symbols should be posted at laboratory entrances. There should be two means of egress from each main lab (labs measuring 900 sq ft or more). Doors should swing out of main labs for safe egress in case of emergency.

In most cases, labs should be organized with the highest hazards (e.g, fume hoods) farthest from the entry door and the least hazardous elements (e.g., write-up stations) closest to the door. Write-up desks and benches should be accessible without having to cross in front of fume hoods. All lab users should be trained in emergency procedures.

Appropriate casework should be provided. Islands are preferable to peninsulas, since islands allow people to walk around benches. A 1 in. high Plexiglas lip along shelves prevents

▼ *Fume hoods located in remote corners.*

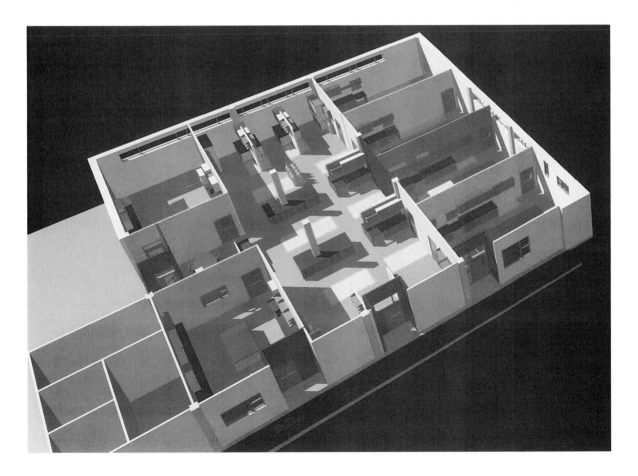

containers from falling off. Where overhead shelving is located above island benches and containers might fall off the back of the shelf, the protective 1 in. lip should be placed there. Personal items and clothing should be kept in lockers outside the lab area. Food and drinks are prohibited in labs.

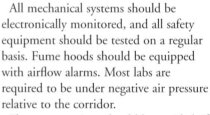

▼ *Protective plastic lip at shelves. Salk Institute, La Jolla, California, Louis I. Kahn, architect.*

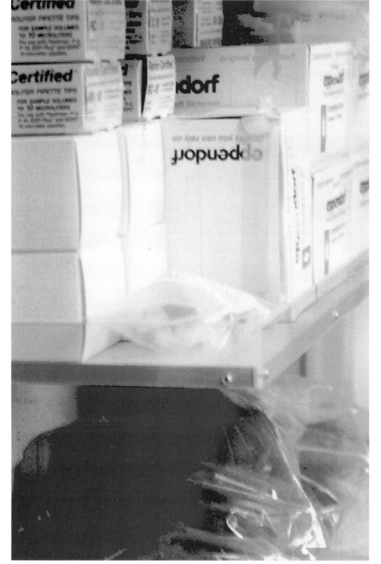

All mechanical systems should be electronically monitored, and all safety equipment should be tested on a regular basis. Fume hoods should be equipped with airflow alarms. Most labs are required to be under negative air pressure relative to the corridor.

Floor penetrations should be avoided, if possible, to prevent chemicals released during a spill or flood from traveling to the floor below. Wet vacuuming should be used instead of floor drains to contain chemical spills. (This can also help in identifying what has been spilled on an individual.)

Designers should consider placing an emergency center in a central location on each floor, to provide easy access for everyone. An emergency center consolidates reagent neutralizers, hand-held sprays, first aid, and fire control equipment in one common area. The center should contain a fire extinguisher with hanger, two 1 gal (3.8 l) plastic bottles, a first aid kit, a fire blanket, and a galvanized sand pail.

Safety showers and eyewashes

According to American National Standards Institute (ANSI) standards, safety showers should never be farther than 100 ft away from any researcher, along a clear and unobstructed path. Locating safety showers within 75 ft is the recommended and safer approach. Safety showers are usually placed in the corridor, highly visible from the lab exits. All safety showers should meet Americans with Disabilities Act (ADA) criteria (described later in this section) and should include an eyewash. Putting a floor drain under the shower is not recommended. A floor drain may create contamination problems in the drain piping or leak down to the floor below. It is better to allow the chemicals at the shower to be mopped up in order to identify what was on the individual.

Deluge showers should flow at a rate of 30 gal of water per minute. All safety showers should provide low-velocity water at 70–90° F. Manual close valves are recommended for all safety showers. A safety shower should be designed with an automatic cutoff, but should deliver at least 50 gal before the automatic cutoff is activated. Safety showers should not be located near any sources of electricity, especially electric panel boxes.

In each lab, there should be an eyewash and a body wash at at least one sink (preferably an ADA-compliant sink). Eyewash units should supply a multistream cross flow of potable water at 65–75° F. Contaminated eyes should be flushed for 15 minutes. Eyewashes should flow at a rate of 3–7 gal of water per minute. Eyewashes are not required by most codes but are highly recommended for safe laboratory practice.

Fume hood height

Another important issue is the height of the fume hood for people who are less than 5'9" tall. The typical fume hood test by the American Society of Heating, Refrigerating, and Air-Conditioning Engineers (ASHRAE) is based on a 5'9" male. When the person is shorter and the sash is lower, then it is more difficult for the hood to operate properly because less air will go through the sash. If the fume hood is left higher to allow for more airflow through the hood, then a person shorter than 5'9" may be at risk, because the person's mouth and nose may be closer to the chemicals being used in the hood. Hoods that can be placed at different heights should be specified.

▲ Emergency center located in a central location. Confidential building.

Chemical storage

Building codes classify a project's "occupancy type" based to a great extent on the quantities of flammable chemicals expected to be kept on hand. Construction costs are directly related to this classification. If the occupancy type can be shifted by reducing storage needs, significant cost reductions can be realized.

A *hazardous chemical* is defined as a chemical for which there is statistically significant evidence that exposure may produce acute or chronic health effects. Storage options include the following:

1. *Supplier warehousing.* Vendors can hold the chemicals for the lab, supplying them on an as-needed or just-in-time basis.

2. *On-site external storage.* An appropriate external storage facility can be any one of a range of prefabricated, self-contained, environmentally controlled hazardous storage containers. The environment must be controllable because many chemicals are sensitive to heat, humidity, and light. Placement and proper management can be just as important as container type.

▼ *Gas cylinder storage in the lab entry alcove. Joslin Diabetes Center, Harvard University, Cambridge, Massachusetts. Ellenzweig & Associates, architect.*

3. *Internal, centralized storage.* Centralized internal facilities usually consist of a designated room for chemical storage, shared by all researchers on that floor or in that building.

4. *Internal, decentralized storage.* In-lab storage may be combined with centralized or external storage. Chemicals are often stored in a special, labeled cabinet in each lab. Some are 7 ft, freestanding cabinets, and others are located beneath fume hoods. All chemical storage cabinets should be exhausted.

In any lab where shelving is used to store chemicals, the shelves should be no higher than eye level. The shelving should be made of a chemically resistant material.

Storage strategies must be compliant with all National Fire Protection Association (NFPA) and Occupational Safety and Health Administration (OSHA) regulations. Flammables must be stored separately in an NFPA/OSHA-approved flammables cabinet, usually beneath a fume hood. Flammables cabinets should be sealed, requiring no exhaust ducting. If flammables storage cabinets are not tightly sealed, volatile fumes can accumulate. Exhaust vents are usually not recommended, because the volatile vapors can escape into the building and some ductwork may not withstand a fire.

Chemical storage rooms should be ventilated by at least 15 air changes per hour and should have dedicated exhaust systems. Chemicals should be stored in plastic or metal containers whenever possible, not in breakable glass. All chemicals should be properly labeled, and should be arranged on the shelf in chemically compatible families, not alphabetically. Chemicals should never be stored in a fume hood or on the floor.

Chemical wastes

It is not permitted to pour chemicals into a drain that flows directly into the public water system. Chemicals must be handled locally in the lab or with dilution tanks in or near the building. Local handling is the most affordable approach: The researcher pours the chemical into a specific container that is later picked up by a waste-management staffperson or by a vendor. If chemicals are allowed to be poured down the drain, then all the drains must be constructed with chemical-resistant piping, which can be very expensive. The holding tanks will take up a few hundred feet, at a minimum, at the basement level.

Security Systems

There are several options to consider for the design of a security system. The least costly, initially, is the lock-and-key system. But there are problems: keys can easily be copied, are difficult to manage, and are costly to replace when lost or stolen.

Access-card systems use identification cards with a magnetic strip, which works as an electronic key. Cards and card-readers are programmed to allow only authorized people into particular areas. When an unauthorized person tries to enter the area, an alarm occurs and the control panel immediately transmits a signal to the host. So-called "smart card" (or "one card") systems can be used for a variety of administrative purposes beyond security—for example, student registration, cafeteria debiting, and so on. Using an access-control system with an integrated database, student and employee status can be updated immediately, without the expense and administrative time necessary to mail new

cards. Other security options to consider are computerized alarm systems, electronic locks, and video surveillance.

The Regulatory Environment

Building and life-safety codes

The following codes and standards may affect the architectural design of lab facilities, depending on jurisdiction:

- Association for Assessment and Accreditation of Laboratory Animal Care (AAALAC) standards
- American with Disabilities Act (ADA) regulations
- American National Standards Institute (ANSI) standards
- Providing Accessibility and Usability for Physically Handicapped People
- ANSI Z358.1 — Emergency Eyewash and Shower Equipment
- ANSI/AIHA — American National Standard Z9.5 for Laboratory Ventilation
- Building Officials and Code Administrators International (BOCA) National Building Code
- Occupational Safety and Health Administration (OSHA) standards
- OSHA Standard 29 — Occupational Exposures to Hazardous Chemicals in Laboratories
- National Fire Protection Association (NFPA), National Fire Codes
- NFPA 101 — Life Safety Code.'97
- NFPA 30 — Flammable and Combustible Liquids Code
- NFPA 45 — Fire Protection for Laboratories using Chemicals
- National Institutes of Health (NIH) 81-2385 — Guidelines for the Laboratory Use of Chemical Carcinogens

- Standard Building Code
- Southern Building Code Congress International (SBCCI)
- Standard Fire Prevention Code, SBCCI
- Standard Gas Code, SBCCI
- Standard Plumbing Code, SBCCI '94
- Standard Mechanical Code, SBCCI

The codes and standards are minimum requirements. Architects, engineers, and consultants should consider exceeding the applicable requirements whenever possible.

Several key building and life-safety code issues must be addressed early in the design process:

1. What is the building classification?
2. What types of hazardous chemicals will be used?
3. What quantity of each chemical will be stored in the building?
4. What is the height of the building?
5. How will chemicals and other hazardous wastes be removed from the lab?

Laboratory construction is typically classified as belonging to one of four types. Types 1 and 2 require noncombustible materials; Type 3 may include some combustible materials; and Type 4 requires exterior walls to be of noncombustible materials. Important considerations in determining the type of construction for a laboratory building are the types and amounts of chemicals stored in the building. The three tables below and opposite list the various types of materials, the class, and use group for construction based on the amount of chemicals stored. Type 4 construction is the least expensive to build, Type 1 the most expensive. In most cases, it is advisable to minimize the amount of chemicals in a building and to order what is needed on a daily or weekly basis from a local vendor.

EXEMPT AMOUNTS OF HAZARDOUS MATERIALS PRESENTING A HEALTH HAZARD (MAXIMUM QUANTITIES PER CONTROL AREA)

Material	Storage[b]			Closed Systems[b]			Open Systems[b]	
	Solids (lb)[cd]	Liquid (gal or lb)[cd]	Gases (cu ft)	Solids (lb)[c]	Liquid (gal or lb)[c]	Gases (cu ft)	Solids (lb)[c]	Liquid (gal or lb)[c]
Corrosive	5,000	500	810[cd]	5,000	500	810[cd]	1,000	100
Highly Toxic	1	(1)	20[e]	1	(1)	20[e]	1/4	(1/4)
Irritant	5,000	500	810[cd]	5,000	500	810[cd]	1,000	100
Radioactive	25 rem, unsealed			100 rem, sealed sources			25 rem, sealed source	
Sensitize	5,000	500	810[cd]	5,000	500	810[cd]	1,000	100
Toxic	500	(500)	810[cd]	500	(500)	810[cd]	125	(125)
Other Health Hazards	5,000	500	810[cd]	5,000	500	810[cd]	1,000	100

[a] Quantities in parentheses correspond to the units in parentheses at the heads of the columns.

[b] The total quantity in use and in storage may not exceed the amount allowed for storage.

[c] The maximum alloved amounts can be increased by 100% in buildings equipped throughout with an approved automatic sprinkler system. Note d also applies and the two allowances are cumulative.

[d] The maximum allowed amounts can be increased by 100% in building equipped throughout with an approved automatic sprinkler system. Note c also applies and the two allowances are cumulative.

[e] Permitted only when stored in approved exhausted gas cabinets, exhausted enclosures, or fume hoods.

[f] 1 lb of black sporting powder and 20 lb of smokeless powder are permitted in sprinkler or unsprinklered buildings.

FIRE RESISTANCE RATINGS OF SELECTED STRUCTURAL ELEMENTS IN HOURS*

	Type of Construction Noncombustible					Noncombustible/combustible		
	Type 1 Protected		Type 2 Protected		Type 2 Unprotected	Type 3 Protected	Type 3 Unprotected	Type 4 (Heavy Timber)
	1A	1B	2A	2B	2C	3A	3B	4
Structural Element								
Exterior walls	4	3	2	1	0	2	2	2
Load bearing	Also must comply with Section 705.2							
Nonload bearing	Must comply with Section 705.2							
Fire and party walls	4	3	2	2	2	2	2	2
	Also must comply with Section 707.1							
Fire separation assemblies								
Exit enclosures	2	2	2	2	2	2	2	2
Shafts (other than exits) and elevator hoistways	2	2	2	2	2	2	2	2
Fire partitions, exit access corridors	1	1	1	1	1	1	1	1
	Comply with Section 1011.4; fire retardant-treated wood permitted for types 1 and 2 if fire resistance rating 1 hour or less is required.							
Interior bearing walls, bearing partitions, columns, girders, trusses (other than roof trusses), and framing								
Supporting more than one floor	4	3	2	1	0	1	0	Section 605 governs
Supporting one floor or roof only	3	2	1.5	1	0	1	0	Section 605 governs
Structural members supporting wall	3	2	1.5	1	0	1	0	1
	Must not be less than supported wall; also exceptions in selected cases							
Floor construction, including beams	3	2	1.5	1	0	1	0	Section 605 governs
Roof construction, including beams trusses and framing, arches and roof deck (15' or less in height to lowest member)	2	1.5	1	1	0	1	0	Section 605 governs

* Abbreviated version of Table 602, BOCA Building Code. This table is included only to illustrate certain possible exceptions, exemptions, or variations permitted depending on other factors.

HEIGHTS AND AREA LIMITS USE CLASS

Type of Construction	Business	Educational	Hazard, H-2	Hazard, H-3
Noncombustible				
1A (protected)	Not limited	Not limited	16,800 5 stories, 65 ft	33,600 7 stories, 85 ft
2B (protected)	Not limited	Not limited	14,400 3 stories, 40 ft	28,000 7 stories, 85 ft
2A (protected)	34,200 7 stories, 85 ft	34,200 5 stories, 65 ft	11,400 3 stories, 40 ft	22,800 6 stories, 75 ft
2B (protected)	22,500 5 stories, 65 ft	22,500 3 stories, 40 ft	7,500 2 stories, 30 ft	15,000 4 stories, 50 ft
2C (unprotected)	14,400 3 stories, 40 ft	14,400 2 stories, 30 ft	4,800 1 story, 20 ft	9,600 2 stories, 30 ft
Noncombustible / Combustible				
3A (protected)	19,800 4 stories, 50 ft	19,800 3 stories, 40 ft	6,600 2 stories, 30 ft	13,200 3 stories, 40 ft
3B (unprotected)	14,400 3 stories, 40 ft	14,400 2 stories, 30 ft	4,800 1 story, 20 ft	9,600 2 stories, 30 ft
4 (heavy timber)	21,600 5 stories, 65 ft	21,600 3 stories, 40 ft	7,200 2 stories, 30 ft	14,400 4 stories, 50 ft

These three tables can be used for review. It is recommended that life and safety professionals be involved early in reviewing the design to make sure it meets health and safety requirements. The design team can build the appropriate building, but the campus health and safety staff will have to oversee the researchers to ensure that the guidelines are met. It is also recommended that local code officials be involved in the review of the design and approach to the construction as it pertains to life-safety issues.

Laboratory classifications

The amount and type of chemicals will determine the building classification. The following are the four laboratory classes, with the special practices associated with each:

1. Low risk. There are no special practices associated with a low-risk laboratory.

2. Moderate risk
   - Work with materials with safety and health ratings of 3 or greater in any category must be performed in a fume hood.
   - Work with substantial amounts of materials with hazard ratings of 1 or 2 must be performed in a hood or in an assembly designed to be safe in the event of a failure.
   - Appropriate personal protective equipment, such as goggles, must be worn in the work area.

3. Substantial risk
   - Specific policies, depending on the nature of the hazard, must be made part of the laboratory industrial and hygiene plan as well as the safety plan.
   - All work that can be completed separately from the laboratory operations should be completed in a separate area of the lab or in a room adjacent to the lab. All paperwork should be performed outside the lab.
   - No safety feature should be altered in any way without written approval.
   - Personal safety equipment must be worn.
   - A laboratory safety committee should review each new experiment planned to determine whether it can be carried out safely.

4. High risk
   - Specific policies, depending on the nature of the hazard, must be made part of the OSHA-mandated laboratory safety plan.
   - All work that can be completed separately from the laboratory operations should be completed in a separate area of the lab or in a room adjacent to the lab. All paperwork should be performed outside the lab.
   - No safety feature should be altered in any way without written approval.
   - Personal safety equipment must be worn.
   - A laboratory safety committee should review each new experiment planned to determine whether it can be carried out safely.

Other typical code issues will have to be studied and resolved. These include exit capacity, travel distance, number and size of fire stairs, door and wall ratings, exit signs, exit lights, emergency power, and rest-room requirements.

Storage of combustible and flammable liquids

The following information is based on NFPA 30, which concerns flammable and combustible liquids. Combustible liquids have a flash point at or above 100°F (37.8°C) and are classified as follows:

- Class II: Liquids with a flash point at or above 100°F (37.8°C) and below 140°F (60°C)
- Class III A: Liquids with a flash point at or above 140°F (60°C) and below 200°F (93°C)
- Class III B: Liquids with a flash point at or above 200°F (93°C)

Flammable liquids have a flash point below 100°F (37.8°C) and a vapor pressure not greater than 40 lbs per sq in. (absolute) (2,068 mm Hg) at 100°F (37.8°C). Flammable liquids are classified as follows:

- Class I A: Liquids with flash point below 73°F (22.8°C) and a boiling point below 100°F (37.8°C).
- Class I B: Liquids with flash point below 73°F (22.8°C) and a boiling point at or above 100°F (37.8°C).
- Class I C: Liquids with flash points at or above 73°F (22.8°C) and below 100°F (37.8°C).

No more than 120 gal (454 l) of Class I, Class II, and Class III liquid may be stored in a storage cabinet. Of this total, no more than 60 gal (227 l) may be of Class I and Class II liquids, and no more than three such cabinets may be located in a single fire area, except in an industrial occupancy, where additional cabinets may be located in the same fire area if the additional cabinets (not more than a group of three) are separated from other cabinets or group of cabinets by at least 100 ft (30 m).

In addition to following the standards above, it will be necessary during the design phase of the project to work closely with the client representatives. The project team may have to incorporate additional requirements as laboratory and support spaces are more definitively outlined.

Fire suppression system

Most lab buildings are designed with a water sprinkler system for code and insurance reasons. In many cases it may be less costly to provide a water sprinkler system than not to do so. Other suppression systems may be necessary, depending on the chemicals being used and the type of research being conducted.

Seismic design

Seismic design is mandated in some areas of the country. Seismic design considerations include the following:

- 3 in. shelf edges for reagent shelving
- 12-gauge metal blocking in walls for wall cabinet attachments
- Earthquake catches for all doors and drawers
- Bolted cylinder straps
- All loose tabletop equipment guy-wired to the tabletops
- All mechanical, electrical, and plumbing equipment double-harnessed to a main structure

ADA Issues

The Americans with Disabilities Act (ADA) is enforced through the U.S. Justice Department and court system, not

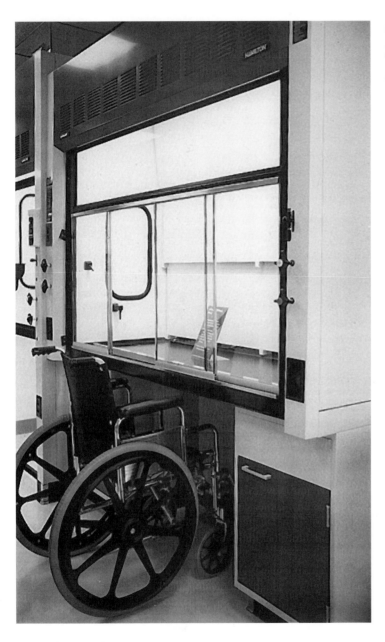

▲ ADA fume hood.

and renovations should take noncompliant elements into account. The following are considerations for accessible design:

- Provide some adaptable furniture systems and adjustable-height work surfaces to accommodate people in wheelchairs.

- Provide one ADA fume hood in each lab. An ADA hood is designed with a sash that opens vertically and horizontally.

- Provide one ADA height (34 in.) sink for each lab. (The Accessibility Board of the Justice Department in Washington, D.C., has stated that a mobile, self-contained ADA sink on each floor is not acceptable as a means to provide access to sinks for students or for any other public use.)

- Provide one ADA workstation/write-up area in each lab.

- Choose emergency shower handles that can be pushed up to stop the flow.

- Install pullout shelves in base cabinets.

- Install a lightweight fire extinguisher within reach of a handicapped workstation.

ADA recommended dimensions and clearances are as follows:

Work-surface height	34 in. max.
Knee clearance	32 in. max.
Work-surface depth	24 in.
Maximum sink depth	6.5 in.
Shoulder-to-hand reach	35–45 in.
Elbow-to-hand reach	22–26 in.
Side reach	24 in.
Reach height	46 in.
Control height	48 in. max, 15 in. min.

by building code officials. Merely obtaining a building permit does not in any way imply compliance with ADA codes and regulations. Any new lab project must consider ADA compliance,

◀ ADA safety shower. Engineering Graduate Research Center, North Carolina State University, Raleigh. Odell & Associates, architect.

▼ Emergency shower maximum reach.

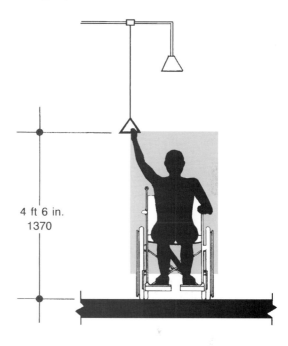

4 ft 6 in.
1370

▼ Laboratory workstation for wheelchair access.

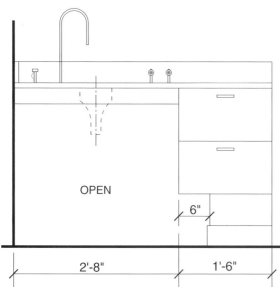

OPEN

6"

2'-8"   1'-6"

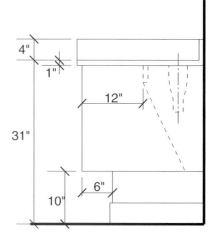

4"
1"
12"
31"
10"
6"

171

Door clearance (requires 36 in. door)	32 in.
Aisle width	48 in. min.
Clearance required to turn wheelchair	60 in.
Clearance from floor to underside of work surface	27 in.
Emergency shower handle height	54 in. high max.

Controls for technology devices in classrooms cannot be higher than 54 in. above the floor and must accommodate a parallel approach by a person in a wheelchair. Private industry may construct labs that can be modified to be accessible for persons in wheelchairs.

WAYFINDING, SIGNAGE, AND GRAPHICS

Wayfinding comprises "the strategies people use to find their way in familiar or new settings, based on their perceptual and cognitive abilities and habits" (Arthur and Passini 1984). These strategies answer three questions:

- Where am I now?

- Where is my destination?

- How do I get there from here?

Wayfinding is facilitated by a communication system consisting of three essential types of information: site and architectural, graphic, and verbal. Each type must reinforce the others in a unified system of environmental information.

Site and architectural information is communicated by the forms, adjacencies, and opportunities for movement in the environment itself. It includes architectural elements, interior design features, corridors, vistas, and other navigational cues.

Graphic information is communicated primarily through the use of signage elements, which provide general information such as directions, regulations, and the identification of destinations. Graphic information may also be presented in the form of directories, kiosks, and bulletin boards.

Verbal information includes printed materials such as maps and brochures as well as spoken instructions by staff and users of a facility.

This information will be even more clearly communicated if supported with the following organizational wayfinding system elements:

- *Naming conventions.* Nomenclature must be simplified and controlled to have distinct, straightforward, and easily recognizable names that will appear in a consistent hierarchy on all sign types.

- *Color coding.* A color-coding system is used to reinforce wayfinding and aid in orientation.

- *Orientation maps.* A representational map of the building is often essential to orient users to their destinations and to illustrate circulation throughout the building.

- *Room numbering.* It is important to design a room-numbering system that clearly communicates location and allows for flexibility, for freedom in department relocation and expansion, and for additional numbers.

Signage

The wayfinding/signage system should be carefully orchestrated to support the major circulation routes within a facility, providing the exact information required for the user at the correct point at which it is needed. Instead of all information being available at all locations, a hierarchy of information with specific signage and/or visual cues is developed within the environment to call out these areas in an appropriate manner. A typical hierarchy of signs encountered by a visitor trying to find a specific room is shown below.

A well-designed signage system incorporates all the information required for each specific sign type into a coherent, distinct, recognizable system that integrates color, graphics, materials, scale, form, and detailing.

Typical lab environment signage consists of informational, directional, identification, regulatory, and code signs:

- *Informational signage* provides information about the facility, including room names and numbers, departments, whether a conference room is in use, and the hours a facility is open.
- *Directional signage* provides directions to users of the facility and includes

ceiling-mounted, wall-mounted, or freestanding signs; building/ department directories; and wayfinding instructions.

- *Identification signage* indicates the name of the building, department, or room. Special identification signs, such as donor- and lab-identity signs, support the unique characteristics of the facility.

- *Regulatory signage* includes signage with regulatory information, such as "No Smoking," "Hazardous Materials," or "No Access" signs.

- *Code signage* is required by city codes and includes stair/level identification signs, rest-room signs, evacuation maps, and occupancy signs.

Modularity within the signage system allows for easy replacement and interchangeability of sign components. Changeable message signs allow for the flexibility of a laser-printed paper insert to provide information that changes

SIGN HIERARCHY		
Narrative	**Signs Encountered**	**Features/Type of Information**
Visitor approaches building	Building ID	Campus and building identification/address
Visitor enters building	Reception area ID	Campus and building identification.
Visitor enters main circulation corridor	Elevator flag sign	Elevator symbol identifies location of elevators.
Visitor approaches elevator and identifies destination	Building directory	Lists departments by name, location (floor), and department number/color.
Visitor exits elevator at proper level	Directional sign	Directs to departments/ features on that level.
Visitor heads toward departments	Department ID	Identifies department by floor number/color.
Visitor approaches door	Department ID changeable insert	Identifies department by name by tactile/braille and floor number/color.
Visitor approaches room number. Room function identified on changeable paper insert	Room ID	Identifies room by tactile/braille room number/color.

frequently. For code compliance, Braille and tactile letters/numbers must be detailed and integrated into signs.

Integration of the signage system with the interior architecture by careful formatting, placement, and selection of materials can create a system that not only supports but also truly enhances the lab environment.

Graphics

The essence of any laboratory is the information that continually flows through it in the form of research, teaching, and regulation, all in pursuit of science and learning. The entire lab community should maintain a certain level of awareness of the proper protocols and of the many threats to health and safety that labs contain.

Complete lab planning includes professionally designed signs, manuals, labels, and other graphic materials for the purpose of maintaining proper communication. It is very important that the presentation of graphic information be as carefully designed and managed as the lab itself.

The efforts of a facility's environmental health and safety (EH&S) office are critical to the safe functioning of the lab environment. A graphic safety master plan can provide EH&S departments with a framework for creating and updating the information program while keeping to an attractive and functional standard. It is important to maintain unity and consistency between the manuals and all other formats. Elements to standardize include language, layout, logos, icons, color coding, typography, software, printing methods, and paper size and weight. It is important that EH&S departments have the means to easily adapt new information to the format. Their active involvement is, of course, crucial in developing the standards.

Lab safety manuals

Planning a graphic safety program may begin with the design of safety manuals. Safety manuals present the official policy of the offices of EH&S and lab management. A manual may consist of a single bound document or a may include a series of documents covering various topics, such as radiation, biosafety, chemical spills, hazardous waste disposal, laser safety, and personal injury. The manuals cover both mandatory safety precautions and emergency responses. All information displayed on signs and labels should relate directly to the contents and style of a facility's manual, to create a sense of unity and consistency. Large institutions commonly maintain their manuals on-line so that they are accessible throughout the campus and can be updated at the source without having to be redistributed.

▼ *Typical lab door signage.*

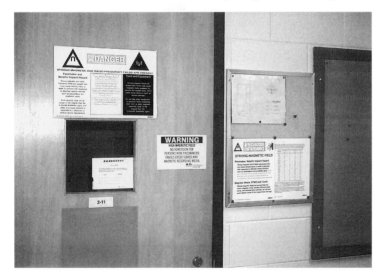

Labels

Labels are critically important in labs where chemicals are used. An unlabeled or improperly labeled container can create an extremely dangerous situation. Hazardous chemical waste must be properly labeled to avoid mixing incompatible chemicals. There are numerous off-the-shelf labels available, but ideally a label would be visually and functionally compatible with the design and format of the facility's manual and signage.

Material safety data sheets

The law requires that material safety data sheets (MSDSs) be present and available anywhere chemicals are used. Their existence is based on the "right to know" law set forth in OSHA's Process Safety Management (PSM) and Programs (29 CFR 1910.119). This law was designed to help local communities protect public health and safety and the environment from chemical hazards. MSDSs are written by attorneys of the chemical suppliers for the purpose of compliance with the law and to avoid litigation. MSDSs are now widely available to the lab community as on-line databases, which are something of an improvement over the paper sheets. The trouble with on-line databases, however, is that the information is "elsewhere" — not necessarily immediately available at the point of contact with the chemicals.

Another format is MSD sign cards. These are individual 4 x 6 in. cards, printed on synthetic card stock, each with highly useful information on several hundred of the most hazardous chemicals used in laboratories. Unlike MSDSs, these cards use concise language and attractive, readable graphics to make the

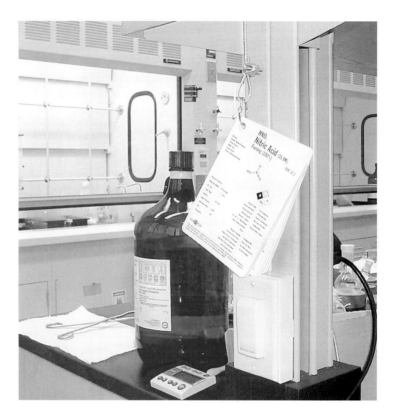

▲ MSD sign cards.

message most accessible. The point of the cards is to have them available in close proximity to the chemicals and their users at the point of interaction, which is not easy with MSDSs, even if they are available on-line. The MSD sign cards are intended for use especially by academic and professional laboratories, where there is a much higher level of training than in a typical industrial setting.

Lab hazard signs

Many local regulations require a certain amount of information to be posted outside lab doors to indicate the types and levels of hazard inside. To mount and be able to update such information easily can be a challenge. The lab hazard sign frame is a device for mounting

▲ *Lab hazard sign frame.*

▶ *Window grid.*

single 8½ x 11 in. sheets, which slip behind the acrylic window. It is a simple yet elegant solution with a neutral, clean appearance suitable for most lab corridors.

The window grid display system is a modular design that allows greater freedom for lab managers to determine the format and quantity of signs they need to display. As information changes, lab managers are able to update each window's content, independent of the others. The appearance of the corridors is greatly improved. Regulators and emergency personnel will have greater confidence in what to expect in terms of hazards. The health and safety message will be conveyed with greater authority.

Life and safety sign book

The life and safety sign book presents the essential messages of safety manuals in an accessible, user-friendly format with as many as ten two-page spreads. The sign book mounts to the wall with adhesive Velcro strips, and the pages are held open with small Velcro tabs. If necessary, the sign book can be removed and taken to the site of an emergency. The sign book, which makes use of graphic icons and simplified language, is much more easily understood in a stressful situation than is a typical safety manual. Its unique design attracts attention and makes the official protocols more of a presence in the laboratory community. The contents of the sign books are completely under the control of lab managers and EH&S officers and can therefore refer users to further information in a manual. Through digital printing, high-quality color graphics can be produced in any quantity.

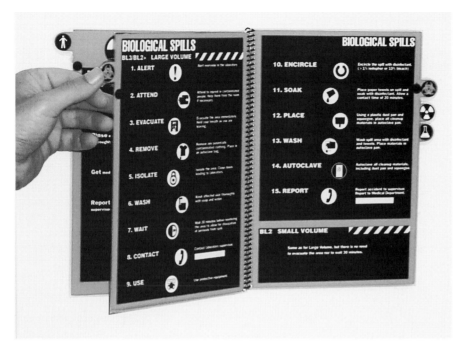

◀ *Life and safety sign book.*

SPECIALIZED LAB AREAS

Biosafety Level Labs

Biosafety Level 2 (BL-2)

BL-2 labs (formerly referred to as P-2 labs) have the following requirements:

- 100 percent outside air

- Exposed surfaces that are smooth and easily maintainable

- Caulking at all furniture-to-wall seams for ease in cleaning up spills

- Autoclaves ("clean" for sterilization of instruments and "dirty" for decontamination)

- Cages decontaminated by autoclaving before they are cleaned

- Protective coats or gowns to be worn at all times and removed before leaving the suite

If a researcher is not sure whether a lab should be BL-2 or a BL-3 (discussed below), the lab should be designed for BL-3 standards. It is very difficult and expensive to convert a BL-2 lab into a BL-3 lab, but a BL-3 lab can be used for either BL-2 or BL-3 research.

Biosafety Level 3 (BL-3)

BL-3 labs are designed to contain the agents used within them. Design issues include the following:

- BL-3 spaces must be accessible only through a controlled entrance. For obvious safety reasons, the general public and nonessential lab personnel must not be allowed to enter.

- BL-3 spaces should be under negative pressure with respect to adjacent areas. If the pressure is compromised, an automatic alarm should sound.

- Liquid-resistant finishes are recommended for walls, floors, and ceilings.

- Any windows in the BL-3 area must be sealed shut.

- Each BL-3 module should have near the exit a hand-washing sink that operates automatically, by foot, or by elbow.

- Because of the possibility of contamination, lab furniture must be easily cleanable.

- Spaces between furniture and equipment must be easily reached for cleaning.

- Work surfaces must be impervious to water and resistant to organic solvents, acids, bases, and heat. Stainless-steel surfaces are recommended.

Biosafety Level 4 (BL-4)

There are fewer than ten true BL-4 labs in the country. BL-4 labs are required when agents pose a high individual risk of aerosol-transmitted laboratory infection and life-threatening disease. This type of containment laboratory must be designed and constructed to specific containment requirements to minimize the potential for personnel exposure and to prevent dissemination of BL-4 organisms to the environment. Personnel enter and leave only through the clothing change and shower rooms. To do any work with animals, a worker must wear a one-piece positive-pressure suit ventilated with a life-support system. Personnel must shower before they leave the facility.

Complete laboratory clothing is provided for all personnel who enter the BL-4 suite.

Supplies are submitted through a double-door vestibule. After the outside doors are secure, personnel inside the facility obtain the supplies. A double-door autoclave is provided for decontaminating materials that leave the facility. There must be a separate individual supply and exhaust system. The exhaust is filtered with HEPA filters before being discharged. Laboratory animals are housed in a Class III biological safety cabinet or in a contained caging system.

Note that once systems are in place and the facility is running, it is very difficult and expensive to renovate, as this requires the lab to be shut down. The lab must be designed right the first time, taking into account any future needs. According to knowledgeable researchers and end users, the following are the key points to consider in designing BL-4 labs:

- Handling of liquid wastes

  Where will liquid wastes go?

  How big is the cooker?

  How long should the wastes be cooked?

  Is there a need for stainless-steel piping and drains?

  Is there a need for easy access to storage tanks to test spour strips?

  Redundancy of mechanical systems

  Duplicate HEPA filters

  100 percent redundancy of air handlers—no downtime

- Safety

  Chemical showers at both means of egress, allowing for equipment to be decontaminated as well

  Alarms and controls located in the BL-4 lab as well as in adjacent spaces to allow for maintenance of the space either within or outside of the lab

  Bag-in and bag-out HEPA filters

  Air pressure and airflow

  Containment

Room within a contained room (building within a building)

Minimal penetrations in the wall

Stainless-steel ductwork and cabinetry

- Comfort

Large shower area to accommodate the entire research team, not just one or two individuals

Rest-rooms for both sexes

Place to get water to drink during the day—difficult to work in space suit without water

Column-free spaces for maximum flexibility

Communication to the suits by people inside the BL-4 lab and by observers outside the lab

Enough space for storage of space suits at the end of the day

- Operations

Full-time person needed to maintain autoclaves, boxes, suits, and mechanical equipment

Training for people to operate a BL-4 lab

The tables below and on the following page give recommended biosafety levels for activities in which experimentally or naturally infected vertebrate animals are used and for infectious agents. The source is the Centers for Disease Control and Prevention.

Clean Rooms

Clean rooms are usually associated with the manufacture of miniaturized components. A clean room is an enclosed area that requires a lower level of airborne particulate contamination than normal

RECOMMENDED BIOSAFETY LEVELS FOR LAB USE OF EXPERIMENTALLY OR NATURALLY INFECTED VERTEBRATE ANIMALS				
Biosafety Level	Agents	Practices	Safety Equipment (Primary Barriers)	Facilities (Secondary Barriers)
1	Not known to cause disease in healthy adults	Standard animal care and management practices, including appropriate medical surveillance programs	As required for normal care of each species	Standard animal facility; nonrecirculation of exhaust air; directional airflow recommended
2	Associated with human disease Hazard: percutaneous exposure, ingestion, mucous membrane exposure	ABSL-1 practice plus: limited access; biohazard warning signs sharps precautions; biosafety manual; decontamination of all infectious wastes and of animal cages prior to washing	ABSL-1 equipment plus primary barriers: containment equipment appropriate for animal species; PPES: laboratory coats, gloves, face and respiratory protection as needed	ABSL-1 facility plus: autoclave available; hand-washing sink available in the animal room
3	Indigenous or exotic agents with potential for aerosol transmission; disease may have serious health effects	ABSL-2 practices plus: controlled access; decontamination of clothing before laundering; cages decontaminated before bedding removed; disinfectant foot bath as needed	ABSL-2 equipment plus: containment equipment for housing animals and cage dumping activities; class I or II BSCs available for manipulative procedures (inoculation, necropsy) that may create infectious aerosols PPEs: appropriate	ABSL-2 facility plus: physical separation from access corridors; self-closing, double-door access; sealed penetrations; sealed windows; autoclave available in facility
4	Dangerous/exotic agents that pose high risk of life-threatening disease, aerosol transmission, or related agents with unknown risk of transmission	ABSL-3 practices plus: entrance through change room where personal clothing is removed and laboratory clothing is put on; shower on exiting; all waste are decontaminated before removal from the facility	ABSL-3 equipment plus: maximum containment equipment (i.e., Class III BSC or partial containment equipment in combination with full body, air-supplied positive-pressure personnel suite) used for all procedures and activities	ABSL-3 equipment plus: separate building or isolated zone; dedicated supply/exhaust vacuum and decontamination systems; other requirements outlined in the text

RECOMMENDED BIOSAFETY LEVELS FOR INFECTIOUS AGENTS				
Biosafety Level	Agents	Practices	Safety Equipment (Primary Barriers)	Facilities (Secondary Barriers)
1	Not known to cause disease in healthy adults.	Standard microbiological practices	None required	Open bench top sink required Basic
2	Associated with human disease Hazard: auto-inoculation, ingestion, mucous membrane exposure	BSL-1 practice plus: limited access; biohazard warning signs; "sharps" precautions; biosafety manual defining any needed waste decontamination or medical surveillance policies	Primary barriers: Class I or II BSCs or other physical containment devices used for all manipulations of agents that cause splashes or aerosols of infectious materials; PPEs: laboratory coats;gloves; face protection as needed	BSL-1 plus: autoclave available Basic
3	Indigenous or exotic agents with potential for aerosol transmission; disease may have serious or lethal consequences	BSL-2 practice plus: controlled access; decontamination of all waste; decontamination of lab clothing before laundering; daseline serum	Primary barriers: Class I or II BSCs or other physical containment devices used for all manipulations of agents PPEs: protective lab clothing; gloves; respiratory protection as needed	BSL-2 plus: physical separation from access corridors; self-closing, double door access; exhausted air not recirculated; negative airflow into laboratory containment
4	Dangerous/exotic agents which pose high risk of life-threatening disease, aerosol-transmitted lab infections, or related agents with unknown risk of transmission	BSL-3 practices plus: clothing change before entering; shower on exit; all material decontaminated on exit from facility	Primary barriers: all procedures conducted in Class III BSCs or Class I or II BSCs in combination with full-body, air-supplied, positive pressure personnel suit	BSL-3 plus: separate building or isolated zone; dedicated supply/exhaust, vacuum, and decon system; other requirements outlined in the text Maximum containment

and generally incorporates temperature and humidity control. These requirements are achieved by purging the room with air that has passed through a filtration and conditioning system. The room should be under positive air pressure to avoid ingress of contamination.

Static pressure regulators should be used to maintain the desired room pressure. Entry design should incorporate air locks or vestibules kept at a slightly reduced pressure. To control temperature fluctuations, small clean-room chambers are recommended over one large clean-room space. The applicable codes and standards for clean rooms are as follows:

- Uniform Building Code (referring to H occupancies)
- Uniform Fire Code (referring to H occupancies)
- Federal Standard 209D (1988)

- American Association for Contamination Control (19970), standard CS-6T
- Institute for Environmental Sciences (1984), Standard IES-CC-RP-006

Clean-room work surfaces should be smooth, easily cleanable, nonabrasive, and chip-resistant. Perforated, high-pressure phenolic laminate on steel or aluminum panels is recommended for return-air flooring. Coating grating with plastic or epoxy is also recommended. If the room contains hydrogen, measures must be taken against the possibility of explosions. Blast-out panels may be necessary.

Darkrooms
Some facilities are using computer imaging, which is replacing the need for darkrooms. Biomedical labs, however, are still likely to need darkrooms.

RECOMMENDED AIR CHANGE RATES AND AIR VELOCITIES		
Room Classification	Air-Change Rate	Air Velocity
Class 100,000	18–30 air changes per hour	—
Class 10,000	40–60 air changes per hour	10 FPM
Class 1,000	150–300 air changes per hour	30–50 FPM
Class 100	400–540 air changes per hour	75–90 FPM
Class 10	400–540 air changes per hour	75–90 FPM
Class 1	540–600 air changes per hour	90-100 FPM

A red warning light outside the door of a darkroom should automatically activate when the room is in use. A double-compartment sink with ample drain board and bench space is required. Stainless steel is recommended for sinks and work surfaces. Cabinets for chemicals and paper storage are necessary. A light filter should be used when developing X-ray film. The switch for the incandescent light should be covered and located 60 in. or more from the floor to prevent accidental operation. A silver recovery unit mounted under the sink may be required to prevent wastewater contamination.

Darkroom design is changing. The traditional system uses a gel to separate radioactive molecules; the gel is exposed to the X-ray film, usually for several days or a week. Next, the X-ray film is realigned with the gel. The density of the spots is determined with the use of a light transmission device, and the image is scanned into the computer.

A new product, called a Multifluor detector, detects radioactivity, fluorescence, and chemiluminescence. It is used for gel imaging and other experimental protocols. The Multifluor detector combines several steps using a screen technology so that the image is detected, scanned into the computer,

quantified, and categorized. The advantage is that researchers can use fluorescence in place of radioactivity. There is a desire to eliminate the use of nuclides and, thus, the care needed in their handling. The Multifluor technology is more sensitive than the traditional X-ray film and exposes the gels for hours in a day, rather than days in a week. Researchers can also analyze X-ray film using the Multifluor system, thus being able to use both options.

It is not necessary to have the Multifluor detector device in a darkroom. A dark area is required, however, for handling the screens. The Multifluor detector device requires no special plumbing or toxic chemicals, as are needed for X-ray development.

Environmental Rooms (Cold and Warm Rooms)

Cold rooms are usually kept at 39°F, which allows people to work in the space for a limited time without becoming too cold. (There are also super-cold rooms at 24°F.) A vestibule may be necessary to minimize temperature loss from the cold room. Warm rooms are commonly designed at 98°F. The key design issues to address in environmental rooms are as follows:

▲ *Entry into a modular cold room.*

- A separate power system with emergency backup should be provided for each chamber.
- Observation windows should be heated triple-pane windows, with the option of a rubber flap.
- All fixtures should be vapor-proof.
- Each chamber must be equipped with a thermometer and a light.
- Freeze-proof, self-closing doors with magnetic gaskets are required.
- To control temperature and humidity fluctuations, each chamber should have only one door unless the chamber is more than 400 sq ft.

Tissue Culture Suites

To control the growth of bacteria, several small chambers are recommended over one large tissue culture area. The chamber should be under positive pressure with respect to adjacent spaces. Flooring should be seamless and easy to clean. A lay-in acoustic tile ceiling is standard. Each biological safety cabinet should have dedicated 115V, 20 amp circuits. All equipment drain pans and incubators must be kept clean and free from mold. An in-swinging, self-closing door with a panic bar on the outside for easy opening is recommended. Laminar flow hoods and glove boxes to contain the tissue culture may be desirable, since special rooms are not needed when the research can be conducted in the specialty equipment.

- Prefabricated environmental rooms usually offer superior performance and greater flexibility than built-in rooms.
- Flammable liquids and gases must not be used inside environmental rooms, as they are not fire-rated.
- Several small chambers are recommended over one large room.

SPECIALIZED EQUIPMENT AND EQUIPMENT SPACES

Sensitive electronic equipment can be affected by magnetic fields. As equipment becomes more sophisticated, tolerances for interference decline. Large currents must be kept away from sensitive equipment such as electron microscopes. Magnetic shielding must be provided when necessary. Sensitive equipment should be kept away from steel columns, magnetized doors, and other metal equipment.

Nuclear Magnetic Resonance Apparatus

Nuclear magnetic resonance (NMR) apparatus should be located on the lowest floor level and the floor slab and structure should be very rigid to minimize vibration. The NMR should be located as far away as possible from elevators or mechanical equipment.

Safety zones should be marked around the NMR, and warning signs placed. Steel objects such as chairs, desks, and tools should be kept outside the safety zone. Utility requirements usually include 208 V, 60 Hz, three-phase, 20 amp electrical power that is grounded; compressed air; and nitrogen and helium gases. Room temperature should be maintained at 74°F (plus or minus 2°F). The humidity should range from 45 to 55 percent relative humidity. There should be at least six air changes per hour.

Electron Microscope Suite

The size of the room will depend on the size and number of electron microscopes. The room must be able to be blacked out. It must have chilled water for cooling the power supply. The suite usually includes imaging, a darkroom, a print darkroom, and a prep area. The room should be stable to

▼ NMRs should be located on lowest floor level to minimize vibration. Biochemistry Building, University of Wisconsin, Madison. Flad & Associates, Inc., architect.

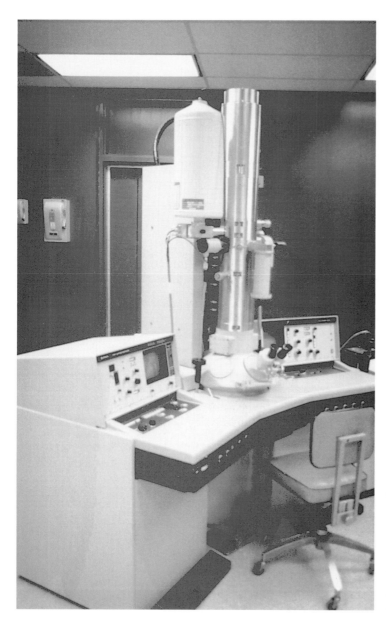

▲ Electron microscopes. Manufacturing Related Disciplines Complex, Phase II, Georgia Institute of Technology, Georgia. Perkins & Will, architect.

Relative humidity should be no greater than 50 percent. There will need to be low-impedance clean ground power supply and room for cylinder gases and for high-voltage electrical services. A dedicated electrical circuit to each electron microscope can help to minimize noise from other equipment. Dimmer room light switches are necessary.

Magnetic Resonance Imagers

Magnetic resonance imagers (MRIs) are computers linked to super-conductive cylindrical magnets into whose magnetic fields the objects to be examined are inserted. The magnetic field should be located so that there is no interference from metal objects. As with an NMR, the radius of the MRI's magnetic field extends around the equipment in all directions. The magnetic field can interfere with heart pacemakers and electronic equipment. There should be at least ten ft of clearance to allow for the refilling of the liquid helium and nitrogen that cools the magnet. Electrical filters are required on all electrical conductors. The MRI units will require clean electrical power and restrictive security.

Lasers

Rooms with lasers must be able to be blacked out. Most researchers prefer laser labs with no glazing. Other issues to consider include these:

- Is a chemical fume hood necessary?
- What are the laser's vibration criteria?
- Is high-voltage electrical power necessary?
- Will the room contain any cylinder gases?

minimize vibration. Vibration damping may be required at the equipment. Air distribution in the room is very important to the performance of the microscopes. There should be 10–12 air changes per hour.

Mass Spectrometry

Mass spectrometry (MS) suites must be isolated to address vibration concerns. Exhausts may be necessary directly over the equipment. Computers will be located in the same room as the MS equipment. A sample prep room is usually necessary for gas cylinder storage. The equipment can be noisy, and noise-control measures must be included in the design of the lab.

Vacuum Systems

Vacuum-pump systems should have water-resistant filters on the suction side. The exhausts should be separate from the mechanical system and should be ducted directly to the outside of the building. The housing for the filters should be easily accessible for maintenance. Some buildings will require a central vacuum system with local filters at the source to service the instruments. Many facilities are locating the vacuum system at the source, forgoing a building-wide system, if this is more affordable.

Equipment Sizes

Most labs are "equipment intensive." It is important to understand the size and service requirements. The tables on pages 186–188 give the sizes of common types of laboratory equipment, as well as some technical requirements.

Lab equipment can be purchased and installed in various ways. The client can purchase and install it after the building is constructed. Or the client can purchase the equipment, and the contractor can install it during construction. A third choice is to have the contractor purchase and install the equipment under the base contract.

VIVARIUM FACILITIES

Vivarium facilities can be very expensive and complex spaces to design. A dual-corridor, clean-and-dirty system should control contamination well in an animal facility. The dual-corridor arrangement eliminates the possibility of mixing clean cages and supplies with soiled cages and refuse, reducing the risk for cross-contamination. The great disadvantage of a dual-corridor arrangement is the additional space and cost required. It should be understood at the beginning of the design process that the greater safety of the dual-corridor system necessitates the additional space and cost. Any human error during operations can render the system invalid. Careful management of the vivarium facility is extremely important for successful research and for the safety of the animals and the people involved.

The design of the circulation space should focus on the movement of cages and animals through the facility. In many instances the animals are delivered to the building, transported to the upper floor via a dedicated elevator, then put in a quarantine room. Animal facilities are typically located in the basement or on the top floor of a building for security, confidentiality, and safety. If there is a choice between a basement and a top floor, the top floor is preferred because of the close proximity to exhaust fans and other mechanical equipment.

After the animals are checked and no longer need to be quarantined, they are taken down the "clean" corridor into a holding room or cubicle. When the racks or cages need to be cleaned, they are taken through the "dirty" corridor to the cage washer. If possible, a pull-through cage washer is preferred to separate the

MOVEABLE EQUIPMENT			
Equipment Item	Typical Size	Electrical Requirement (volts)	Comments
Alpha, beta, and gamma counter	40 x 25 x 21"	110	
Balance table	24 x 35 x 41"		
Centrifuge	63 x 36 x 51"	208	Sizes can vary, but most can be accommodated in a space 4' wide x 3' deep. Ultracentrifuges may need cold water and a floor drain. They are usually run under continuous vacuum.
Computers and printers	varies		
Fermenters (benchtop)	19 x 19 x 21"	120	Electric service with gas, as required.
Freezer			
Upright	26 x 36 x 84"	208	An upright type freezer occupies the same space as a refrigerator. Freezers will need 6–8" of clearance to minimize overheating. The intake air filters need to be cleaned regularly. A freezer should be on coasters for ease of movement and access to filters.
Chest	6' wide		
Gas chromatograph (benchtop)	60 x 30"	110	Nitrogen and air hookups necessary. Chromatography is a standard method of protein purification. The work is completed in a cold room or chromatography cabinet (refrigerator).
Gas cylinders			
HPLC setup (benchtop) High-pressure liquid	60 x 30"		
Hydraulic press	varies	208	Possibly requires special structural system.
Incubator	40 x 30 x 86"	110	Incubators may be bench mounted or floor standing, each about 2' square. Carbon dioxide or possibly oxygen may also be required.
Infrared spectrometer	varies	110	Exhaust.
Lyophilizer	48 x 30 x 48"	110 or 208	
Optical table	3–5 x 4–8'		Typical services include air and vibration-sensitive pads.
Oven	20 x 20 x 27"	110	Drying ovens are typically mounted above a sink. Vacuum is necessary.
Refrigerator, standard upright	34 x 36 x 84"	110	
Scintillation counter	36 x 34 x 26"	110	A scintillation counter may be bench mounted or floor standing.
Shaker (small)	varies	110	
Ultraviolet spectrometer	varies	110	Exhaust.
Vacuum pump	10 x 18 x 20"	110	

FIXED EQUIPMENT

Equipment Item	Typical Size	Electrical Requirement (volts)	Comments

Autoclave
  Small chamber
  Medium chamber
  Large chamber
	20 x 20 x 38"
	24 x 36 x 35"
	48 x 84 x 48"
			An autoclave is usually located in the wash area, where specimens can be heated to a very high temperature to kill all organisms. Electric service, steam, and a floor drain are necessary.

Biosafety cabinet, floor standing	48, 60 or 72 x 30–34 x 80–90"		
Bottle washer	71 x 39 x 80"	208	Electric service, hot water, steam, floor drain, and exhaust are typically necessary.
Dishwasher	30 x 30 x 36"		A lab dishwasher is similar to a residential dishwasher, but permits higher temperature and deionized water to be used for lab supplies.
Electron microscope	10 x 14'		Size and services vary. Usually has its own transformer, which should be located outside the electron microscope room. Cooling water may be required. Cold water, floor drain, exhaust, relative humidity control, and magnetic and mechanical isolation are factors that must be addressed.
UHV spectrometer	10 x 8'	110 or 208	Exhaust and magnetic sensitivity must be considered.
Fume hood	48, 72 or 96 x 32" x varies		
Fermenter (14 liter)	30 x 24 x 32"		
Flammable liquids storage cabinet	35, 47, or 60 x 18 x 44 or 60"		
Flow cytometer	84 x 60"	110 or 208	Usually located in a separate lab, in a biological safety cabinet if the cells to be separated are possibly pathogen infected.
Glass washer	42 x 40 x 90"	460	Usually located in a central wash-up room. A purified water supply, compressed air supply, and floor drain will be necessary.
Glassware dryer	37 x 32 x 96"	460	
Ice machine	39 x 32		Floor mounted; water supply connection and floor drain required.
Mass spectrometer	15 x 15'	208	Electric service, cold water, exhaust, and humidity and temperature control are typically required.
MRI (magnetic resonance imaging)	varies	110 or 208	Electric service, cold water, exhaust, humidity and temperature control are typically services needed.

FIXED EQUIPMENT (cont.)			
Equipment Item	Typical Size	Electrical Requirement (volts)	Comments
NMR (nuclear magnetic resonance)	varies	110 or 208	Electric service, nitrogen, air, humidity, and temperature control, and magnetic isolation are required.
Rack washer	84 x 82 x 99"	460	Electric service, hot water, steam, floor drain and a pit will be necessary.
Spectrometer	4 x 9'	110 or 208	Electric service, nitrogen, air nitrogen, and exhaust are typically required.
Shakers (large)	42 x 30 x 52"	208 or 440	
Tunnel washer	40 x 288 x 73"	440	Electric service, hot water, steam, and floor drain are required.

clean and dirty sides. To reduce chances of cross-contamination, multiple barriers can be provided, such as vestibules at the entry, anterooms before entries to specific rooms, cubicles or ventilated racks in the animal rooms, and, at the cage level, micro-isolation racks that may be individually ventilated. The air pressure should be positive on the clean corridor and negative along the dirty corridor.

Facilities in which live animals are housed range from rooms for small species (mice, rats, hamsters) to central quarters for small and large animals, including cats, dogs, primates, sheep, and cows. A central animal facility, such as that needed for a medical school, may include the following:

- Receiving and examination areas for animals, food, and supplies
- Quarantine area
- Housing for animals, with provision for separation of species and isolation for individual projects
- Facilities for washing, sterilizing, and storing cages and equipment
- Storage rooms for food, supplies, and bedding

▼ *Clean/dirty corridor concept for a vivarium facility.*

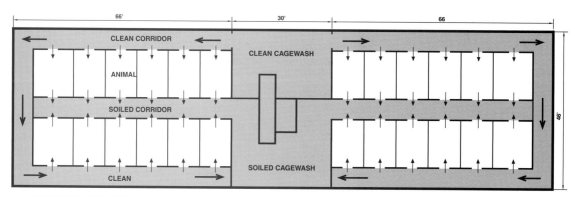

CAGEWASH FLOW DIAGRAM

- Laboratories for surgery, radiology, necropsy, and other procedures
- Administrative offices
- Showers, lockers, toilets, and lunchroom for personnel

Planning Issues

The receiving area should not be easily visible from areas visited by the public or nonprofessional staff. Proper separations must be provided between clean and contaminated areas and between personnel areas and spaces housing animals. Because of the danger of interspecies infection, animal species must be separately housed.

Ensuring the lowest per diem costs for animals while providing improved researcher access to animals is a critical issue in the development of future animal facilities.

Special controls are necessary for experiments involving hazardous agents. Safety measures specified by regulatory agencies provide for different levels of containment. Positive/negative air pressures, high-efficiency particulate air filters, air locks, decontamination areas, closed and ventilated cage systems, double-door autoclaves, and other measures may be required to maintain the necessary containment. Facilities for aseptic surgery are planned with separate areas for preparation, surgery, radiology, recovery, and support, including storage, washing/sterilizing, and lockers. The facilities must comply with all codes, including those applying to safety measures for the use of anesthetic gases.

Air

The supply air equipment for the system should be designed to provide a sufficient volume of 100 percent outside air for adequate ventilation and temperature and humidity control of the animal rooms. It is not acceptable to use recirculated air to or from animal facilities. To maintain a pathogen-free environment, 12–15 air changes per hour are required. Airflow should be controlled with dampers to prevent reversal or back flow. Airflow monitoring and control devices should be provided in the supply and exhaust ducts to maintain the proper supply and exhaust air quantities. Balancing dampers, flow measuring devices, and control devices should be installed on all air supply and exhaust ducts to monitor the status of the duct airflow and pressure. There should be access panels in the ceiling to allow for reasonable maintenance. Controls are best located above the corridors and away from the animal rooms. Animal room exhausts should be of the sidewall type, mounted near the floor in the corners of the room. Filters must be installed in the exhaust ducts to capture animal hair, dander, and other airborne solids and prevent them from being exhausted to the exterior. Air should flow in a downward direction to protect personnel from aerosolized particles.

Mechanical Systems

The average cost of the heating and ventilating systems for an animal facility is three to six times the initial operating cost for a generic wet lab. All systems must be designed for 24-hour operation. Redundant air supply and exhaust systems with filter banks must be provided to ensure continuous service and operation in the animal facility. If the animal facility is part of the research laboratory complex, a separate emergency power system is required to maintain system operations during power interruptions or failures.

Temperature and humidity will depend on the animal species to be housed in each animal room. Separate environmental controls are recommended for each animal room. Sensors to monitor temperature, humidity, and room pressure should be included; sensors and alarms should be connected to a control panel centrally located in the animal facility, to be monitored by the staff on continuous duty and by the institution's main security office. Knockout panels (minimum of two per animal room) should be provided at the ceiling for flexible duct connections to accommodate ventilated animal cages;

the area required varies with the species and the size of the cage racks.

Plumbing

A standard hose bib with threaded hose connection should be provided near the holding rooms. There should be enough hose bids to allow hoses to have access throughout the animal facility. A 6 in. diameter (minimum) floor drain with strainer, solids trap, disposal unit, and threaded cover, and a 6 in. diameter (minimum) drain pipe, sloped floor to drain should be provided for the holding rooms. A trap should be installed to prevent back flow into the room. Floor drains are not required for rodent rooms (which can be wet vacuumed or mopped).

▶ Trench drain in remote corner. Animal Facility, Clemson University, Clemson, South Carolina. GMK, architect.

Lighting

Lighting fixtures should be waterproof, surface or pendant type. (Recessed fixtures may be difficult to seal against infiltration of insects and vermin.) Controls should be provided for a diurnal lighting cycle. Illumination levels for small animals range between 60 and 80 footcandles, depending on the species. Automatic lighting control is recommended in cage rooms to provide adequate periods of darkness and light. Day/night automatic lighting controls should have manual override, timers, and alarm systems.

Acoustical Considerations

The noise level should be controlled at 65 to 75 dB maximum where animals are located. Animals should be isolated from noisy activities, and soundproof doors should be used in the cage room. Loud, sharp noises can be extremely damaging to animals, both psychologically and physiologically. However, the necessity of using hot water to clean spaces and of providing materials resistant to a wide variety of chemicals and surfaces that withstand abusive treatment requires that interior finishes be hard, rigid, smooth, and chemically resistant. This environment makes it impossible to control sound reverberation completely.

Almost all available acoustical materials are soft and porous. Such materials absorb moisture and water, and thus lose their acoustical properties. The materials with the better acoustical ratings are ideal environments for the growth of bacteria, fungi, and other organisms. There are two solutions. The first is to pour sand into the concrete block walls. This is easier to do, from a structural point of view, on the ground floor. The additional weight of the sand will be a significant increase to this structural system of any elevated floor. The second solution is to use acoustical baffles such as those used in dog kennels. These can be hung from the ceiling; they are cost-effective and absorb some sound.

General Finishes

Wall, floor, and ceiling finishes in the animal areas should be smooth, hard, impervious, seamless, and capable of withstanding frequent hot water or steam wash-downs.

Floors should be concrete, trowel or brush finished, with specified sealers and hardeners in animal rooms and in cage washing and feed storage areas. Seamless vinyl (with chemical or thermal welded seams) is satisfactory for other areas, including laboratory, service, and support spaces. Floor slabs in multistory animal facilities should be constructed with a waterproof membrane underlayment. Floor loading should be 125–150 lb/sq ft minimum.

Masonry partitions should be provided in animal holding rooms, cage washing areas, shipping and receiving, feed processing and storage, surgery, preparation, and recovery, with a sealed troweled epoxy finish to withstand hot water wash-down. Masonry (concrete) blocks are perhaps the most durable and effective material for partitions in animal rooms and cage washing and feed storage areas. Blocks should be solid or filled to prevent infiltration of insects or vermin. The block face should be sealed and smooth epoxy finish applied. The base should be integral with the floor and wall, forming an impervious, jointless finish. Reinforced wall-mounted cage rack bumpers should be provided to protect wall finishes and reduce equipment noise. Work surfaces in animal support rooms should be nonmagnetic stainless steel.

Ceilings should be constructed from hard and impervious materials—generally waterproofed gypsum board with sealed joints and an epoxy finish,

though hard plaster or Kenne's cement may also be used. Exposed concrete (underside of a structural slab) is also satisfactory if the finish is smooth. Exposed pipes and fixtures are not acceptable, because they provide a surface for dust accumulation and may cause other problems.

All floor, wall, and ceiling penetrations, including outlet boxes and light switch boxes, must be sealed to prevent insect and vermin infestation and air leakage. The ceiling height should be 9 ft minimum for most animal care spaces. Corridor ceiling heights should be 7 ft clear minimum.

Waste Management

Waste solutions from cage-washing areas must not drain directly into the sanitary sewer system. All fluid wastes from the animal spaces must be directed to holding tanks for processing. Bedding and animal waste may have to be autoclaved prior to disposal. If the animals are used in research involving radioactive materials, the waste may have to be held until half-life decay is within safe limits. Many institutions contract with licensed waste-management firms to manage and dispose of hazardous waste materials.

Animal Housing Systems

Cage racks for small animals vary in size from 24" deep x 36" wide x 60" high to 32" deep x 60" wide x 72" high. Wheel locks should be provided to prevent the racks from rolling.

Ventilated cages are being used more frequently. Because they are, in essence, individual environments, they may allow more than one species to be housed in the same animal room. They may contribute to energy savings by reducing

▼ *Small Animal holding rooms. Animal Facility, Clemson University, Clemson, South Carolina. GMK, architect.*

the number of air changes required in animal rooms. They may also provide a higher-quality environment for the animals because of the immediate removal of ammonia fumes from the cages.

There are many reasons not to transport animals to other areas of a research facility (e.g., cross-contamination, trauma to the animals, difficulty in containing odors, etc.). Therefore, the use of ventilated cage rack systems is increasing, and research laboratory work space is included as part of the animal facility. The basic laboratory module can then be applied as the basic building block for the animal facilities. This standardization and use of modules of the same dimensions permits efficient and economical integration of animal facilities within the framework of the total research facility. The ventilated cage rack, or micro-isolator cage, provides HEPA-filtered air to the cages and includes a self-watering feature. With micro-isolator cages, the double-corridor, clean-and-dirty concept is no longer necessary.

Ventilated cages have an airflow rate of 30–60 changes per hour, and the cages can maintain the microenvironment at a very stable rate. A ventilated cage should last four to five years longer than traditional static cages because of its stronger construction and because it does not have to go through the cage washer as frequently. The use of ventilated cages should reduce direct personnel labor costs by approximately 50 percent.

Transgenic Facility Systems

Recent developments using animals as carriers of human genes have produced experimental techniques to model various human characteristics for medical purposes. The animals used have become accurate models for a wide range of gene research. Human genes are injected into the animals to produce the desired effects. These animals transmit the gene characteristics to their offspring, producing a unique transgenic line of animals. The animals are, however, subject to cross-contamination and the usual maladies that may infect any breed. Special micro-isolator cage systems have been developed to house these animals. The cage systems provide a high level of protection and permit the animal to be transported to other laboratory areas for research and experimentation.

The micro-isolator cage provides a barrier at the cage level, protecting the animal from contamination. The spent air may be emitted into the cage room and exhausted or connected to a duct for exhaust directly to the exterior. The bedding may be changed every two to three weeks to reduce the ammonia buildup from animal waste. The animal is transferred to another sterilized micro-isolator cage in a clean room or to a biosafety cabinet environment. The animal may be exposed in a biosafety cabinet or worked on in a class 100 special procedures room.

Specific Rooms

Procedure rooms

Animal procedure rooms are adjacent to a group of animal holding rooms. A procedure room may have a fume hood or biosafety cabinet, stainless-steel cabinetry, sink, table, and exam lights, usually hung from the ceiling. Surgery for small animals can be done in a procedure room.

▼ *Procedure room.*

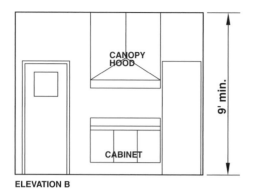

CANOPY HOOD

CABINET

9' min.

ELEVATION B

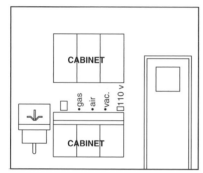

CABINET

gas • air • vac. 110 v

CABINET

ELEVATION A

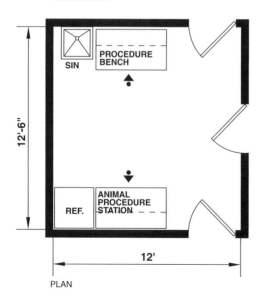

SIN

PROCEDURE BENCH

12'-6"

REF.

ANIMAL PROCEDURE STATION

12'

PLAN

Surgical suites

A surgical suite should be isolated from potential sources of contamination. It consists of a prep area, scrub room, operating room, and recovery room. Lockers should be adjacent to the surgical suite to allow personnel to change before and after surgery. The prep room is a holding and prep area for the animals. There should be a vacuum at the table to dispose of shaved hair. The prep room should have interior glazing to allow viewing into the operating room.

Necropsy

The necropsy area is for the examination of deceased animals. There should be a downdraft table, stainless-steel casework and sink, and a freezer for carcass storage. The necropsy room is potentially one of the most hazardous rooms in the vivarium suite. It should be physically separated from the animal holding areas and the main circulation paths.

Receiving room

A receiving room should be located near the elevator to receive new animals before they are put in quarantine. There should be an exam table and light in this space.

Quarantine room

Most animals will be quarantined before they are placed in an animal holding room. Cubicles are suggested if there will be frequent shipments of animals into the facility.

Small animal holding rooms

Small animal holding rooms typically house mice, rats, hamsters, guinea pigs, or rabbits. Each species must be held in a separate holding room.

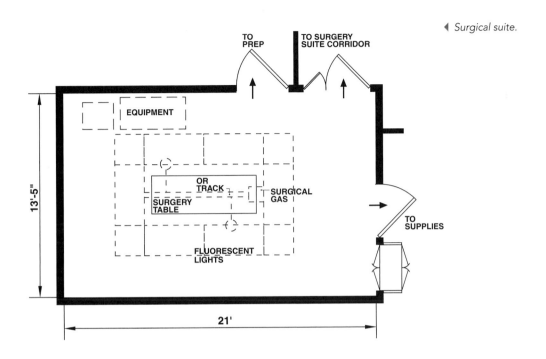

◄ *Surgical suite.*

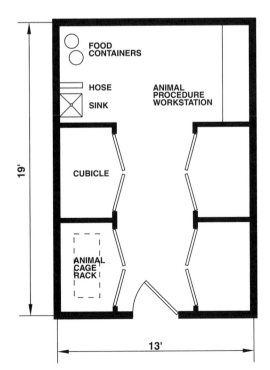

◄ *Cubicles, rather than holding rooms, are an option.*

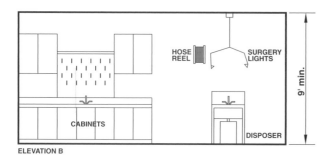

ELEVATION B

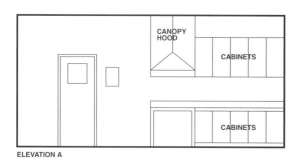

ELEVATION A

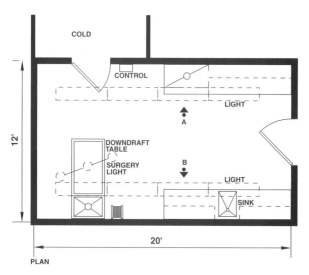

PLAN

▲ Necropsy room.

Large animal holding rooms

Large animal holding rooms may house cats, dogs, pigs, or primates. Large animals can be noisy and should be isolated from the small animal holding rooms. Each cage should have an automatic watering system. Self-cleaning drains may be preferred. Dogs will require runs for daily exercise.

Cubicles

The basic concept of animal cubicles is to divide large rooms into smaller animal housing units (animal cubicles) that share circulation and service space in order to maximize the number of small, isolated housing spaces that can fit within a given area.

A cubicle typically houses one cage rack. Some cubicles should be designed to accommodate larger cages for rabbits and cats. If there is enough space, the cubicles should be sized to hold both smaller and larger cages. Cubicles can be used as holding rooms, and they are better than holding rooms if the objective is to provide the maximum number of isolated housing spaces. Another benefit of the cubicle is that it provides another containment barrier.

Feed and bedding storage

Feed and clean bedding materials should be stored on racks off the floor. All cracks and openings must be sealed to prevent penetration of insects and vermin. Doors should be provided with seals. Air changes should be between 12 and 15 per hour.

Cage washers

There are three common types of cage washers used for the sanitation of cages and racks:

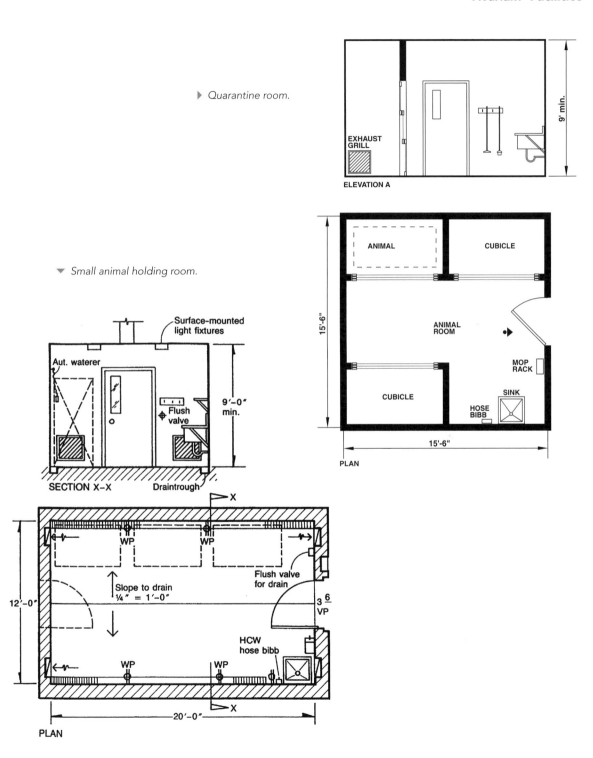

▶ *Quarantine room.*

EXHAUST GRILL

9' min.

ELEVATION A

▼ *Small animal holding room.*

Surface-mounted light fixtures

Aut. waterer

Flush valve

9'-0" min.

SECTION X–X   Draintrough

ANIMAL

CUBICLE

ANIMAL ROOM

MOP RACK

SINK

HOSE BIBB

15'-6"

15'-6"

PLAN

X

WP   WP

Slope to drain ¼" = 1'-0"

Flush valve for drain

12'-0"

3 6/VP

HCW hose bibb

WP   WP

20'-0"

X

PLAN

- *A rack washer* can hold one or more cage racks. Rack washers are either front-loaded or pass-through. The pass-through machine works well for a "clean and dirty" facility.

- *A cabinet washer* is smaller than a rack washer and can accommodate only cages. The racks must be cleaned by some other method.

- *A tunnel washer* allows small cages or equipment to be put on a conveyor belt. It is usually more efficient than a cabinet washer.

Cage washers can be run on steam or electricity. It is important to understand the amount of labor necessary to run a cage washer. A larger, more expensive unit may take less time or fewer people to operate. The cost of manpower should be greater than the cost of the equipment.

The appendix contains a list of Web sites to consult for further information on vivarium facilities.

▼ Cage-wash area with exhaust ducts above soffit. This arrangement pulls steam up and off the glass washer, so that steam does not fill the room. Animal Facility, Clemson University, Clemson, South Carolina. GMK, architect.

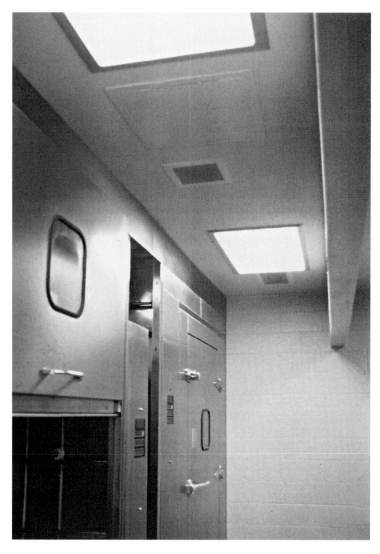

CHAPTER 4
ENGINEERING DESIGN ISSUES

The coordination of engineering systems design ensures a successfully operating laboratory facility. The design of the engineering systems should be based on the lab module. This chapter will cover engineering design issues, options, and how to coordinate all engineering and architectural issues throughout a building. Specific engineering issues are discussed in the following order:

- Structure
- Mechanical systems—general design issues
- Fume hoods—mechanical system design issues
- Electrical systems
- Lighting design
- Telephone/data system
- Information technology
- Closets
- Audiovisual engineering for presentation rooms
- Plumbing systems
- Commissioning
- Renovation/restoration/adaptive reuse
- Facility management issues

STRUCTURAL SYSTEMS

After the basic lab module is determined, the structural grid and location of beams should be evaluated. In most cases, the structural grid equals two basic lab modules. With a typical lab module of 10' 6" x 30', the structural grid would be 21' x 30'. A good rule of thumb for lab buildings is to add the two dimensions of a structural grid; if the sum equals a number in the low 50s (e.g., 21' + 30' = 51'), then the structural grid should be efficient and cost-effective.

Longer spans can also work successfully but may make it more difficult to control vibration in the building, may cost more money, and may require a greater floor-to-floor height. A few buildings have been built with large trusses that span the entire length of the lab, creating column-free spaces. The Salk Institute is an example. The openings in the truss allow the mechanical ductwork to go through in the interstitial space. This arrangement is considered ideal in some cases, but it is more costly and usually not necessary. A long-span Vierendeel truss can increase the cost of the structural system by at least 10 percent, adding 2–3 percent to the overall building construction cost. Concrete column sizes are typically 18–24 in. square, and steel columns 10–15 in. square. The estimated sizes and depths of framing given in this chapter are intended to be guidelines only; such dimensions must be studied in detail for each specific project.

Key design issues to consider in evaluating a structural system include the following:

- Framing depth and effect on floor-to-floor height
- Ability to coordinate framing with lab modules
- Ability to create penetrations for piping in the initial design, as well as over the life of the building
- Potential for vertical or horizontal expansion
- Vibration criteria
- Cost

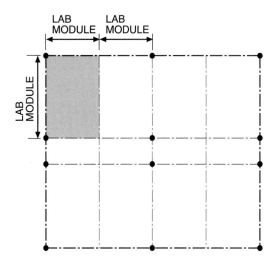

▲ *Structural module.*

When deciding on a structural system, the local construction market, the availability of labor, and the expertise of the contractors should be evaluated. Two questions must be resolved:

- Should the building be constructed of steel or concrete?
- What are the contractors and subcontractors most familiar with?

The answer to the first will partly depend on where in the country the lab facility is being built. For example, in the Northeast, steel construction is generally preferred; concrete construction is preferred in the Southeast. The choice between steel and concrete is usually decided on the basis of competitive prices from contractors in the area, and local preference may override one or more of the preceding key design issues. If the system chosen is one with which the contractor has direct experience, then choosing that system will likely result in cost and scheduling benefits. Reviewing the structural system with the local contractors should occur in the schematic

design phase, because the overall massing, design, and cost will be affected by the selection. Common options for structural systems are discussed below.

Steel

In most parts of the country, laboratories are commonly constructed with structural steel wide-flange beams and columns. Although metal deck slabs, which span between steel beams, can, with an adequate thickness of concrete topping, achieve fire separations between floors, it is important to understand how to fire-rate the steel framing while allowing for space and sequencing of the other trades.

Here are a number of other issues related to steel construction that must be considered:

- In high seismic zones, steel construction may be preferable to concrete because of its superior ductile behavior.
- For greatest economy, steel framing systems may require diagonal bracing in a vertical plane, which must be coordinated with architectural layouts.
- Steel systems that span more than 30 ft may require special attention in design to meet vibration criteria. Steel joists are typically not recommended at floors because the joist stiffness may not be adequate to control floor vibration.
- Steel beams will have to be fire protected, which means that lay-in ceilings will be necessary.

Steel construction requires approximately the same depth as concrete construction. The height and mass of the building are basically the same for steel and concrete construction.

Cast-in-Place Concrete

Several cast-in-place concrete systems are available. One-way beam systems and joist and slab systems are common, and their economy depends largely on formwork requirements and repetition. Spans for these systems can easily reach 40 ft, with beam depths approximately equal to the length of the span divided by 20; slab depths are typically determined by fire-rating requirements. A longer span means an increase in the size of the beam (width, depth, or both).

Two-way cast-in-place systems (such as flat plates and flat slabs) are also common, with span limits of about 30 ft in each direction. The slab thickness is about the length of the span divided by 30 but is thicker at drop panels at columns.

Structural depths and concrete quantities can be reduced if a concrete system utilizes posttensioning, which precompresses the concrete and helps in resisting applied loads. Beam or joist depth can be reduced to about span length divided by 30, and two-way slab depths can be about span length divided by 40. Posttensioned slabs are difficult to core through after they are constructed, because of the potential of cutting the post-tensioning tendons. It is very difficult to renovate a posttensioned slab by cutting holes in it for ductwork or plumbing pipes. Posttensioning is therefore not commonly used for laboratory construction.

Pan-joist system

The pan-joist system consists of secondary beams every 3–6 ft between primary beams, which frame the columns. This is a common structural system for laboratories because the

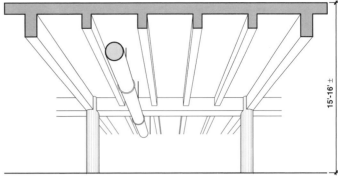

SECTIONAL PERSPECTIVE · DUCTWORK UNDER PRIMARY BEAMS REQUIRES TALLER STRUCTURE

15'-16' ±

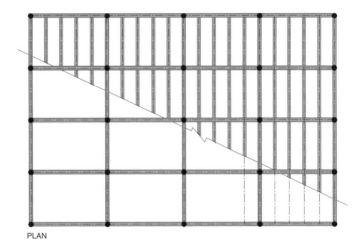

PLAN

▲ *Pan-joist system.*

inherent stiffness and mass of the concrete addresses concerns about vibration. A problem with this system is the difficulty in coring holes for roof and floor drains, because as much as 25 percent of the floor area has beams or joists below it. The cores should occur between beams, not at a beam. Another problem is that the subcontractor has to supply pan forms based on the lab module to coordinate with the rest of the building. Many subcontractors have standard pans that are not based on the lab module. The design team should talk with the local subcontractors in the

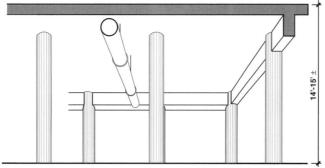

SECTIONAL PERSPECTIVE DUCTWORK UNDER FLOOR SLAB REDUCES FLOOR TO FLOOR HEIGHT

14'-15' ±

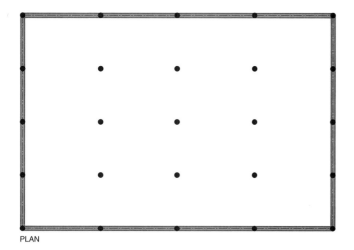

PLAN

▲ Flat-plate system.

around the perimeter of the lab building. The edge beam aids in lateral load resistance and cladding attachment. This system works well because there is typically no need for interior beams and the floor-to-floor height needs to be only 14–15 ft. The slab is also easy to penetrate for drains or vertical risers. For the structure to work most efficiently, the building grid should basically be a rectangle and bays should be as nearly square as possible.

The flat-plate or flat-slab structural system can reduce floor-to-floor height from 1' to 1'6", which should result in significant cost savings on the project. Not only may this structural system cost less than other options, but also there is less exterior skin and fewer vertical risers. This reduction of materials can produce a reduction of 1 percent or more in the construction cost. The flat-plate or flat-slab design should work well for most research laboratory structures because both require a rectangular floor plan to be efficient.

design phase to coordinate the pan size and spacing with the lab module and engineering systems. A typical floor-to-floor height for a building with a pan-joist system is 15–16 ft.

Flat-plate or flat-slab system
The flat-plate or flat-slab system can be appropriate if the contractor and subcontractor are used to this method of construction and the lab modules are compatible with span limits. Flat slabs have a drop panel below the slab and around the columns, whereas flat plates do not. There may be an edge beam

Post-and-beam blank system
The post-and-beam blank system is being used in south Florida today. The concrete beams are precast, then set on the site. The beams can be cut on site to whatever length they need to be. After the first floor of columns and beams has been set, plywood forming is constructed to allow for the pouring of the floor slab. The poured slab helps to create a single composite structural system. The advantages are that the members can be precast, the beams can be cut, and it is easy to make penetrations through the floor slab. The typical floor-to-floor height is 15–16 ft.

Columns

Staggered columns

Staggered columns with angled beams allow vertical risers to occur at each lab module without any interference from a column or beam. The typical floor-to-floor height is 15–16 ft.

Columns at corridors

Columns can be located in the lab, in the corridor, or in the center of a partition. If the columns are located in the lab, then the corridor can have a clean, column-free appearance and the design of the corridor can be more flexible. Locating the columns in the lab usually requires some custom detailing of the casework, and columns may create problems in teaching labs. If columns are located in the corridor, then repetition may be desired from an aesthetic point of view. The location of columns outside the lab will make it easier to lay out casework and to make changes in the lab. The disadvantage of locating the columns in the corridor is that the clear area for equipment and people to pass through may have to be increased, resulting in a less efficient building design.

Some labs are designed with the columns located on the centerline of the wall. The theory behind this approach is that the wall may not be necessary and, if it is not, then casework can be lined up back to back. If the wall is necessary, then it is simply located between the casework components.

Vibration Control

Vibrations caused by footfalls require both structural and architectural solutions. Footfall-induced vibrations, important for above-grade floors, can be reduced by placing sensitive equipment near columns, keeping as much distance as possible between heavily traveled areas and sensitive equipment, and minimizing the length of spans.

Control of structure-borne vibration can be enhanced by locating highly sensitive equipment on a grade slab and isolating the portion of the slab directly below the equipment from the rest of the structure.

Vibration is alleviated by increasing the stiffness of the floor slab. The stiffness can be increased by providing a combination of mass and/or depth for above-grade slabs. Cast-in-place concrete

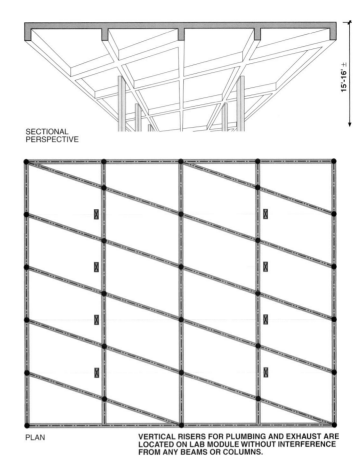

SECTIONAL PERSPECTIVE

15'-16' ±

PLAN

VERTICAL RISERS FOR PLUMBING AND EXHAUST ARE LOCATED ON LAB MODULE WITHOUT INTERFERENCE FROM ANY BEAMS OR COLUMNS.

▲ *Staggered columns.*

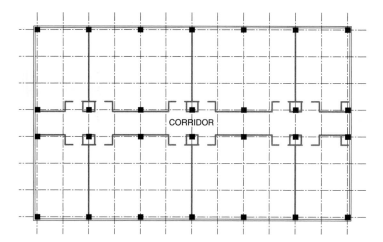

▲ *Columns at corridor.*

natural frequency of the system between column supports, "f," and static stiffness at the center of the bay, "k."

Laboratories should be designed for 125 lbs per sq ft live load throughout the laboratory areas for vibration considerations.

MECHANICAL SYSTEMS— GENERAL DESIGN ISSUES

Shafts and Ductwork

After the structural system is determined, the location of the main vertical supply and exhaust shafts must be studied, as must the location of the horizontal exhaust and supply ductwork. To minimize the floor-to-floor height, it is important to minimize the number of times that exhaust and supply ducts overlap.

Access to all mechanical systems is very important. First, there must be space to allow for servicing the parts and adjusting of dampers. Second, there must be access to the control valves and electrical breakers. Third, there must be space and access to allow changes and additions to utility services. If the design of the building addresses these issues in the initial construction, then much time and cost can be saved when maintenance and renovations occur over the life of the building.

There are several options for locating the main shafts. Key issues to take into consideration are these:

• Efficiency of engineering system design

• Initial costs

• Long-term operating costs

• Building height and massing

• Design image

has characteristics and mass advantages that assist in vibration reduction. To the extent possible, mechanical and electrical equipment should be isolated from the structure by placing such equipment in separate structures or by using slab joints and vibration isolation supports for the equipment (i.e., spring/damper systems). Special tables or pads can also be used to isolate sensitive equipment from the supporting floor.

Air-handling ductwork must be designed to minimize vibration. Supply and exhaust air fans, compressors, pumps, and other noise and vibration producing equipment should be located in mechanical rooms with protective wall construction.

Special local vibration control devices may be utilized for any highly sensitive equipment, such as optical benches and analytical instruments. Instruments that are extremely sensitive to vibration should ideally be located on slab-on-grade construction to minimize transient structure-borne vibration.

Vibration criteria for areas intended to accommodate sensitive equipment are based on the product of two factors: the

The various options are as follows.

Shafts at the end of the building

Vertical distribution is through the shafts, and horizontal distribution is in the ceiling.

Advantages

The labs are unobstructed, with the shafts at the end. The concept is reasonable in cost, and this concept works well with a manifolded exhaust system.

Disadvantages

Access through the ceiling tile or via an open ceiling in the lab may conflict with research activities. The roof equipment and ductwork may have to be spread across the entire roof to provide access to the shafts at the end. The main exhaust and supply trunk lines may be larger than required in other options.

Shafts in the middle of the building

This option is similar to the first, except that the main shafts are located in the middle of the building.

Advantages

The shafts will have short, efficient runs to distribute and exhaust the air. The concept is very cost-effective. The mechanical equipment (air handlers and exhaust fans) can be centrally located on the roof, minimizing the massing of the penthouse. In addition, this concept works well for a manifolded exhaust system.

Disadvantages

Access through the ceiling tile or in an open ceiling in the lab may conflict with research activities. Locating the shafts in the middle divides the lab into two areas, limiting flexibility in the future.

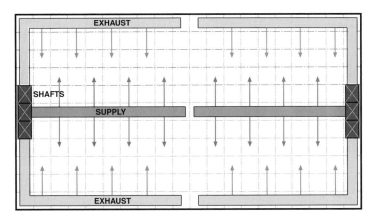

▲ *Shafts at the end of the building.*

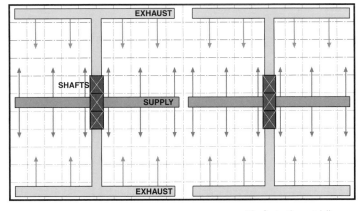

▲ *Shafts in the middle.*

Shafts at the end and supply in the middle

Advantages

The shafts will have short, efficient runs to distribute and exhaust the air. The concept is reasonable in cost, as compared with the other options. The exhaust and supply ducts generally do not overlap, minimizing the floor-to-floor height. This concept also works well for a manifolded exhaust system.

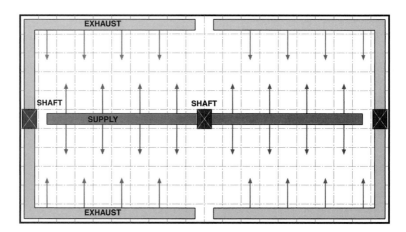

▶ *Exhaust shafts at the end and supply in the middle.*

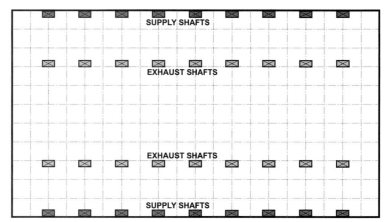

▶ *Multiple internal shafts.*

Disadvantages

Access through the ceiling tile or in an open ceiling in the lab may conflict with research activities. The central supply shaft may limit floor-plan layouts by creating a "large mechanical column."

Multiple internal shafts

Several shafts, usually one for each lab module, distribute much of the utilities vertically.

Advantages

The shafts will have short, efficient runs to distribute and exhaust the air. The floor-to-floor height is lower because the size of the horizontal ductwork is much less than in the other options. In addition, the horizontal ductwork should be able to run between the beams. The floor-to-floor height can be reduced at least 2 ft or more. Renovations can easily be made outside the lab, in the people corridors. The shafts can also be designed to accommodate process piping and the risers and stacks for floor and roof drains. This concept works very well if several dedicated exhaust shafts are required. It also works well for older buildings that were not originally constructed as laboratory facilities and that have floor-to-floor heights of less than 15 ft.

SHAFTS

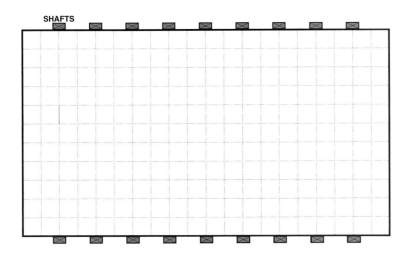

◀ Shafts on the exterior.

Disadvantages

More floor area is required for all the shafts. The floor plans will not be as efficient, requiring more gross area to service the net usable spaces. The shafts become obstructions, like columns, limiting the changes that can occur throughout the life of the building. There will be fewer opportunities for interior glazing.

Shafts on the exterior

Shafts are located on the exterior, freeing the entire interior space for laboratories.

Advantages

The horizontal runs required to serve the building are shorter. There is maximum flexibility in the laboratory zone inside the shafts. A minimal floor-to-floor height is required. This concept may work well for the renovation of older structures if such buildings are not considered historically significant.

Disadvantages

It is difficult to access the shafts. Access is usually at the interior common wall between the lab and the shaft. Consequently, any renovations would interrupt the research being conducted in the lab. The shafts on the exterior will limit the views and amount of glazing. The exterior shafts will make a strong aesthetic statement. (This may be preferred or undesirable.) More floor area is required for all the shafts. The floor plans will not be as efficient, requiring more gross area to service the net usable spaces. The shafts will have to be insulated.

Service corridors

The laboratory spaces adjoin a centrally located corridor, where all utility services are located.

Advantages

Facility engineers are afforded constant access without their having to enter the lab. Shutoff valves and electric panel boxes are easily accessible. Material handling is separated from people corridors. If the service corridor is 10' 6" wide or greater, it can be used as an equipment corridor.

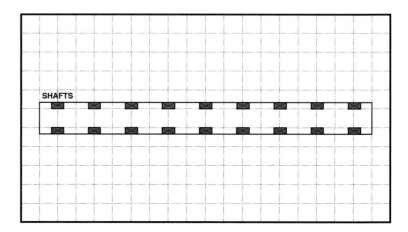

SHAFTS

▶ *Service corridor.*

Disadvantages

The gross area is greater, and planning efficiency can be 5 percent less than in the options already discussed. The lower the building efficiency, the higher the cost per net sq ft (NSF). Building flexibility is limited. The building is split in half, which does not encourage communication among all researchers. There is minimal natural light into the lab spaces, because a people corridor is required around all labs to allow the researchers into their labs.

Interstitial space

An interstitial space is a separate floor located above each lab floor. The services drop down into the laboratory. Interstitial space is used very selectively because of its higher initial cost.

Advantages

The use of interstitial space allows the building to accommodate change very easily and gives it a longer useful life. The labs are unobstructed by shafts and can be renovated quickly, cheaply, and with very little (if any) interruption. The system is cost-effective over the life of the building if the labs will have to be renovated at least every five to ten years. Construction time can be reduced, because the mechanical, electrical, and plumbing services can be installed in the interstitial space at the same time the lab is being finished. There should be much less conflict among the trades during construction. Higher initial costs can be reduced by allowing work on the mechanical and electrical systems to be undertaken concurrently with the laboratory buildout, and the construction process can be easily fast-tracked. The full, walk-on interstitial floor saves time and money by enabling subcontractors to work without scaffolding.

Disadvantages

The volume of the building increases, and the initial cost is higher than that of the other options (up to 5 percent of the construction cost). This option affords the lowest net-to-gross efficiency and the highest cost per NSF. Additional sprinklers are required for the interstitial spaces.

These disadvantages, however, may be offset in both the short and long term.

◀ *Partial interstitial space. NIH Building 40, Bethesda, Maryland. HLM, architect. Courtesy NIH.*

▼ *Interstitial space.*

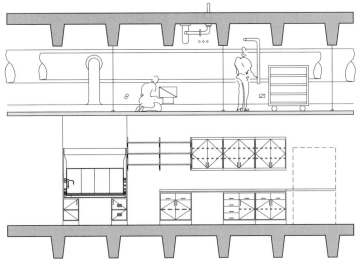

Guy Ott, vice president of facility operations at the Fred Hutchinson Cancer Research Center (FHCRC) in Seattle, stated that the construction of interstitial space added 2.6 percent to the initial construction costs of that facility but realized a 2.3 percent savings due to shortened construction time. FHCRC expects renovation costs to be half of what they would be if there were no interstitial space. The interstitial space gives FHCRC the flexibility to incorporate new scientific techniques and equipment as they become available.

Partial interstitial—two rows of columns along the corridor

In many cases, spacing columns every 30–35 ft across the depth of a building will not fully coordinate with the corridor and lab module. Should there be a row of columns on both sides of the corridor? An additional row of columns along the corridor would allow for column-free laboratories but may increase the cost of the structural system and limit future modifications to the building. One design option is to have a row of columns along both walls of the corridor, with no beams across the corridor. This concept allows for much

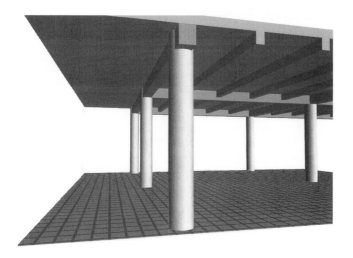

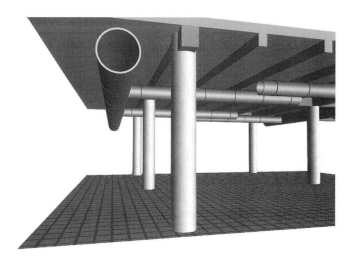

Architectural and Engineering Coordination Case Study

All vertical risers must be coordinated with the architectural design and lab module. The illustrations at left and right demonstrate one way to fully coordinate the architectural and engineering systems in a laboratory building.

Mechanical Equipment

Mechanical systems belong to two general categories:

- *Primary*—centralized equipment to generate utility sources such as steam and chilled water
- *Secondary*—largely ventilation and exhaust systems

Primary systems

Primary mechanical equipment systems include the boilers, chillers, cooling towers, and air compressors. A key design issue is whether the primary equipment should be in a central plant or within the building as a stand-alone facility. The advantages of a central plant include operational costs that are more economical in the long term (diversity provides an opportunity for higher efficiency at centralized equipment). There is no rule of thumb for the amount of savings produced by a centralized plant because savings depend on the degree of centralization. There are two key elements involved in operating cost efficiency: energy and labor. Energy economies can be achieved by larger equipment, better balancing of loads with equipment capacity, and single-point metering. Labor economies can be achieved by reducing the total number of staff necessary to maintain and operate the plant. Reduction in labor is usually the more significant consideration.

⬆ *Architectural and engineering coordination. Design of the structural system should be the first step.*

⬆ *Locate mechanical ductwork next.*

of the engineering system to run horizontally in the corridor ceiling. Because there is no beam in the corridor, there is more space to maintain the control boxes, shutoff valves, and so on. This concept is commonly referred to as a "partial interstitial," because the area over the corridor is used for servicing the engineering systems.

There is also a potentially lower first cost (economy of scale versus distribution cost). A central plant is more reliable, easier to maintain, and incorporates redundancy with minimal additional capital costs. Emissions are at one location, and extra capacity is available throughout the facility.

The main disadvantage of a central plant is the higher cost for initial construction resulting from high distribution costs. In a large development that is constructed at one time, a central plant is usually less costly to build than regional plants or stand-alone buildings. Most research campuses, however, are developed in phases. If a central plant is built in the first phase, the initial cost of the first phase is higher, because the central plant must be large enough to accommodate all further development. If the first phase is one-third to one-half of the total development and the distribution distances are reasonable, the first phase premium can be as low as 25 percent. If there are existing stand-alone buildings, then the new services will have to be fed from the central plant to the existing structures. The existing building services are tied into the central plant, usually at the end of the life of the original systems or if new ownership takes over.

Several factors come into play in determining the location of the primary equipment, including proximity to support utilities such as gas, electricity, water, and sewers.

The distance of distribution systems (ductwork for heating and cooling) from the central plant to the laboratory structure, as well as their size, will also determine the location of the central plant. There usually is

the need to isolate the equipment from the structural system to control vibration and noise. Most equipment should be located where space is available for expansion. Effluent cross-contamination and prevailing winds will impact the location of the exhaust and supply air intakes. Convenient vehicular access for service and maintenance should not be forgotten.

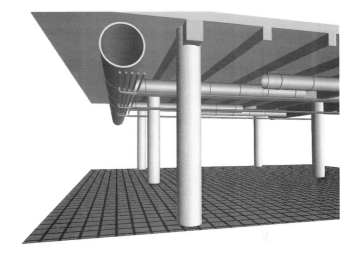

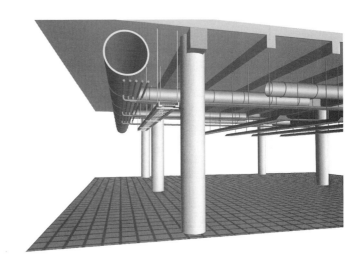

⏶ *The third step is to locate process piping.*

⏶ *Fourth, locate cable trays and lights.*

When sizing the equipment the following design considerations should be addressed:

Safety factor

A safety factor of 1.0 (that is, 1.0 times the calculated load) is usually sufficient for mechanical, electrical, and plumbing (MEP) design, although in some research facilities each component and system should be evaluated individually. For example, heating and cooling load calculations are performed at "design conditions," which are regularly exceeded in a given year. In a research laboratory, with 100 percent outside air, any variation in outdoor air temperature or humidity is immediately sensed by the heating and cooling equipment. Therefore, consideration should be given to safety factors for these systems.

Redundancy and standby capability

Redundancy and standby capability can be addressed either at the component level or at the system level, depending on the criticality of the loads served. Although no universal standards exist, some rules of thumb may apply. For office areas, redundancy and standby capability are usually not needed, except for heating systems in freezing climates (so that the building does not freeze). For ordinary laboratory facilities, systems should have either $n + 1$ system redundancy (i.e., the ability to meet the design load if one component fails) or multiple components, so that if one component is lost the load can still be served, at least in part. For critical functions, like clean rooms, animal holding facilities, manufacturing facilities, and so on, consideration should be given to $n + 1$ component redundancy where 100 percent "extra" capacity is not

available in a separate piece of equipment for each major component.

Diversity

Diversity is the actual anticipated peak divided by the calculated peak. For example, diversity = number of hoods in use/total number of hoods. The diversity range may be anywhere from 70 to 90 percent, reflecting the fact that less than 100 percent of the hoods will be used at the same time.

Optimum efficiency

In determining optimum efficiency, the designer must recognize that laboratories experience a wide range of actual operating conditions throughout the course of a year. For example, in the heating season, electrical loads are substantially lower during unoccupied hours than at design conditions. Similar situations exist with other systems. Therefore, it is not enough to simply choose equipment to meet the peak load; the designer must be careful to select equipment that performs efficiently under all operating conditions. This often means using multiple components, so that not all need to be in operation to run efficiently at lower loads.

Future loads

During the design process, the desired future capacity for the building should be determined, then the primary equipment and ductwork should be designed to accommodate the future needs. This is a key issue in the design of most laboratory buildings. As we tour structures built 10–20 years ago, the main complaints we hear are about insufficient electrical power or the need for additional hoods. If the primary equipment had been designed with greater capacity in anticipation of future requirements, the labs would meet the research needs of today.

Secondary systems

Design issues related to the secondary mechanical equipment systems include the following:

- System selection criteria
- Building system options
- Local laboratory control system options
- Fume hood control options
- Individual versus central exhaust systems
- Fume exhaust ductwork options
- Energy recovery
- Environmental criteria
- Location of equipment

In many cases, the secondary mechanical systems offer the best opportunities for energy conservation.

Location of Air-Supply Grilles

The location of the air intake is also another important design issue. The air-supply louvers will require a large area on the exterior facade. Most louvers are approximately 50 percent open. If a building requires 100 sq ft of open area, then the total louver area will have to be approximately 200 sq ft. The size and location of the air supply louvers will have an impact on the aesthetic image of any wet laboratory facility. There are basically two choices, as discussed in the following paragraphs.

At ground level

Advantages

Air handlers located low in the building (at ground level) are easier to maintain.

Disadvantages

The louvers should be at least 4 ft off the ground to minimize the chance of pulling in bad air from grass clippings during mowing, exhaust fumes from automobiles or from trucks at the loading dock, or odors from trash bins. Locating louvers low also may create a noise problem for pedestrians. The louvers will take up a substantial amount of area, diminishing the pedestrians' aesthetic experience as they walk around the building.

At the roof penthouse

Advantages

The ground floor can be used for program space. A recent National Institutes of Health (NIH) computer-modeling study indicated that often the best place to locate the air intake is directly below the exhaust stacks. The exhaust stacks usually push the air up and away from the building.

Disadvantages

Extra roof structure is required to support the air handlers. When they are placed on the top of the building, air handlers are, in a sense, taking up prime real estate better suited for offices and labs. The building will appear more massive. The supply grilles may conflict with the exhaust stacks. Wind-wake studies should be modeled to minimize the risk of conflict between the air supply and exhaust.

Secondary Containment

Secondary containment is created when the laboratory space is under negative pressure relative to corridors and surrounding nonlaboratory spaces. Because the negative pressure must be maintained in the laboratory, the lab cannot have operable windows or doors to the exterior. Interior doors to laboratories must remain closed as much as possible, should be equipped with closers, and should not be held open. If the direction of airflow is deemed critical, monitoring devices are used to signal or alarm an improper pressure relationship between adjacent spaces.

The laboratory spaces are continuously ventilated 24 hours per day, seven days a week. Supply air must be effectively distributed to all parts of the laboratory space from the ceiling, without creating drafts at exhaust hoods. The maximum supply air velocity in the vicinity of fume hoods and biological safety cabinets should be 50 cu ft per minute (cfm) at 6 ft above the floor.

Air from wet laboratories and other spaces that might contain hazardous materials must be exhausted out of the building and not recirculated. Air from offices and other "clean," nonhazardous areas may be recirculated or directed toward negative-pressure laboratories.

Ventilation Considerations

Proper ventilation is a must for every lab because of the chemical and biological contaminant sources generated in lab activities. Improper ventilation can contaminate not only the lab but the entire facility. Air from wet labs should not be recirculated into other rooms in the building. Most wet labs should be under negative air pressure when in use. To accomplish this, exhaust air volume must exceed supply air volume. Fume hoods are recommended for activities that generate unacceptable levels of exposure to toxic or objectionable airborne materials.

In many wet labs, 10–12 air changes per hour are recommended, with 10 air changes as the minimum threshold. The lab must be designed for the number of air changes necessary. Too many air changes will require more from the mechanical systems, and add more cost to the budget. Too few air changes will result in a problem with odors in the lab and in the building.

Location of Controls for Ductwork

The laboratory HVAC system should be properly controlled to be compliant with regulations, ensure operational safety, satisfy process constraints, and enhance occupants' comfort. A well-controlled system will provide flexibility and minimize the operating cost of the building.

A typical control system should provide the following minimal safety requirements in response to abnormal situations:

- Announce equipment failure to a monitoring center and turn on the existing standby equipment.

- Maintain relative levels of pressurization in the laboratories.

- Stop the air supply to the laboratory, resulting in an increased negative pressurization level, in case of fire or smoke detection in the laboratory. Exit doors must open easily under such situations.

The long-term maintenance and operation of a research laboratory must be understood in the initial design of the project. Will the facility engineers have access to the lab for maintenance? What is the additional cost for locating all controls in the corridor?

These questions must be answered before the ductwork can actually be designed. Ideally, if the controls can be located in the corridor, then maintenance can occur with minimal or no loss of time to the research team. The problem with locating all controls in the corridor is that additional building height may be necessary to accommodate the crossing of exhaust and supply ducts; more ductwork may be necessary to service the building; or the corridor ceiling may have to be lower.

Controls for the mechanical systems include the following:

- The lab exhaust box, which balances the fume hood exhaust and general exhaust air and modulates the supply air terminal
- The fume hood exhaust controls, which control exhaust air to maintain a constant face velocity at the hood
- A thermostat that controls the room temperature

Fume hood exhaust controls and the thermostat are usually located in the lab at a wall near the entry door.

The location of controls for mechanical equipment is always a design consideration, usually driven by balancing the cost of additional space with accessibility and reduced long-term operational costs. In many research facilities, both private and academic, the scientists secure their laboratories in a manner that makes it difficult for service technicians to access control components. In these settings, the control components should be external to the labs. When the controls are located outside the labs in the corridor, there is usually a need for additional ductwork and sometimes more area in the building. Controls cannot be located outside the labs in buildings with low floor-to-floor heights or with narrow corridors. The tradeoffs

must be studied and evaluated at the beginning of the project.

Noise Control

Noise control requires specific attention to design and construction details. Several factors should be addressed in the design of the mechanical and electrical systems to minimize noise problems. Fan noise, for example, may be transmitted to spaces through the duct system or through the building structure. This noise is characterized by a low-frequency rumble and often includes annoying pure tones. Labs with exposed ceilings are often noisy—a result of noise generated from the ductwork and/or the equipment in the room. In such situations it is very difficult to minimize the noise generated by equipment because the floor, walls, and ceiling services are constructed of materials with hard surfaces.

Noise generated by the excitation of duct wall resonance produced by fan noise, by pressure fluctuations caused by fan instability, and by high turbulence caused by discontinuance in the duct system can be a concern. Noise of mid- to high-frequency can also be generated by air flowing past dampers, turning vanes, and terminal device louvers. Additionally, noise and vibration can be caused by out-of-balance forces generated by the operation of fans, pumps, compressors, and so on. All these situations require special acoustical or, possibly, structural solutions.

Elevator equipment noise from motor generators, hoist gear, and counterweight movement or from hydraulic pump systems must be isolated.

Conduits should not directly link noise-sensitive spaces, nor should they mechanically bridge vibration-isolated building elements using a rigid connection. Flexible conduit must be used for connections to isolated floor slabs, walls, and vibration-isolated mechanical/electrical devices. Duct silencers should be considered when duct distance is not sufficient to provide adequate acoustical separation.

The *ASHRAE Handbook* recommends the following as acceptable sound levels for laboratory spaces:

Space Usage	Room Criteria Noise Level
Testing/research, minimal speech communication	45–55
Research, extensive telephone use, and speaking	40–50
Group teaching	35–45

FUME HOODS—MECHANICAL SYSTEM DESIGN ISSUES

Labs that contain fume hoods have special mechanical system requirements, related to

- Face velocity and static pressure
- Fume hood exhaust
- Fume hood sash options
- Fume hood risers

Face Velocity and Static Pressure

There must be an adequate "pull" of air (known as face velocity) to move fumes from the hood through the ductwork. Face velocity of approximately 100 ft per minute (fpm) is generally recommended. To maintain consistent face velocity, a certain quantity of air, or exhaust volume, is required. Exhaust volume is measured in cfm. Both face velocity and exhaust volume are affected by the type of hood selected, its location in the lab, and the room's heating, ventilation, and air-conditioning system (HVAC).

Sash position also affects face velocity. The sash is a transparent glass panel set in the fume hood face that provides access to the hood interior while protecting the user from contact with dangerous chemicals and fumes.

The air foil influences the patterns of airflow into the hood. Located just beneath the sash, the air foil decreases the turbulence of air entering the hood, resulting in improved efficiency and better fume containment. (Some fume hoods feature air foils on the left and right sides of the sash, as well.)

Static pressure is the resistance created as air moves through a fume hood. Sometimes referred to as static pressure loss, it is measured in inches of water. Fume hoods operate more efficiently and with less noise at lower static pressure values.

Obviously, the amount of air passing through a hood (exhaust volume) and the speed at which it enters (face velocity) will affect static pressure values. There are a few other hood design characteristics that also affect static pressure:

- Larger baffle slots make it easier for air to move through the hood.
- A larger exhaust outlet enables more air to pass through at lower velocity.
- A tapered exhaust collar reduces turbulence.
- Together, the exhaust collar and the baffle configuration affect the system's static pressure.

The static pressure rating of a hood, which is very important in determining the correct sizing of the blower system, should be provided to the HVAC engineer to ensure a properly sized exhaust fan. A low static pressure rating indicates that the hood is offering minimal resistance to airflow, resulting in reduced noise and requiring a smaller exhaust fan.

Fume Hood Exhaust Systems

There are two types of fume hood exhaust systems:

- Constant volume (CV)
- Variable air volume (VAV)

Either system can be used with individual or manifold duct and blower configurations. A lab's fume hood exhaust system must be compatible with the room's HVAC system.

Constant volume exhaust systems

CV fume hoods maintain consistent exhaust volume regardless of sash position. Face velocity must therefore be regulated by some other means. A CV system does not allow much flexibility to accommodate different requirements. If there are few hoods in the lab facility, then a CV system may be more cost-effective than a VAV system. Another advantage is that the CV system is easier to run and maintain because it has simpler controls. Three types of hood can provide constant volume function: bypass, auxiliary air, and restricted bypass.

Bypass fume hoods with CV exhaust systems

Incorporating a bypass (an additional source of exhaust air when the sash is lowered) is one way to keep face velocities within an acceptable range, while maintaining balance between the room ventilating system and the hood's exhaust

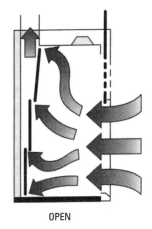
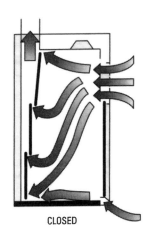

OPEN   CLOSED

volume. CV hoods are equipped with bypass louvers located above the sash, which open as the sash is lowered, allowing additional air to enter the hood.

Auxiliary air fume hoods with CV exhaust systems

When there is insufficient room air to supply a fume hood with its exhaust volume requirements, an auxiliary air hood may be recommended. Air is brought in from the outside, heated to room temperature in winter or cooled

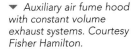

▲ *Bypass fume hood w/constant volume exhaust systems. Courtesy Fisher Hamilton.*

▼ *Auxiliary air fume hood with constant volume exhaust systems. Courtesy Fisher Hamilton.*

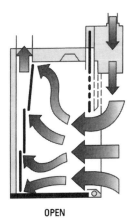
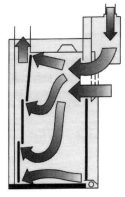

OPEN   CLOSED

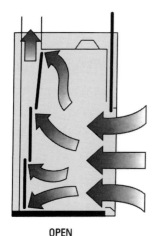

OPEN

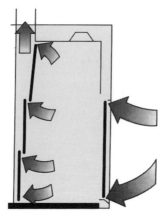

CLOSED

▲ Restricted bypass fume hood with constant volume exhaust systems. Courtesy Fisher Hamilton.

▼ Restricted bypass fume hood with VAV exhaust systems. Courtesy Fisher Hamilton.

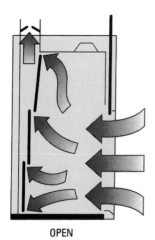

OPEN

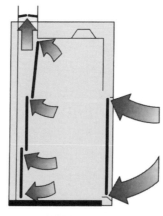

CLOSED

to ± 20° F of the room temperature in summer, then supplied to the fume hood. When the sash is raised, auxiliary air is directed to the fume hood face. When the sash is lowered, auxiliary air enters the hood from above.

Operating with 50–70 percent auxiliary supply air, these hoods use significantly less room air, which can result in energy savings. Supply air temperature and moisture content must, however, be carefully controlled to prevent containment problems or adverse effects on work performed in the hood.

Undesirable turbulence at the hood face can be prevented by careful balancing of the hood with the room's ventilation system.

Restricted bypass fume hoods with CV exhaust systems

Constant volume operation can be achieved when restricted bypass hoods are equipped with "face opening reducing devices" and postless sashes. These modified sash designs can reduce exhaust volumes by as much as 30–60 percent. This reduced exhaust volume enables the bypass to be reduced, achieving constant volume operation without excessive increase in face velocity.

Variable air volume exhaust systems

VAV systems maintain constant face velocities by varying the exhaust volume in response to changes in sash position. A maximum amount of air is exhausted when the sash is fully open; a minimum amount of air is exhausted when the sash is completely closed. A minimum flow of 20 percent total exhaust volume should be maintained to achieve optimum containment and satisfactory dilution with the sash closed.

VAV technology has become more refined over the past decade or so. Although VAV is more sophisticated and requires more hardware than a CV system, results can be beneficial in certain circumstances. Today, an increasing number of facility engineers have the ability to maintain and operate VAV systems.

Restricted bypass fume hoods with VAV exhaust systems

All VAV systems should be used with a restricted bypass fume hood to maximize energy savings and safety. Because only the amount of air needed to maintain the specified face velocity is pulled from the room, significant energy savings can be realized with the sash in a closed position. Either vertical or horizontal sash configurations can be used effectively in VAV applications.

Sash Options

There are three types of sashes: vertical, horizontal, and combination.

Vertical sashes

Vertically rising sashes present several design issues to consider.

Advantages

Vertical rising sashes are less expensive than other types of sashes. They allow researchers unrestricted access to the interior of the fume hood.

Disadvantages

Face velocity of 100 fpm may be required over the entire open area of the sash, resulting in 1,200 cfm exhaust for a standard 6 ft general chemical fume hood. The amount of exhaust air used requires more energy to move, increasing the costs by requiring larger, more expensive supply and exhaust air systems.

Horizontal sashes

The horizontal sliding sash is another option.

Advantages

Only a portion of the face area can be open at any time for a four-panel hood, reducing exhaust air and associated energy requirements. The horizontal sliding panels can serve as face and body shields.

Disadvantages

A horizontal sash is more expensive than a vertical sash. It is more restrictive for researchers, because it provides less access to the hood area unless the panel is removed. In some cases, users remove panels for setup purposes without replacing them, resulting in hood velocities that are low and unsafe.

Combination sashes

The combination sash, or dual sash, is a relatively new design that is being installed in many labs today.

Advantages

With the use of a combination sash, as compared with a vertical sash, exhaust air is reduced as much as 40 percent—up to 500 cfm for a 6 ft hood—with a resulting reduction of energy requirements. The horizontal sliding panels can serve as face and body shields. The vertical sash can be raised during setup to provide full access to the hood interior at reduced face velocity.

Disadvantages

The initial cost of the combination sash is higher than that of either the vertical or horizontal sash (but combination sashes are more cost-effective over the long run).

Fume Hood Risers

There are basically two approaches to exhausting fume hoods: the dedicated (individual) exhaust system and the manifolded system. The choice must be evaluated early in the project, because the decision will have an impact on the floor-to-floor height, long-term operating and maintenance costs, and the exterior image of the building.

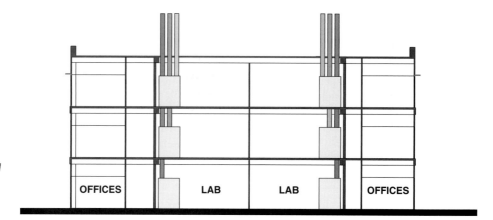

▶ *Individual dedicated exhaust system.*

OFFICES | LAB | LAB | OFFICES

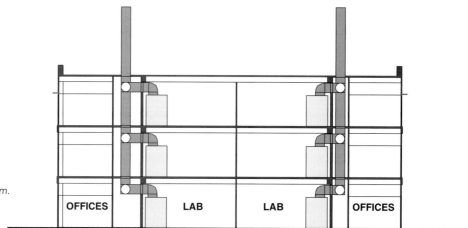

▶ *Manifold exhaust system.*

OFFICES | LAB | LAB | OFFICES

Individual exhaust system

The risers for the fume hood exhaust ducts will have to be close to the hood if a dedicated exhaust system is required. The shaft has to separate the different exhaust ducts, as stated in the building codes. When each dedicated exhaust duct reaches the roof, it is tied into an individual exhaust fan or manifolded to a central location that is on the roof and outside the building. The use of individual stacks and fans can require more maintenance because of all the additional parts.

Advantages

There is more ability for control or treatment. There is no mixing of fumes from different hoods or labs. Exhaust ducts are vertically exhausted directly to the atmosphere. This system is less expensive if there is a small number of hoods (ten or fewer).

Disadvantages

This system requires a considerably greater number of individual fans, more ductwork wiring, and more roof penetrations, which together typically increase first costs and maintenance costs. The system is much more difficult to balance, and reduction of exhaust air quantities during unoccupied operation is costly. Energy recovery systems are not practical.

Manifolded exhaust system

If there is a central manifolded fume hood exhaust system, then the exhaust can tie into a main duct at one location on the floor. There are several options for a manifolded system. In many cases, a manifolded system is designed so there may be a need for dedicated exhaust for special requirements, such as radioisotope and perchloric hoods.

Advantages

Exhaust air is well diluted before it is raised to the atmosphere. The central exhaust approach is very dependable, with redundant fan capacity. Energy consumption can be reduced with energy recovery and VAV controls.

Disadvantages

This system should *not* be used with hoods handling radioactive materials, perchloric acid, strong oxidizing agents, highly reactive chemicals, or biological hazardous materials (BL-3) or with hoods requiring water wash-down. Duct runs are longer and have the potential for spreading fire.

ELECTRICAL SYSTEMS

Site and Building-wide Issues

Load estimation

The load estimation process typically includes conceptual load estimation, program-based load estimation, and applied demand factors. The conceptual load estimation takes into account basic rules of thumb for good practice. For example, in lighting design, the following standards are recommended:

- 1.5–2.0 watts/sq ft in labs
- 1.3 watts/sq ft in offices
- 0.8 watts/sq ft in corridors

The program-based load estimation for electrical services typically takes into account lighting, ventilation, air conditioning, pumping, laboratory equipment, receptacles, and elevators.

Site distribution concepts

Site distribution concepts are generally based on master-planning issues and recommendations of the local utility agency. In talking with a local agency, two questions should be asked:

- What voltage (480 V, 5 kV, 15 kV, 25 kV, or higher) is available?
- What rates (secondary versus primary metering; independent power suppliers' rates) are available?

Secondary metering generally entails less capital expense and higher energy costs; it is usually right for smaller clients. For primary metering, the customer must purchase or lease transformers, switchgear, and so on. There is a primary discount and future flexibility in negotiations with independent power suppliers.

Level of system redundancy

The most important place for system redundancy is usually at the site distribution level. Annual maintenance is required at the medium-voltage switch gear and must be accommodated in the design. The costs and benefits must be analyzed to design for the most appropriate system redundancy. A good rule of thumb is to provide 25 percent spare capacity for the electrical panel board loading.

Analysis of electrical system redundancy focuses on two points: probability of failure and incremental cost. Probability of failure is predicted by statistics. For example, a cable termination has a much higher probability of failing than a protection device, which in turn has a higher probability of failing than does a transformer. The electrical supply (electric utility) has the highest probability of failure.

Failure analysis leads to conclusions about the components and systems that would be best served by redundant capabilities. This information must then be balanced against the cost of the redundancy, which is harder to provide the closer you get to the load. In other words, redundant building entrance equipment is less expensive than redundant service to each duplex receptacle. The normal break point is at the unit substation level. In laboratories, it makes sense to regularly "double-end" unit substations and all of the distribution before them, and to single-end the service thereafter.

Power quality

Power quality has to do with the compatibility between the requirements of the equipment and the characteristics of the serving system. This compatibility is defined in two ways:

- *Frequency compatibility.* Frequency compatibility problems are rare in utility-based systems. Problems are more common in engine/generator-based systems.

- *Waveform compatibility.* Distortion is caused by "nonlinear loads" from electronic ballasts, computers, variable frequency drives, and uninterruptible power supplies.

Interior distribution concepts

Typically in the United States, a 480/277 volt load center supports major HVAC and elevator loads at 480 volts and nonincandescent lighting at 277 volts. Systems using 240 volts should be avoided.

For interior grounding, the grounding electrode system should be robust. An equipment grounding conductor should be specified in every branch circuit and feeder conduit, and all equipment and boxes should be grounded.

Emergency/Standby Power Requirements

It is important to understand the requirements for a laboratory's equipment and research before determining the standby power. It is necessary to know whether the equipment can sustain short- or long-term interruptions.

Code-required loads for the emergency system must be identified, as must optional standby loads. It is also important to understand the National Electrical Code/Segregation requirements.

Three types of power are generally used for most laboratory projects:

1. Normal power circuits are connected to the utility supply only, without any backup system. Loads that are typically on normal power include some HVAC equipment, general lighting, and most lab equipment.

2. Emergency power is created with generators that will back up equipment such as refrigerators, freezers, fume hoods, biological safety cabinets, emergency lighting, exhaust fans, animal facilities, and environmental rooms.

3. An uninterruptible power supply (UPS) is used for data recording, certain computers, microprocessor-controlled equipment, and possibly the vivarium area. The UPS can be either a central unit or a portable system.

A generator protects against prolonged utility outage; a UPS system protects against any disruption in electricity supply. In other words, a generator is available to provide electricity in the event utility service is lost, after a momentary delay. A UPS system prevents the load served from experiencing any interruption in the electricity supply, regardless of its origin.

At the outset of a project, it is critical to define the loads to be served by an emergency generator and potentially by a UPS. This is because the emergency load tends to grow as the project planning is completed, and it is important to ensure that the installed generator capacity can serve the loads that are ultimately connected to it.

Very few laboratory facilities employ facility-wide UPS systems. A UPS is usually provided at an individual laboratory or suite of laboratory levels, often locally. A central UPS will have a higher initial cost but lower long-term operational costs. The failure of a single central UPS, however, can be much more costly than the loss of one portable UPS. Portable UPSs are more costly in the long run but provide greater flexibility. Individual units can be relocated as equipment is moved. Either UPS option will typically provide power for 10–15 minutes, after which emergency or normal power will have to be operating. Receptacles should be color-coded to distinguish between normal, emergency, and UPS power.

Special electrical systems may be needed for hazardous locations, locations with high or low temperatures, and unusual voltage or frequency applications.

Locate at 36 in. maximum centers for outlets in instrument-usage areas. Requirements for 110V, 208V, 220V, and so on must be verified. All electrical outlets in the lab should be ground-fault interrupters (GFIs). Areas where GFIs are required must be verified by referring to applicable codes. If GFIs are required at hoods, they must be specified separately.

Electrical Cable Trays/Panel Boxes

Electrical components tend to be easier to coordinate than plumbing or mechanical systems because the wire they use is flexible and requires a relatively small amount of space.

Cable trays are usually located on a raceway for easier maintenance. Electrical and data wires usually need to be run and modified often through the life of the building because of additional needs for computers, telephones, and equipment. Easy access is therefore very important.

Cable trays are usually located in the corridor below the ceiling, at the same height as the ceiling, or just above it.

Panel boxes are located either in zones on each floor or at the entry alcove to each lab. An adequate number of extra breakers must be included in each panel box to accommodate future needs.

LIGHTING DESIGN

Lab spaces are at times generic in layout, but often they are unique to the research and experimentation they serve, or at least possess certain unique elements. Therefore, it is vital that the lighting designer understand the laboratory environment, the purpose it serves, the way its users work, and the physical properties of each space, including the opportunities for and limitations on various lighting systems.

No matter what the differences from one laboratory to the next, there is a common and essential need: the ability to perform a variety of detailed tasks quickly and accurately without eyestrain or visual discomfort. Above all, the intent of the laboratory lighting system is to produce a visual environment that enhances productivity, increases a sense of well-being, and fosters creativity in the workplace. To achieve these high standards, lighting design must be visually comfortable, aesthetically appealing, affordable, and easily maintainable.

There is a misconception that lighting quality has only to do with controlling glare and/or providing a certain quantity of light. Both are important, without question. These are only two of numerous factors to consider, however. Others include direction of light, light-source color, the ability to render colors accurately, contrast, uniformity, and surface reflectance.

Daylight is the standard for color quality in lighting, with a color-rendering index (CRI) of 100. Daylight is obviously the most energy-efficient source of illumination.

Key Issues

The first chapter of this book discusses sustainability issues in lighting design. The following paragraphs cover some of the other key issues.

User expectations

Minimal glare and uniform lighting levels are essential for visual comfort. Indirect lighting, or a combination of indirect and direct, should be considered. A ceiling height of at least 9' 6" is necessary for indirect lighting. When indirect light fixtures are used in main lab areas, task lighting is usually required, which adds cost to the project. Fluorescent lay-in light fixtures with parabolic louvers can also be used to minimize glare.

Illumination levels

Too often, an overwhelming emphasis is placed on quantity of light as measured in footcandles by an illuminance meter. Although illuminance is a useful metric for analysis, it is important to understand the limitations of this tool. Illuminance is the measure of light arriving at a surface, not what is actually seen. More important is the amount of light reflected by that surface that actually reaches the eye, measured as luminance. Therefore, illuminance has no practical meaning without the knowledge of the reflectance and light-dispersing properties of surface materials within the space. With this knowledge, the designer can provide an amount of light appropriate for the task to be accomplished.

User requirements for lighting levels must also be considered, as well as any state or local energy codes that may limit the total lighting-power budget. Recommended illumination levels, according to the Engineering Society of North America, are as follows:

Most labs	75–100 footcandles
Tissue and reading cultures	150–200 footcandles
Offices	50–75 footcandles

Uniformity

Lighting for laboratory workspaces should provide high visibility while reducing glare, extreme contrasts, and harsh shadows. Lighting that is uniform reduces the amount of adaptation a person's eye must endure when switching between tasks, thereby reducing the potential for eyestrain and increasing productivity.

Horizontal illuminance is used to establish the "base" level of light on a horizontal work surface. Uniformity of horizontal illuminance is important to allow for a high level of task mobility and flexibility. Uniformity of vertical illumi-nance lets researchers perform three-dimensional tasks at multiple levels with-out encountering harsh shadowing or high contrast from one work zone to the next.

Uniform ceiling luminance helps to blend daylight with artificial lighting, thereby reducing extreme contrasts and glare. Uniform ceiling luminance, combined with light colors and highly reflective room surfaces, also increases the overall perception of the brightness and spaciousness of a room.

Methods of light distribution

Two primary methods of light distribution are commonly used in laboratory environments to produce ambient (general) lighting. These are (1) indirect/direct distribution, a combination of downlighting and uplighting of the ceiling surface; and (2) direct distribution, or downlighting.

Indirect/direct distribution

Indirect/direct lighting distribution typically involves the use of fluorescent sources for spaces with higher ceilings. A minimum ceiling height of 9' 6" is recommended in order to suspend luminaires at a distance from the ceiling that is sufficient to create uniform ceiling luminance without compromising the use of equipment space below. Ideally, luminaires are located so as to provide uniform ceiling luminance while concentrating the direct lighting component on the work surface.

The benefits of indirect/direct distribution include a substantial reduction in distracting shadows over work surfaces and an increased sense of brightness without overlighting the space. It is not uncommon that the level of illuminance required with this strategy is less than that needed for direct distribution to perform tasks equally well, and often with increased lighting quality.

Direct distribution

Direct distribution is commonly used with fluorescent sources in spaces with ceiling heights lower than 9' 6", in areas of high equipment density where users do not spend an extended duration of time except for experiment preparation and cleanup, and where the ability to suspend luminaires is compromised. Direct lighting is most successful when more luminaires are used, each having a smaller light output. This layout results in better

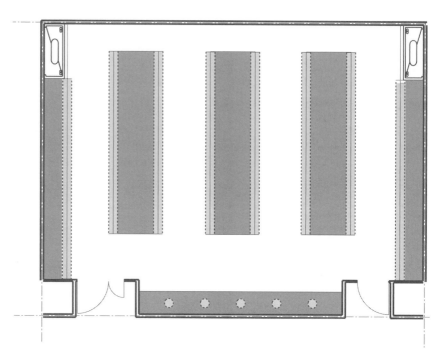

▶ *Lighting parallel to casework.*

control of glare, reduced shadowing, and increased uniformity. The two most common luminaire types used with direct distribution are lensed fluorescent and parabolic fluorescent luminaires:

• *Lensed fluorescent luminaires* produce a brightly lighted lab environment but do not provide any control of direct glare for the user or of indirect glare on visual display terminals. The direct-only distribution also creates shadows on horizontal work surfaces, thereby reducing visibility.

• *Parabolic fluorescent luminaires* have louvers that reduce light output at high angles. The louvers offer glare control, but, because of high light-source cutoff, often result in dark vertical surfaces, including room walls. This tends to produce a cavernous effect and greatly reduces the sense of room brightness. As with

lensed fluorescents, there will be shadows on horizontal work surfaces because of the direct distribution.

Luminaire location and orientation
Minimizing shadows on a work surface will improve visibility and comfort, thereby increasing lighting quality. When a luminaire with direct distribution and a parabolic louver is chosen, the layout of the light fixtures is particularly important. If the light source is behind the user standing at the lab bench, that person's own shadow is cast on the work surface.

When luminaires are oriented parallel to the lab bench, they should be aligned near the front edge of the bench to allow maintenance from the aisle space and to provide light distribution on the work surface in front of the lab user. When orientating luminaires perpendicular to the lab bench, they should extend 12–18 in. beyond the edge of the bench.

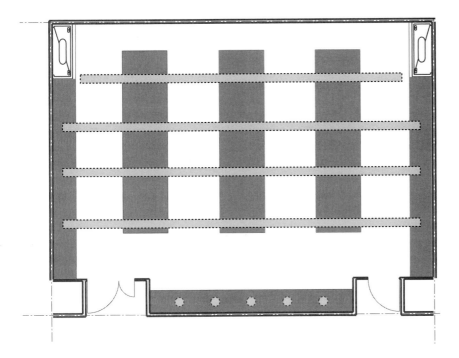

◀ *Lighting perpendicular to casework.*

Laboratories can be successfully lighted with luminaires oriented parallel or perpendicular to the lab bench. Each laboratory should be studied and the best determination made after a consideration of all factors, including the dimensions of the lab module, equipment layouts, and the luminaire selected. If possible, the best method for making a final decision is to build a full-scale mock-up of one or two lab modules and install different lighting options.

When locating luminaires, consideration should also be given to the ease and cost of maintenance. Lab benches are typically covered with equipment, glass elements, chemicals, and other objects that maintenance staff prefer not to disturb when having to replace a lamp or ballast. If luminaires are run parallel to lab benches, it is recommended not to locate them directly over the benches but where they can be maintained from the aisle space. When luminaires are oriented perpendicular to lab benches, only a portion of the light fixture should extend over the lab bench so as to allow maintenance from the aisle space.

Lighting Design for Specific Spaces

In a flexible environment where team and individual seating arrangements change, an appropriate solution is indirect lighting, with most of the light reflected off the ceiling from pendant-mounted fixtures. Pendant fixtures are typically mounted 18–24 in. below the ceiling. Because light is reflected, an efficient installation requires 80 percent reflectivity for ceiling materials and 65 percent reflective paint for major walls.

The separate switching of selected rows of fixtures allows for a more efficient use of lighting resources. For example,

227

fixtures running adjacent to a window wall can be switched separately; during most seasons and most hours of the day, illumination is provided by daylight, and these fixtures are not needed. Another switching option involves multiple ballasts; with a three-lamp fixture, a user may turn on one row of lamps, two rows of lamps, or all three.

Cost

Lighting quality is closely linked to fixture cost and efficiency. Prices vary, depending on the area of the country and other specific issues related to the design of the building. For example, lay-in fixtures with acrylic prismatic lenses cost about $35 for a 4 ft fixture. Their efficiency is 50–70 percent, and they are generally thought to provide poor-quality light. A similar fixture with a parabolic louver produces less glare and can be purchased for as little as $50. Pendant fixtures that create indirect light start at $80 each. The efficiency of a pendant indirect fixture is 70–85 percent, but because the light is indirect there is a good chance that task lighting will be necessary in labs using pendant indirect fixtures. Pendant fixtures with both direct and indirect light start at about $140. The efficiency of a bidirectional pendant fixture ranges from 80–95 percent. Even though they cost more initially, pendants will outperform lay-in fixtures for the life of the building and provide superior lighting quality.

Light-Source Options, Including Daylighting

Today the T-8 electronic ballast system is entrenched as the system of choice. Refinements are being researched for the T-8 system to provide for better lumen maintenance, more precise fixtures, better ballasts, and less mercury. T-5 and T-2 lamps are on the horizon. T-5 lamps for general lighting are 18 percent more efficient than the T-8s and are less expensive, provide better optical control, and offer better design opportunities. Some states currently allow a T-5 ballast system to be used. T-2 lamps are appropriate for task lighting and display cases.

On an average winter day there are more than four hours of sunshine that is usable for natural daylighting of interior spaces; on an average summer day, about ten hours. During winter, when more artificial lighting is used, the additional heat generated by this lighting is usually beneficial for the building. In the summer, peak cooling requirements may be reduced with the use of more natural daylight.

TELEPHONE/DATA SYSTEM

The telephone/data system consists of wall outlets in all occupied spaces, including offices, laboratories, secretarial and clerical support areas, and conference rooms. These outlets are then connected in separate telephone and data rooms via conduit and cable tray system. A central telephone and communication room (used for data acquisition and security) should be provided, usually in a central location on the lowest level. Combination voice/data equipment rooms (VDERs) should be provided on each floor, usually in a central location to minimize the length of run for the wire. Telephones should be provided at the exits of mechanical and electrical rooms. A single conduit should be run from each wall outlet box to the cable tray above an accessible ceiling. A prewired building telephone and data cabling system is usually purchased and installed by the owner.

INFORMATION TECHNOLOGY

Computer networks must be flexible, manageable, and easily expandable. It is critically important that the design team have the ability to communicate, comprehend, and document an understanding of a facility's unique systems, operations, and startup requirements and to translate those needs to construction bid documents. It is only by focusing on the specific requirements that these goals will be satisfied. Getting qualified information technology (IT) consultants on board early in the project can add value to the design process and can reduce overall project construction and facility startup expenses.

Today, effective design for technology means much more than just placing voice and data outlets in convenient locations. It calls for a comprehensive, "whole network" approach to communication technologies. Voice, data, video, access systems, security cameras, closed circuit TV (CCTV), and cable TV (CATV) all affect the building process and require coordination with other building systems and elements (e.g., door schedules, conduit and j-boxes, ergonomic and functional furniture selection, etc.).

Making efficient use of telecommunications utility spaces and accommodating future changes in equipment and/or services require thoughtful planning. Of course, saving construction dollars is important, but the impact the design will have on operating budgets is just as critical a consideration.

Fiber-Optic Infrastructure

The TIA/EIA-568-A Commercial Building Telecommunications Cabling Standard recognizes 62.5/125 μm optical fiber as the fiber-optic cable of choice for premise networks. As the need for higher data rates increases, however, facility planners and IT managers may wish to deviate from this industry standard and install 50/125 μm fiber-optic cable instead.

The decision will be based on bandwidth, distances, advancing technology, and money. For fiber-optic infrastructures, the amount of data that can be transmitted basically depends on two factors: the wavelength of the signal and the "loss budget" established for the fiber-optic network design.

Speed and bandwidth

Since the 1980s, network data rates have increased so quickly that we have "added a 0 — 10 Mbps, then 100 Mbps, then 1,000 Mbps — approximately every five years. Once only imagined, Gigabit Ethernet is now a reality, and 1.2 Gb/s (Gigabits per second) ATM (asynchronous transfer mode) is also a leading contender for high-speed backbones. In terms of future planning, no one can predict with certainty which technology will prevail, but if present trends continue, the need for more bandwidth will continue to drive technology and put heavy demands on a building's infrastructure.

We need more bandwidth — or we predict that we will need it in the not-too-distant future. We also desire low cost. Data rates of more than 622 Mbps cannot be achieved using 62.5/125 μm multimode fiber while applying the distance limitations as specified by current Telecommunications Industry Association/Electrical Industry Association (TIA/EIA) and International Standards Organization/International Electrotechnical Commission (ISO/IEC) standards.

Interestingly, we can achieve more bandwidth, over greater distances, and with some surprising cost savings by deviating from today's published standard and installing 50/125 μm multimode fiber to support some applications.

Vertical cavity surface emitting lasers (VCSELs) have been developed as a lower-cost light source, supplementing LEDs and single-mode lasers in higher-speed applications. Through extensive testing by the 802.3z committee (Institute of Electrical and Electronics Engineers, IEEE), which has put together specifications for running Gigabit Ethernet traffic over fiber-optic cable, 50-micron multimode optical fiber cable has proved superior in its ability to support Gigabit Ethernet. Fifty-micron optical fiber has the ability to support Gigabit Ethernet up to the recommended 500 in both long and short (1300 nm–850 nm) wavelengths. The result will probably be that VCSELs rather than LEDs will be used in Gigabit transmissions, and 50-micron fiber has an advantage at these speeds and distances.

Cost

Not only is 50/125 μm about 10–12 percent less expensive than 62.5/125 μm, but it uses the same form factor connectors. TIA/EIA has accepted a proposal to include 50-micron fiber in the upcoming TIA/EIA-568b cabling standard, and the ISO/IEC have recognized 50-micron fiber for some time in the ISO/IEC-11801 international cabling standard.

In new installations, 50-micron optical fiber is an intelligent choice because of its lower cost and better performance. In existing networks where there may be a large installed base of 62.5-micron fiber there are aperture mismatch issues that will have to be considered.

CLOSETS

Electric, data, and custodial closets—typically 65–100 NSF each—are usually located near one another at the center of each lab zone. It is more efficient and cost effective to locate the closets centrally, but in many facilities that location is within the lab zone. Data closets are typically bigger than other closet types, and more of them are needed than in the past because of the high requirements for information technology. All closets of the same type should be located directly above each other for efficiency.

AUDIOVISUAL ENGINEERING FOR PRESENTATION ROOMS

Presentation rooms (including classrooms) must be designed for displaying images and reproducing audio program material in a manner that can be accurately perceived by the viewer. This requires proper attention to the facility's space arrangement, acoustics, and lighting.

Projection Screens/Viewing Areas

Space planning for front projection involves placement of an opaque, reflective surface so that projected images can be clearly seen by all viewers. Appropriate viewing-area design encompasses a number of interrelated factors, including screen size, placement, and material.

Screen size is determined by the type of media being presented and by the distance to the farthest viewer. If the images are to include dense text, a ratio of 1:6 should be used. This means, for example, that if the distance to the farthest viewer is 48 ft, the screen should be 8 ft tall for dense text such as spreadsheets or document displays.

Screen width is based on screen height and is determined by the image format to be displayed. Normal television and computer images have a 4:3 image width-to-height ratio. For most rooms, a minimum screen dimension of 60 in. high x 80 in. wide should be specified. Distance to the nearest viewer is also a concern. With higher resolution computer video display images, the nearest viewer should be no closer than two times the screen height.

The viewing-area width depends on the placement of the screen and the type of screen material used. Projection screens should typically be centered on the front wall of the space. In general, matte white projection screens should be used because their characteristic even diffusion typically offers the widest and most consistent viewing areas. Although the optimum maximum off-axis angle is about 30 degrees, the practical limitation is an angle of about 50 degrees off-axis. (Note that the viewing angle should be measured from an axis placed at the far edge of the screen.)

Depending on ceiling height, the number of rows of seats, and whether the floor in the seating area is flat or tiered, the screen's bottom edge should be 42 in. (tiered seating) to 48 in. (flat seating) above the floor. Screen size and placement can also be limited by the ceiling height. At least 6 in. of space

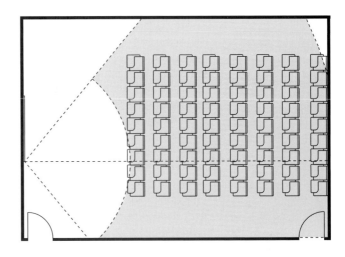

Projection screen in deep room.

should be maintained between the ceiling and the top edge of the screen's projection area. In a typical flat-floored classroom with a 5 ft high screen, the ceiling height will have to be at least 9 ft. Most rooms have a 9–10 ft ceiling height, so a 5 ft high screen should work well.

Another option to consider is a computer board. Computer boards are approximately 3 ft high and 5 ft wide and can be viewed in small- or medium-size rooms. Larger rooms will require

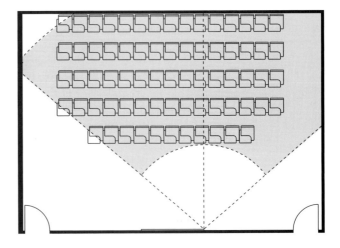

Projection screen in wide room.

monitors to be added so that everyone can easily view the presentation. Computer boards can be written on and networked to others.

Document cameras allow a presenter to display a three-dimensional object, a photograph, a sheet of paper, or any simple text document on a large screen, using a ceiling-mounted video/data projector. A document camera does not require as much space as an overhead projector. Document cameras can be permanently mounted in the ceiling, with controls located in the media panel near the front corner of the room. Calculate 1.5 times the width of the screen to approximate the distance between the screen and the document camera.

For additional flexibility, one or two screens may be added on either side of the center screen. Some rooms will lend themselves to an additional corner screen at a 45-degree angle.

Presentation Space Acoustics

Speech intelligibility can be degraded by excessive reverberation (and/or echoes) and excessive background noise. Traditionally, classrooms have been constructed with minimal amounts of acoustically absorptive materials, and acoustical deficiencies have been tolerated. In presentations where there is no live presenter, the clarity of the program is dependent on the quality of the audio recording, the audio playback system, and the acoustics of the space.

Excessive reverberation is an especially common acoustical deficiency. Reverberation can be controlled by using acoustically absorbing materials such as mineral fiber or fiberglass ceiling tile, fiberglass wall panels, and carpet. Carpet can also reduce noise caused by students

shifting in their seats. Note that the front third of the ceiling should be hard surfaced (e.g., gypsum board) to help reflect sound from the presenter to the listeners.

A related common acoustical deficiency is flutter echo. This deficiency is characterized by a "hollowness" in the sound that is caused by its being reflected multiple times between parallel walls. Splayed wall panels can minimize the problem created by flutter echo. Another related problem is "slap back," an echo caused by sound being reflected off the rear wall. The problem can be addressed by installing acoustically absorptive materials, such as 1–2 in. thick fiberglass wall panels on the rear wall.

Wall construction with a sound transmission class (STC) of 57 or better should be used to separate rooms equipped with audio program playback systems.

Presentation Space Lighting

Control of ambient light is critical. Ambient light falling on a screen will be reflected back to the viewers, washing out projected images. Because the area around the projection screen must be able to be darkened while maintaining necessary lighting levels at student and instructor positions, careful control of room lighting and daylight entering through windows is essential.

Diffuse indirect lighting is desirable for general classroom use, but indirect lighting should not be used during presentations where front projection is required. A direct, controlled lighting component must be provided for use during these presentations. To minimize direct light on the wall and ceiling surfaces during presentations, direct lighting in audience areas should provide reasonable cutoff characteristics, with glare and lamp image cutoff angles of 45–55 degrees. Illumination levels (footcandles) for general lighting should provide 70 horizontal footcandles (maintained) at work surfaces. Lighting on the speaker should be tightly controlled and provide 75–100 vertical footcandles from a front overhead angle of approximately 45 degrees.

Incandescent sources should be avoided for general lighting. However, accent lighting at the speaker's station and other critical locations requiring directional and glare control may be incandescent. In general, such accent lighting should use quartz and/or halogen (PAR) lamps for good light control and extended lamp life. Fluorescent lamps should have color-rendering indexes (CRI) of 70 or better.

Lighting fixtures should be grouped in zones to allow various areas of the room to be controlled separately. Accent lighting, step lighting, and lighting for other specific areas should also be in separate zones. The lighting zones should enable the area around the projection screen to remain darkened (and thereby minimize stray light falling on the projection screen) while illuminating a presenter at either side of the screen. The zoning should also allow sufficient light to remain on over seating areas so notes can be taken. Zoning is appropriate for lecture halls and classrooms with front-screen video projection. Lighting fixture locations will have to be coordinated with ceiling-mounted video projector placement and monitors.

Budgeting

Accurate budgeting for presentation systems has long been problematic. Not only are historical cost data for

audiovisual technologies limited, but the technologies are advancing at such a pace that such historical data as do exist are potentially misleading.

The available data, however, indicate that adding instructional presentation systems can increase the overall cost of a new building project by 8–15 percent. This cost impact results from the installed cost of the cable plant, equipment and its installation, and design. Provisions for specialized lighting and acoustical treatments must also be considered. The computer furniture discussed in chapter 1 will also add cost to the furniture budget.

In addition to the costs associated with the design and installation of instructional presentation systems, there is a potentially significant administrative burden. Technical staff to assist in the setup and operation of the systems will be required. Furthermore, presentation systems require routine maintenance and, over time, may have to be upgraded.

PLUMBING SYSTEMS

Floor Drains, Roof Drains, and Sprinklers

Roof and floor drains can be tricky to coordinate. Usually it is good practice to minimize the number of drains in a lab, which provides fewer opportunities for leaks in the rooms below. Ideally, the horizontal piping from a drain should go directly to the outside wall or to an interior chase via a "wet" column, then down the building to the building-wide drain system. When the drains are adjacent to the columns, care must be taken to coordinate the drain and horizontal piping with the beams and interior walls. The vents should be handled in the same manner as the drains and should be tied into a wall or "wet" column. Some labs require dedicated drains for radioactive materials and certain chemicals that must be handled with special tanks and dilution systems. The plumbing risers should be located on a modular basis to address future needs and lab renovations. The slope of the piping will have to be coordinated to make sure the length of the pipe is not too great and that there is enough space to accommodate the slope without conflicting with the ductwork, other piping, or wiring.

Roof drains are sometimes forgotten until the end of design. A roof drain can easily be 6 in. in diameter, which will not fit in most interior walls (usually less than 4 in. clear). Roof drains are often coordinated with the fume hood or plumbing risers in a common chase located either along the corridor or on the outside wall at most structural bays. Again, the vertical risers for the roof drains should be organized according to the lab module at the beginning of the project. The wet piping for the drains, sprinklers, and the process piping is usually located below the ductwork and above the electrical systems.

Sprinklers require a modest pitch. If there is a ceiling, the sprinkler heads will have to go under the ceiling. If there is no ceiling, the sprinkler heads will have to be at the underside of the structure to cover the entire volume of the space below.

Laboratory Piping Systems

Process piping is usually installed on racks horizontally or vertically. If the racks are horizontal, there is usually less conflict with the other engineering systems. The location of the shutoff valves for the process piping is important. Maintenance

staff and researchers need direct access in case of an emergency or to make easy modifications to the lab. Options include the following:

- Shutoff valve boxes in the lab or at the lab entry alcove
- Above the door at the entry alcove
- Where the piping comes into the bench
- Behind the casework at the rack

There are several key design goals to strive for in designing laboratory piping systems:

- Provide a flexible design that allows for easy renovation and modifications.
- Provide appropriate plumbing systems for each laboratory based on the lab programming.
- Provide systems that minimize energy usage.
- Provide equipment arrangements that minimize downtime in the event of a failure.
- Locate shutoff valves where they are accessible and easily understood.
- Accomplish all of the preceding goals within the construction budget.

Laboratory Waste and Vents

There are a variety of pipe materials to consider for laboratory waste and vents:

- *Flame-retardant polypropylene* is a very stable material with high corrosive resistivity. Installation cost is relatively low. Hangers are necessary every 5 ft on center. This material has low tolerance to high temperatures.
- *Borosilicate glass* is also a very stable material with high corrosive resistivity. Borosilicate does have high tolerance

to temperature and can be finished in plenum spaces. Disadvantages include high installation costs, high material costs, and construction with a mechanical joint (which is less reliable than a polypropylene fusion joint).

- *Duriron* is most commonly used below ground. It has a high tolerance to temperature, but installation costs are extremely high. Duriron also has corrosive reactions with ketones and strong bases.

There are various means of dispensing of laboratory liquid waste. Neutralization of waste disposal can occur in four different ways:

- Passive neutralization with no monitoring
- Passive neutralization with monitoring
- Active neutralization with monitoring
- Passive and active neutralization with monitoring

Hot Water

Water-system options for hot-water maintenance include heat tracing, recirculation, and the use of local water heaters. The advantages of local water heaters include the reduction of piping and lower first costs. The disadvantages are the large electrical draw required for the local water heaters and the cost of maintenance. Local water heaters do make sense for domestic water and for some lab water requirements.

Vacuum

Local vacuum systems can be employed where the need for vacuum is limited and relatively distributed through the facility. Central systems should be employed in facilities where the need for vacuum is

great or vacuum is required at all laboratories. Three notes of caution are in order:

1. Make sure that central vacuum systems are not used for housekeeping purposes; they should be used for scientific purposes only.

2. The vacuum system's effluent can be subject to environmental regulations. If this is the case, a central system generally is most appropriate, enabling treatment to be performed at a single point.

3. If an especially deep vacuum is required, a local system should be considered. Equipment and distribution costs can rise geometrically for central systems with deep vacuum requirements.

The decision to centralize a vacuum system often rests on operational issues. Vacuum pumps consume space, generate noise and effluent, and are somewhat maintenance-intensive. As a result, systems are often centralized.

Piped Gases

There are several options for locating the piped gases needed to service a laboratory. The central location within the building can serve large areas, but the amount of usage must be justified financially. Local closets can serve multiple labs; they usually need to be fire rated for code compliance and may require an auto-switchover, and the contractor will have to install the piping. Locating the piped gases in the lab near the door is another approach. The piping can serve multiple benches. This option requires the contractor to install the piping but may not require an auto-switchover. Locating piped gases in the lab at a bench will take more program space, but this option is very flexible and it will not require the contractor to install the piping. Local generation of the gases with cylinders eliminates the need for contractors and provides a flexible system.

Typically, gases are supplied either through central systems or via gas cylinders stored in or near the laboratories. If cylinders are used, they should be restrained—that is, anchored to a wall, a wall rack, or a bench. In addition, some provision must be made for storing incoming cylinders and waste cylinders at the receiving dock. Storage must also be provided for cylinders delivered to the labs or to the lab floor.

Numerous code requirements, such as those issued by the National Fire Protection Association (NFPA) and the Occupational Safety and Health Administration (OSHA), govern gas systems. These governing codes should be identified for each gas system early in the design process.

Compressed air

Compressed air is another important requirement for many laboratories. Pressure regulation can be at the compressor, by the floor, or by the lab. Compressed gases are similar to compressed air.

Storage of gases and cryogenic liquids
Oxygen

Oxygen can be provided by an outside vendor, with a bulk storage tank that is located on the site. Cylinders can also be used in or near the labs.

Nitrogen

Nitrogen can be supplied in a bulk liquid nitrogen storage tank by an outside vendor, or in cylinders located

in or near the labs.

Natural gas

Natural gas can be provided by an on-site gas utility or from a bulk propane gas storage tank located on-site.

Hydrogen

Hydrogen is provided by an outside vendor, usually in bulk storage located on site. A second option is manifolded cylinders, also provided by an outside vendor.

Cryogenic liquids

Cryogenic liquids (nitrogen, argon, and carbon dioxide) can be stored in bulk tanks or liquid dewars.

Laboratory Water Supplies

Four types of water are typically supplied to laboratories:

- *Chilled water* provides cooling for special equipment (such as an electron microscope). A chilled water system is typically constructed as a part of the central building system.

- *Potable water* is provided for laboratory work areas and rest rooms.

- *Domestic water* is used at drinking fountains, emergency showers, eyewashes, break rooms, and janitor's closets.

- *High-purity water* is required for many research processes. High-purity water systems are dealt with below.

High-purity water systems

High-purity water is classified into three types: Type I, Type II, and Type III.

Type I water

Type I water is used in numerous critical

laboratory applications. Inorganic analysis applications include inductively coupled plasma spectrometry (ICP), ion chromatography (IC), atomic absorption spectro-photometry (AA), and electrophoretic procedures (EP). Organic analysis applications include liquid chromatography (LC), high performance liquid chromatography (HPLC; higher restrictions, such as "organic free," may be imposed), gas chromatography (GC), and mass spectroscopy (MS).

Type I water is also used for biological applications, fermentation systems, in vitro/in vivo fertilization, general microbiology, recombinant DNA, tissue culture, and immunological applications.

Type II water

Type II water is purified water that meets the requirements of most routine clinical laboratory methods in chemistry, immunology, hematology, and so on. It is the type of water used in reagent preparation and glassware rinsing.

Type III water

Type III water is general laboratory-grade water. This class of purified water is used for qualitative procedures, glassware washing, and preliminary rinsing. Final rinsing water should match water intended for glass-washer use.

These are the basic methods used for water purification:

- Reverse osmosis, producing RO water
- Distillation, producing distilled water
- Deionization, producing deionized water
- Deionization combined with reverse osmosis

A combination of these methods and additional purification processes are

necessary to meet levels required by Type I water.

The first of these processes, known as RODI (reverse osmosis deionization), is used most often. Its advantages are low installation cost and maintainability. Its disadvantages are that it wastes a significant amount of water (approximately half the total) and that the water comes in direct contact with a membrane. The equipment used for distillation can result in water with higher purity and is used in regulated applications, such as water for injection for pharmaceutical facilities. However, this process is maintenance-intensive.

Case study

A key issue in designing most laboratory facilities is to decide whether the water-purification system should be a central system, with water piped throughout the building, or a local point-of-use system at the sink. What follows is a summary of a study recently conducted for a new teaching laboratory of approximately 110,000 gross sq ft (GSF). The central and point-of-use approaches are both evaluated.

The building occupants require pure water at a CAP Type II standard of quality. This grade of pure water maintains 1,000 colonies of bacteria per ml of water maximum, and the electrical resistance of the water may not drop below 2 Megohms at the outlet. In the event that an end user requires higher-quality water, a secondary form of polishing will be provided.

The present number of desired pure-water outlets within the building is 80. The biology and chemistry programs account for all these outlets. The teaching labs require more than one outlet to serve

POINT-OF-USE (POU) VERSUS CENTRAL HIGH-PURITY WATER SYSTEM		
Number of Outlets	38	80
Approach:		
Central System		
First Cost	$165,000	$200,000
Annual Maintenance	$5,100 / yr	$6,000 / yr
Point Of Use		
First Cost	$56,900	$100,000
Annual Maintenance	$17,000 / yr	$24,000 / yr
Simple Payback:		
Central over POU	9 yrs	5.1 yrs

students. The total number of labs served by pure-water is approximately 38.

There are two ways in which the college may approach the pure-water provisions.

The first is as defined in the conceptual program, which calls for point-of-use polishing. Within each lab, a point-of-use polisher (POP) is installed to feed one or more outlets. The polisher is connected to the laboratory cold-water system. If the polisher feeds more than one outlet, multiple outlets can be provided at the station. Point-of-use polishers are connected in series when more stringent water quality is required. POPs typically have a low first cost of installation, but when multiple units are installed serving the same purpose, annual maintenance costs become high.

The second approach is to make use of a centrally piped system. The central system groups the polishing equipment in one location and pumps the polished water out to multiple outlets throughout the building. To achieve consistent water quality throughout the system, water from outlets is continually returned to the central apparatus. When multiple outlets

are required within the building, this approach becomes attractive due to lower annual maintenance costs. First costs of a central system are usually higher than those of a point-of-use system.

To evaluate the cost-benefit ratio of using point-of-use polishing versus a centrally piped system, two schemes with different numbers of intended outlets were developed to understand their cost implications to the building. The first design scheme assumes the desired 80 outlets installed in the building. It is evaluated as both a centrally piped system and a point-of-use system. The second scheme takes liberty in the number of actual required outlets. It assumes that the total number of polishing stations is 38— one per lab on average, with more in the teaching labs and none where not required.

The table above illustrates both pure-water approaches. Dollar amounts listed are for the analysis only and should not be used for budgeting. All costs associated with the pure-water equipment, either central station or point-of-use, have been confirmed with a local pure-water systems vendor.

The table assumes that the point-of-use polishers are leased and maintained by a pure-water vendor for the college. The lease is a one-time first cost. The first cost associated with the polishers is not a purchase cost of the equipment; it represents installation cost only. Costs developed assume some contractor markup as well as contractor supplied items such as distribution piping for the central system and hoop-up for each polisher.

It is clear from the table that the fewer the outlets, the more attractive the point-of-use polishing system becomes. Consideration to the number of pure-water outlets the college actually needs must be applied. The point-of-use polishing approach involves a lower first cost with no reduction in the quality of the water. Additionally, if a point-of-use system is chosen, the expense of the system can be deferred incrementally by the number of units not needed directly after construction. As a station becomes needed, the college can then lease the unit. The entire first-cost burden of the central system is incurred at the time of construction.

This type of analysis should occur on each project. When there is a significant need for high-purity water and outlets, then a central system may be the more cost-effective approach, based on both initial and operating costs.

Other Plumbing Considerations

Other plumbing-related design considerations include the following:

- Provide spare plugged tees in water and gas lines.

- Specify handles instead of knobs on gas stopcocks.

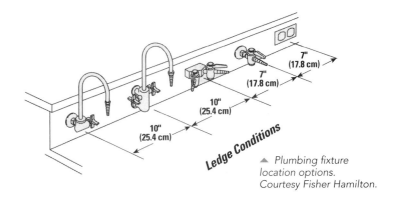

▲ Plumbing fixture location options. Courtesy Fisher Hamilton.

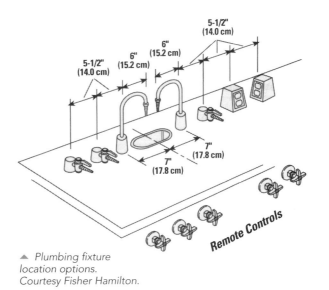

▲ Plumbing fixture location options. Courtesy Fisher Hamilton.

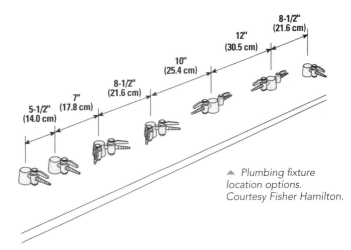

▲ Plumbing fixture location options. Courtesy Fisher Hamilton.

- All fixtures should be color-coded to clarify service.
- To prevent contaminating the water system, include vacuum breakers on all water fixtures that allow the attachment of a hose.
- Provide an electrical outlet near deionized water systems so that purity-level warning lights can be utilized.
- Provide a master control valve for gas.

COMMISSIONING

Commissioning is the process of documenting that all building systems and critical components are properly installed and placed in service and verifying that they operate according to the design. Commissioning is necessary for user acceptance, to minimize risk, and for due diligence. The purpose of commissioning is to minimize the risk of critical component failure or malfunction and to bring the facility to a fully operational status in an orderly and expedient manner. Also, commissioning can ensure that the facility design and construction respond to facility functional requirements.

The following lab facility systems and components are typically commissioned:

- Fume hoods
- Control systems
- Waste treatment systems
- Standby power systems
- Safety devices (showers, eyewashes, etc.)
- Environmental rooms
- Life-safety and alarm systems
- High-purity water systems

- Fire suppression water systems
- HVAC equipment (air-handling units, boilers, chillers, pumps, and fans)
- HVAC distribution components and systems (air valves and control devices)
- Power distribution and circuit protection
- Lighting controls with occupancy sensors

The scope of commissioning should be decided at the beginning of the project. Several tasks must be accomplished in each of these phases to ensure that commissioning can be effectively performed.

Commissioning ensures that each piece of equipment and each control operates properly and in the right sequence with all the other components in the building. Commissioning puts the HVAC system through detailed operational tests. An independent consultant or the engineering design team will verify that all components are working as designed and meeting the manufacturers' specifications. The cost of commissioning is approximately 1–3 percent of the cost of the mechanical system. Many owners find this outlay to be a good investment. Without commissioning, there may be major problems that go undetected for a period of time.

It is also important to equip facility operators with the necessary training to operate the facility properly.

RENOVATION/RESTORATION/ ADAPTIVE REUSE

Historically, more money has been spent each year on renovating labs than on constructing new laboratory space. In addition, more than half of the research being conducted today is housed in facilities that are more than 20 years old. Many renovation projects are modest in size and are usually taken care of by architects and engineers from the institution itself. Larger renovation projects usually involve outside consultants. The renovation of laboratory facilities is usually necessary for one of the following reasons:

- To accommodate growth in staff or to rearrange the lab for more efficient work space. A group of labs may also have to be modified to allow the research team to work more efficiently.

- To improve and update the visual appearance of the lab and building to provide a higher-quality work environment.

- To meet new casework, equipment, or utility service requirements.

- To upgrade the utilities in the lab—increasing electrical power, adding data ports, instituting energy conservation controls, or installing more efficient exhaust systems.

- To address code requirements, such as life-safety codes or the requirements of the Americans with Disabilities Act (ADA).

- To upgrade the building to be more energy efficient. Lab buildings have always been energy hogs, and if a lab building is 20–30 years old, much of the main equipment may have to be replaced.

One of the most difficult aspects of a renovation project is the need to phase the work without interrupting day-to-day research operations. Phasing adds cost to any renovation project. If possible, a swing space should be identified into which researchers can temporarily move while their labs are being renovated. It is best to move the people no more than two times: once into a temporary space and then into their finished, renovated lab.

Another difficult aspect of renovating projects is the unknown. Initial observations or information may not be complete. A contingency should be maintained for unforeseen conditions.

The most difficult lab buildings to renovate are those that were not originally designed as labs. These structures must be thoroughly evaluated to see whether it is more affordable to renovate or to construct a new building, if that is an option. The renovation cost should include an estimate of the cost of lost time and disruption to the research. Some research cannot be interrupted and cannot have any downtime.

Before a renovation is undertaken, the building's structural system and the existing mechanical systems, process piping, and electrical system must all be evaluated.

Structural System

The structure of a building is the least forgiving system and the most difficult to change. If a building was originally constructed for a different use, there is a good chance that its structural system is not really appropriate for laboratories and that final lab design will be inefficient. Columns may not be in the best locations, producing a less efficient layout of casework or location of doors into the lab. The structural system may not be designed to meet vibration requirements. This problem may be resolved by using isolation pads at the source, under the equipment, or by thickening the basement concrete slab. If the basement slab can be upgraded, the sensitive equipment may have to be located in the basement.

Other key issues include whether the floor slab can sustain more penetrations and whether there are areas where new vertical risers can be located. If there are few areas available for penetrations, the renovation may not be possible or it may require another, more complex solution, which may be more costly.

Mechanical Systems

A building's mechanical systems may be quite difficult and expensive to upgrade. Do fume hoods need to be replaced? Is the exhaust system working properly for the lab? For the hoods? Does a heat recovery system make sense? Do the building systems have the capacity to run more fume hoods? Can the hoods be relocated to other areas of the building? One frequently overlooked way to increase the number of hoods without making major changes to the mechanical systems is the use of horizontal/vertical (HV) sash hoods.

If the existing lab has vertical sash hoods as well as 100 percent outdoor air systems, it may be possible to replace the room exhaust air registers with HV-sash hoods. If the lab has vertical sash hoods, it may be possible to increase the hood count by replacing the existing hoods with HV-sash hoods. In some cases, it may be possible to reduce costs further by retrofitting existing hoods with HV sashes.

The amount of outside air and the number of air changes required will have to be studied. In many older buildings, the air is recirculated, which is unacceptable in many wet labs today. The air handlers will have to be evaluated to see whether they can move the correct amount of air through the building.

Process Piping

The location, amount, and type of process piping must be evaluated. If the vacuum, deionized water, air, and other gases are on a central piping system throughout the building, these systems may have to be repaired or replaced. The location of the shutoff valves must be determined, as well as the extent of the area covered by those shutoff valves. For example, if a shutoff valve is located on every floor, then the entire floor will have to be shut down during renovation, which obviously can be a problem. If there are shutoff valves for each lab, it should be easier to phase the renovation.

Electrical System

Electrical power to the building or the lab may have to be increased. Additional breakers may be required to accommodate the more equipment-intensive labs of today. Many older buildings may have panel boxes in a central location. Usually it is more appropriate to have one panel box for one or two main labs (approximately 1,200 NSF). Light fixtures and the lighting design should be reevaluated. Light fixtures are usually easy to replace, and a short-term payback on investment can be realized with today's more energy-efficient fixtures.

FACILITY MANAGEMENT ISSUES

The design team must understand the capability of the owner's operating and maintenance staff and how operating and maintenance expenses are budgeted. Generally, laboratories operated by public institutions are not able to provide the same level of operating and maintenance support as private companies. In addition, energy costs are often funded by a separate, campus-wide budget; if so, the benefits of system enhancements—for example, reduced energy use—may be offset by increased operation and maintenance challenges. Therefore, there is a valid rationale for utilizing simple, straightforward systems in public facilities and reserving those with greater levels of technical complexity and challenge for private companies that have the organization in place to manage them.

In the 21st century, cost savings will be a main focus for facility managers. Facility managers will need to transform functional facilities into buildings that are consistently improving in performance and production, and they will be expected to develop preventive and predictive maintenance plans proactively to minimize the number of emergency repairs and reactive maintenance requirements. The facility manager will need to be able to extend the life cycle of equipment and to forecast equipment needs at least two to three years ahead, to allow projected costs to be incorporated in capital budgets.

▲ View of MRDC II, Georgia Institute of
Technology, Atlanta, from the campus's
engineering quadrant. Perkins & Will, architect.

▲ Materials Science & Engineering lab at MRDC II
with 6 ft ADA fume hood. Perkins & Will, architect.

◀ The atrium of MRDC II is a
great place for special events.
Perkins & Will, architect.

◀ A Mechanical Engineering lab at MRDC II with views north toward Atlanta's skyline. Perkins & Will, architect.

▼ A Materials Science and Engineering laboratory at MRDC II. Perkins & Will, architect.

◀ The three-story atrium of MRDC II features a curved curtain wall with fritted glass for sun shading. Perkins & Will, architect.

▶ The exterior image and massing of the Biomedical Research Building, University of Rochester, Rochester, New York, creates the gateway to the entire medical campus. Perkins & Will, architect.

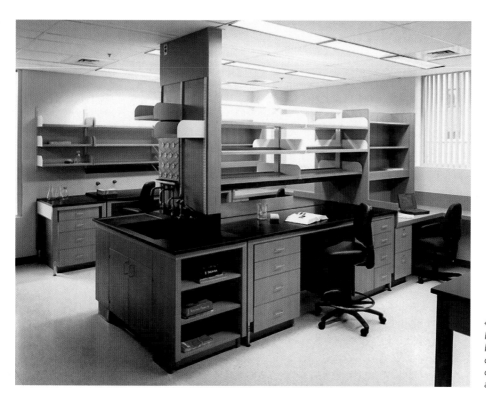

◀ The generic labs of Rochester's Biomedical Research Building are designed with mobile casework. Perkins & Will, architect.

◀ The curved ceiling and spacious corridors of Rochester's Biomedical Research Building allow for comfortable circulation. Perkins & Will, architect.

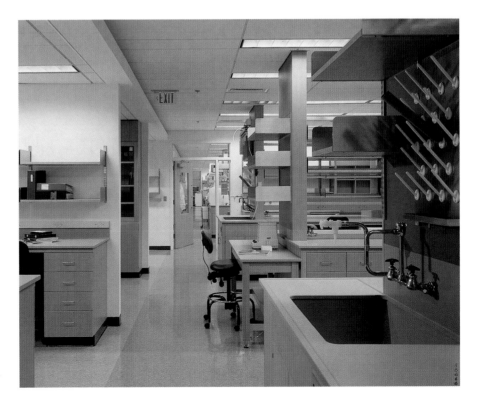

▶ Natural light enters the large open lab spaces of the Biomedical Research Building II, School of Medicine, University of Pennsylvania, Philadelphia. Perkins & Will, architect.

▲ Located in downtown Philadelphia, the new Thomas Jefferson University Cancer Center will enhance the university's position as a prestigious center for cancer research, diagnosis, and treatment. Perkins & Will, architect.

◀ One intent of the exterior image of Penn's Biomedical Research Building II is to architecturally express the university's leadership in research and technology. Perkins & Will, architect.

▲ *The Dongbu Central Research Institute, Taejon, Korea, with its bold arc of laboratories, administrative pavilion, and reflecting pool, creates a dramatic presence for the Institute at the main intersection of a research park. Perkins & Will, architect.*

◀ *The two-story atrium welcomes users and visitors to the Dongbu Central Research Institute. Perkins & Will, architect.*

◀ *A ghost corridor within an "open" lab. Chemical and Life Sciences Building, University of Illinois, Urbana-Champaign. Perkins & Will, architect.*

▼ *Flexible casework in a wet lab. Chemical and Life Sciences Building, University of Illinois, Urbana-Champaign. Perkins & Will, architect.*

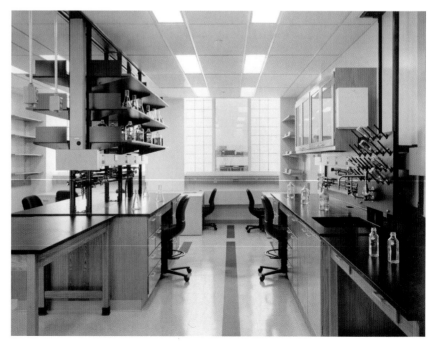

▲ Chemistry lab of the Science Center, Spelman College, Atlanta, Georgia, with the write-up area in the center and the fume hoods around the perimeter. Perkins & Will, architect.

▶ Biomedical Research Building, Washington University, St. Louis, Missouri. Perkins & Will, architect.

▲ Natural light into the two-story study/lounge area of Washington University's Biomedical Research Building. Perkins & Will, architect.

▲ *Equipment corridor in Washington University's Biomedical Research Building. Perkins & Will, architect.*

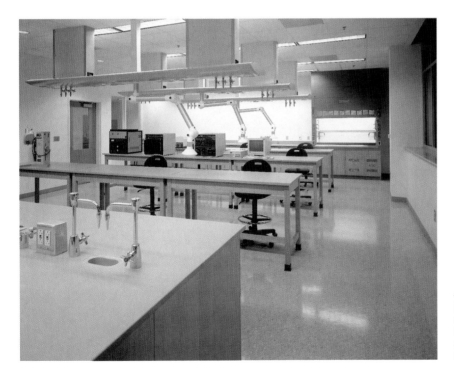

◀ *Advanced instrument chemical lab with overhead service wings for easy access to utilities. Technology Enhanced Learning Center, State University of West Georgia, Carrolton. Perkins & Will, architect.*

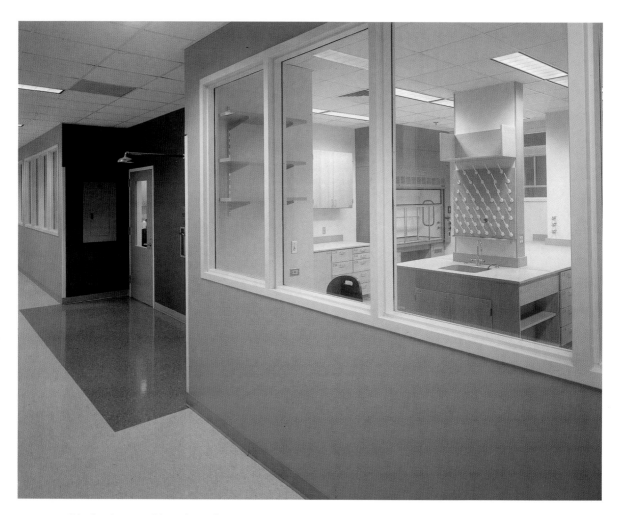

▲ *Window between lab and corridor creates a visual link while allowing daylight to penetrate through the building. Technology Enhanced Learning Center, State University of West Georgia, Carrolton. Perkins & Will, architect.*

CHAPTER 5

COST GUIDELINES

Laboratory buildings cost more than most other types of buildings, for several reasons:

- They require specialized rooms, specialized equipment, and casework.

- Lab buildings are usually constructed with a certain level of flexibility to accommodate different types of research in the future. The cost of this built-in flexibility may be from 5–15 percent of the budget. Measures to enhance flexibility may include mechanical systems designed to accommodate additional fume hoods or the relocation of hoods, redundancy in air handlers, and change in air pressure (5–15 percent of the budget); greater floor-to-floor height for allowances to maintain the engineering systems (0.25–1 percent); additional electrical power for future needs (2–5 percent); and mobile casework (2–5 percent).

- Labs are "energy hogs," requiring special mechanical equipment and a great amount of electrical power.

- The structural system must be designed for heavy loads and vibration control.

- There are usually several systems for piped gases, vacuum, and deionized water.

- Backup generators are usually required for fume hoods, environmental rooms, vivarium facilities, and other special rooms and equipment.

- Safety features—such as eyewash and body wash at sinks, safety showers at least every 75 ft, and safety cabinets— are required.

- The building net-to-gross efficiency is usually low because of the amount of space necessary for mechanical, electrical, and plumbing equipment.

- Most labs require 100 percent outside air.

The following percentages represent the typical portions of a laboratory construction budget allotted to each component:

Mechanical/ electrical/plumbing	30–50 percent or more
Casework	7–12 percent
Fixed equipment	5–10 percent or more
Structure	15–20 percent
General construction	20–25 percent

PROJECT COSTS

The goal is to design the highest-quality building within the budget. The design team must work closely with the client throughout the planning and design process to balance quality expectations with budget constraints. Initial macro-decisions (size of program, corridor arrangement, flexibility desired, cost of land, initial cost versus long-term operating cost) will have the greatest impact on the construction budget. It is imperative that the decision makers have input early in the planning and design process and clearly understand the designer's options before making decisions.

Construction Costs

On most projects, construction costs amount to 70–80 percent of the project

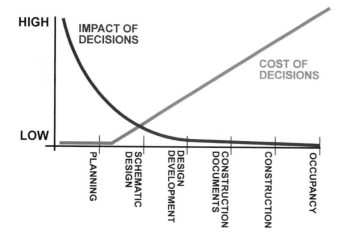

HIGH

IMPACT OF
DECISIONS

COST OF
DECISIONS

LOW

PLANNING
SCHEMATIC DESIGN
DESIGN DEVELOPMENT
CONSTRUCTION DOCUMENTS
CONSTRUCTION
OCCUPANCY

▲ The impact of decisions.

cost. Construction costs include bricks and mortar, demolition, site development, and utility services. Total project costs (see below) include everything necessary to build the facility.

There are a variety of ways to calculate construction cost, including cost per gross sq ft (GSF) and percentage of total project cost. An analysis of academic research buildings from *The College and University Science Facilities Reference Book* is shown in the table below. Approximately 100 laboratory projects were included in the analysis.

It is very difficult to compare the construction costs of laboratory buildings, for several reasons:

- The cost of labor varies depending on where the lab is located and whether union labor is required.

- If the construction market is especially hot when the price of the building is decided, the price may be higher than in a more competitive market.

- The quality of the finishes for the building can make a significant difference in the construction cost.

- The proportion of lab and nonlab space varies from project to project. Lab space generally costs at least twice as much as nonlab space.

- Site and infrastructure costs vary from project to project.

- If all engineering rooms are located in the building (either in a basement or in a roof penthouse area), the building cost per sq ft will be less because the engineering rooms will cost less than office and laboratory spaces. Unfortunately, the building area (GSF will be more, making the construction cost higher than if the engineering equipment is in a central plant or located outside the building.

- Different types of lab differ in their requirements and cost. Wet labs cost more than most dry labs because of the cost of plumbing and fume hoods and because of the greater number of air changes required.

COST ANALYSIS OF 100 LABORATORY PROJECTS

	Average	Maximum	Minimum
Construction cost ($)	36,567,800	116,000,000	14,000,000
Construction cost/sq ft ($)	204	302	110
NSF	108,800	260,000	43,650
GSF	182,600	384,000	68,600
Net/gross (efficiency, %)	0.6	0.9	0.52

* Based on 100 projects built by 1998.

- Vivarium facilities and clean rooms require special finishes and engineering services, making these spaces more expensive than almost all other types of laboratory-related spaces.
- The amount of corridor space in the building has an impact on cost per sq ft. More corridors increase the overall construction cost but reduce the cost per sq ft because corridor space costs less than office and laboratory spaces.

A breakdown of construction cost percentages, based on three recently completed laboratory buildings in Georgia, is shown at right. In 1998 dollars, costs ranged from $128.26 to $175.60 per GSF.

A breakdown of construction cost percentages based on recent laboratory buildings at four of the country's top medical schools is shown at bottom right. In 1998 dollars, costs ranged from $146.00/GSF to $289.00/GSF. This shows that, even among buildings with similar programs, the cost per GSF can vary significantly.

Total Project Costs

Total project costs include construction costs, consultant fees (including architects' and engineers' fees), furniture, equipment, and usually a 5 percent construction contingency. Project costs may also include the following:

- Custom furniture and equipment
- Unusual site conditions (e.g., wetlands) and special construction (retaining walls, structural requirements) that unusual site conditions may require
- Landscaping
- Relocating equipment and furniture

COST COMPARISON OF THREE LAB FACILITIES IN GEORGIA		
	Cost/GSF ($)	Percent of Total
General conditions	14–20	10–12
Foundation/substructure	5–7	3–5
Superstructure	17–19	10–14
Roofing	2–2	0.02
Exterior enclosure	12–15	7–11
Interior enclosure	14–18	10–14
Lab equipment	5–10	4–11
Vertical circulation	1	0.01
Mechanical/plumbing	20–48	22–27
Fire protection	2	1–2
Electrical	10–15	7–0
Site	2–8	3–8
Communications/IT	3–4	2–3
Average	148	

COST COMPARISON OF LABORATORY FACILITIES FOR MEDICAL INSTITUTIONS		
	Cost/GSF($)	Percent of Total
General conditions	12–18	5–8
Foundation/substructure	12–14	34–0
Superstructure	17–30	8–12
Roofing	1–3	1–2
Exterior enclosure	20–30	12–21
Interior enclosure	14–31	10–11
Lab equipment	11–24	7–1
Vertical circulation	2–5	1–4
Mechanical/plumbing	31–100	21–257
Fire protection	2–4	1–2
Electrical	17–33	0–12
Site	Varies	1–0
Average	227	

- Asbestos removal (on renovations)
- Surveys
- Soil borings
- Materials testing
- Commissioning
- Reimbursable expenses such as travel, courier services, reproduction, etc.
- Project management

Efficiency of different corridor designs.

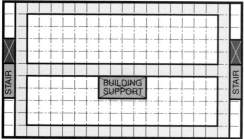

THREE CORRIDOR

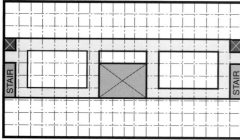

TWO CORRIDOR

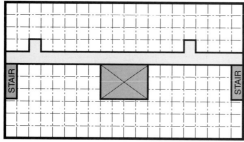

SINGLE CORRIDOR

Capital Costs

Capital costs typically include the cost of land, legal fees, moving expenses, and financing. Project costs are approximately 80 percent and capital costs 20 percent of a total project budget. Other types of costs to consider are life-cycle costs, operating costs, and maintenance costs.

There are some hidden costs that must also be taken into account. The researchers and other professionals employed by the research institution will have to be involved in the design and move-in phases. This cost can add up quickly, but their involvement in the design process should have a long-term payback in a more efficient laboratory building. Move-in costs can be 5 percent or more of the construction cost: equipment must be moved and commissioned; computer systems may have to be modified; and research time can be lost.

AFFORDABILITY/VALUE ENGINEERING

Value engineering reduces costs without compromising quality.

The efficiency of the floor plan is an important cost issue. The net-to-gross ratio can indicate how efficient a lab facility is. Typically, laboratory space has a net-to-gross efficiency of 50–60 percent. The corridor arrangement has a more significant impact on efficiency than do most other program requirements. A single-loaded corridor is the most cost-efficient, and a three-corridor layout (with the service corridor in the middle) is the most costly.

In addition to creating an efficient floor plan, value engineering seeks to minimize the extent of the exterior facade and the level of detail on the facades, as well as the volume of the building. The larger the massing of the building, the greater the construction costs will be. Laboratory program space is more expensive than office space because of the intensive mechanical, electrical, and plumbing requirements as well as the structural vibration criteria.

Lab versus Nonlab Zones

One value engineering option is to separate nonlab space from labs. Zoning the building between lab and nonlab spaces will reduce costs. The appropriate utilities are provided for each zone, and the building codes for two different categories of construction may be used. At least 25 percent of the area must be nonlaboratory space to allow for different mechanical systems. The labs can have 100 percent outside air, and the nonlab spaces can be designed cost-effectively with recirculated air, like an office building.

The nonlab area may include research and administrative offices, meeting rooms, rest rooms, main circulation areas (including stairs and elevators), break rooms, classrooms, utility closets, cafeteria, auditorium, storage rooms, mail rooms, some teaching labs, and mechanical spaces. Assuming that 40 percent of a lab building is nonlaboratory space and 60 percent is laboratory space, separating lab and nonlab spaces can result in cost savings of as much as 15 percent.

Besides reducing costs, locating the offices in a different zone from the labs permits windows in offices to be operable—something that many people desire.

Other General Value Engineering Options

A number of other general value engineering options should be discussed and evaluated in the initial programming and design phases:

▼ *Lab and nonlab zoning for more affordable construction. College of Engineering, Phase 1, North Carolina State University, Raleigh. Perkins & Will, architect.*

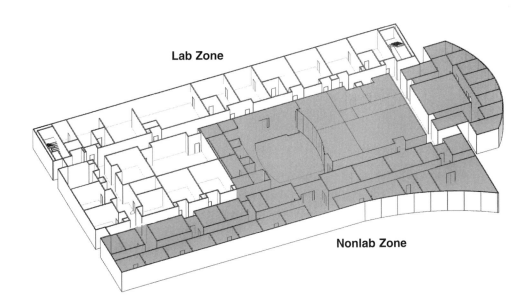

Lab Zone

Nonlab Zone

- Try to design with standard building components instead of customized components.
- Identify at least three manufacturers of each material or piece of equipment specified to ensure competitive bidding for the work.
- Locate fume hoods on upper floors to minimize ductwork and the cost of moving air through the building.
- Evaluate whether process piping should be handled centrally or locally. In many cases it is more cost-effective to locate gases, in cylinders, at the source in the lab instead of centrally.
- Create equipment zones to minimize the amount of casework necessary in the initial construction.
- Provide space for equipment (e.g., ice machine) that also can be shared with other labs in the entry alcove to the lab. Shared amenities can be more efficient and cost-effective.
- Consider designating instrument rooms as cross-corridors, saving space as well as encouraging researchers to share equipment.

COMPARABLE LAB PROJECTS

PROJECT	GSF	NSF	Efficiency (%)	Type of Corridor	MECHANICAL PENTHOUSE OR BASEMENT Comments
Georgia BOR Projects					
West Georgia TELC	114,470	65,560	57	double	mech. basement
Georgia Tech. MRDC II	151,581	85,222	56	double	penthouse
North Georgia Nat. & Health Sci.	100,000	56,515	56	to be determined	to be determined
Georgia Tech. MARC	133,037	87,947	66	double/suite	mechanical in atrium
Georgia Tech. MRDCI	116,923	69,219	59	single	
Georgia Tech. BioSciences				double	
Georgia Tech. Environmental Sc.	286,263	166,243	58	double	penthouse
Other Georgia Projects					
Spelman Science Center	115,876	64,988	56	double	
Emory Woodruff Building				three	
The Southeast					
Univ. of Florida Brain Inst.				double	
Univ. of Florida Vet. School				single	
MUSC Thurmond/Gazes Res. Bldg.	193,615	109,100	56	double	penthouse
Univ. NC Biological Res. Center	120,000	70,180	58	double	penthouse
Wake Forest Human Nutrition	270,000	134,000	50	double	penthouse
Duke Neurobilogy Res. Bldg.	165,000	90,831	55	double	penthouse
Florida A & M Eng. & Science				double	penthouse
Univ. of Alabama Revill Bldg.	245,000	138,000	56	single	penthouse
Univ. of Florida Academic Res.				double	penthouse
Vanderbilt Wilson Hall				double	
Wake Forest Hanes Res. Center	141,000	86,496	61	single	penthouse

Open labs, no corridor, 60–70% efficient; single-corridor plan, 57–62 efficient; two-corridor plan, 50–58% efficient; three-corridor plan, 45–50% efficient

◀◀ Shared deionized water and ice machine on each floor. Stevenson Center Complex Chemistry Building, Vanderbilt University, Nashville, Tennessee. Payette Associates, Inc., architect.

◀ Instrument rooms as cross-corridors. Vanderbilt University, Nashville, Tennessee.

▼ Exposed engineering systems in corridor.

- Design easy-to-maintain, energy-efficient building systems.

- Expose mechanical, plumbing, and electrical systems for easy maintenance access from the lab.

- Locate all mechanical equipment centrally, either on a lower level of the building or on the penthouse level.

- Stack vertical elements above one another without requiring transfers from floor to floor. Such elements include columns, stairs, mechanical closets, and rest rooms.

Value Engineering Options by Construction Division

The following outline, arranged according to the typical construction divisions, provides some ideas for reducing costs in the construction budget.

Division 1: General conditions

- The contractor may be able to suggest cost-reduction ideas here.

Division 2: Foundations/substructure

- Minimize excavation and cut-and-fill.
- Minimize blasting of rock.

Division 3: Superstructure

- Space columns efficiently.
- Use one row of columns along the corridor instead of two.

Division 4: Roofing

- Specify less expensive materials for the penthouse.

Division 5: Exterior enclosure

- Evaluate the amount of glass on the exterior facade and interior walls.
- Evaluate the cost-effectiveness of a metal stud backup system rather than concrete block for a brick exterior facade.

- Consider using screens around mechanical equipment at the roof instead of enclosing the area and creating a penthouse.

Division 6: Interior enclosure

- Minimize interior glazing at walls and doors.
- Create two-story (instead of three-story or higher) atriums. This will eliminate the need for a smoke evacuation system.
- Use as many standard details as possible.

Division 7: Lab equipment/casework

- Choose cabinets that are modular and repetitive in design. The benefit of selecting casework that is all on the same module is similar to that of basing the building design on a lab module: it creates a flexible lab where the casework can be changed easily.

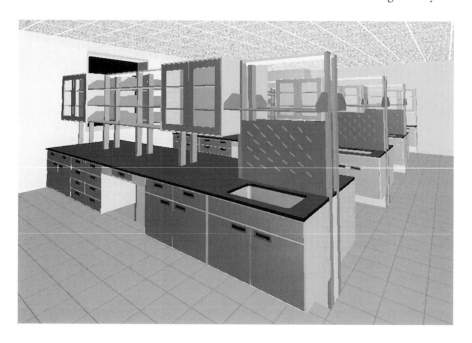

▶ *Design with modular casework.*

Purchasing the same size casework will also save money. Always try to use a manufacturer's standard system, because this is the most cost-effective approach. A 3 ft module, coordinated with a standard knee space, is recommended.

- Purchase casework directly from the vendor, eliminating the contractor markup (approximately 10 percent). Purchasing the casework separately may, however, create some coordination problems during construction if the general contractor is not responsible for overseeing the installation.

- Purchase casework when the actual needs have been identified, reducing the amount of casework included in the initial construction budget.

- Specify movable casework. This will cost more initially but should save money over time.

- Identify storage space outside the lab, which may be more affordable than storage in the laboratory space itself.

- Buy in bulk and construct central stock and storage rooms. Researchers can purchase what they want on a daily basis and can be billed each month.

- Provide continuous flooring first, then locate the casework.

- Specify casework with doors rather than drawers. Doors are more cost-effective, producing a savings of approximately 40 percent. Another option is to design baskets behind the doors when drawer space is necessary. Baskets may be placed on full-extension shelves to minimize the need for drawers.

- Specify plastic laminate tops for dry benches. Wet benches require epoxy resin countertops, which cost slightly more. (Black resin tops are the most cost-effective. Other epoxy colors will increase the cost by 5 percent or more, depending on the color.)

- Use 3' 6" doors instead of 3' doors with 1' (or larger) movable sleeves. A 3' 6" door is wide enough for most equipment to pass through, and a single door has half the hardware and costs approximately 20 percent less than the two-door arrangement.

- Use adjustable shelving rather than wall cases (which can be 83 percent more cost-effective).

◀ Doors are more cost-effective than drawers.

- Specify metal cabinets rather than wood casework. The price will vary depending on demand, but metal cabinets are usually slightly cheaper.
- Note that the costs of wood finishes vary: maple is least costly; red oak is more costly (as much as 35 percent more); and white oak is the most expensive (as much as 70 percent more than maple).

Division 8: Vertical circulation

- Use the freight elevator as a passenger elevator as well.
- Build an architectural stair next to the passenger elevator instead of building two passenger elevators.

Division 9: Mechanical/plumbing

- Keep the wet services along the outside wall. Center islands are more cost-effective as dry areas for instruments and for high concentration of electrical services.
- Determine the number of labs that will need 100 percent outside air. Most dry labs should not need 100 percent outside air.
- Evaluate the possibility of using a heat-recovery chiller, a building management system, and electronic ballasts to conserve energy.
- Use large, manifold exhaust fans instead of small, individual exhaust fans.
- Locate the mechanical shafts so as to eliminate lengthy horizontal duct and piping runs.
- Review the need for ducted versus nonducted returns.
- Evaluate the number of system redundancies needed.
- Reduce the number of zones that require thermostats.

- Allow nonwelded fittings for chilled water and hot-water piping.
- Consider welded versus nonwelded ductwork.
- Reduce the number of control points for process piping.
- Eliminate branch piping valves, and provide the valves in the corridor only.
- Provide a duct leak test only for welded ducts in labs.
- Require competitive bidding (three bids or more) for the controls system.
- Utilize spot welding of continuous weld, and use an approved duct sealant.
- Provide PVC instead of cast-iron piping in the building and for underground services.

Division 10: Fire protection

- (No cost-reduction suggestions.)

Division 11: Electrical system

- Determine the type and number of light fixtures. Minimize the types of light fixture in the building to simplify long-term operations and maintenance.
- If possible, use electric outlet boxes, which are more affordable than raceways.
- Wire light fixtures continuously instead of individually.
- Review the amount of emergency power and the number of uninterruptible power sources needed.
- Locate the transformer outside the building envelope.
- Substitute rated cable for conduit for the fire-alarm wiring.
- Consolidate panel boards at labs.

Division 12: Site

- Obtain a soils report early.
- Balance the amount of cut and fill required to eliminate the need to move soil from the site or to bring soil onto the site.
- Reduce the amount of rock excavation.

Division 13: Special construction (communications/IT)

- Install conduit in the initial construction. Run the wires where they are needed, when they are needed.

PROJECT DELIVERY OPTIONS

How a project is bid and constructed—the project delivery method—can influence cost. The following paragraphs discuss the main options:

Conventional Bids

The conventional bid process (design/bid/build), which allows all contractors a fair chance to bid and to be awarded a project, is common in many state and federal projects. Some projects, like laboratory facilities, may require the contractors to prequalify. This means that each contracting firm that wishes to bid must first submit information about its experience, as well as a list of the people proposed to work on the project. The architect reviews the information. If there is a strong enough reason not to allow a contractor to bid, then the architect must present the findings and allow the client to make the final decision.

The architects and engineers prepare drawings that contractors review before submitting their bids to do the work. The qualified contractor with the lowest bid is awarded the project. Because the lowest bid wins the award, contractors will estimate what is clearly documented, then submit for additional fees for what is not documented. Most architects and contractors consider the conventional bid process to be the least desirable option because of the high number of change orders that usually result. The change-order process is costly for everyone on the team, and it creates division as people debate what is a change order and what is not.

Construction Management

In the construction-management option, an outside firm serves as the general contractor or the owner's management consultant, or both. A construction manager (CM) manages the overall schedule and budget. There are two types of construction managers: those "at risk" and those "not at risk." The "CM not at risk" management process can be used for any project delivery method, including design/bid/build, multiple prime, design/build, or even CM at risk. (In this last option, the CM starts out not at risk; then the client asks the CM to commit to a price rather than having others bid for the project.) The "CM at risk" provides a guaranteed maximum price (GMP), is responsible for the successful performance of each trade, and guarantees the schedule for completing the project. The CM may be both responsible for project management and at risk for the financial performance of the project delivery.

Negotiated Bids

Negotiated bids allow the owner to discuss, review, and evaluate the project with a contractor after bids are received. Usually, add alternates or deduct alternates are estimated. The owner can negotiate with the contractor he or she is most comfortable working with and is not necessarily obligated to accept the lowest bid.

Design-Build

The design-build procedure is usually led by a contractor, who typically provides a GMP at the end of design development. There is currently a trend toward architect-led design-build teams. The design-build process is often preferred by private-sector companies for the following reasons:

- The schedule is accelerated.
- The owner wants to avoid the problems associated with the bid process.
- The owner wants to finalize the cost early in the process.
- The owner is comfortable with a particular contractor.
- Coordination of drawings can reduce change-order costs.
- The owner seeks sole-source responsibility.

TRENDS IN PROJECT FINANCING

Projects can be funded through public agencies, the private sector, donors, or any combination of these. There is an increase in partnering between academia and the private sector, with private-sector companies paying for some research spaces and sometimes funding equipment purchases. Baby boomers are beginning to donate to their alma maters (including medical schools and other research institutions), and some state legislatures are encouraging public universities to seek donors more aggressively by pledging to match their contributions. (This can speed up the state appropriations process and give institutions another avenue to raise funds to meet their construction needs.) Some institutions are trying to pay for some of their construction and operation costs with research grant money. It is difficult to fund an entire building with these resources, but it may be possible to fund a portion of the construction.

SUMMARY OF COST ISSUES

The value and cost-effectiveness of every building component must be challenged and weighed. This evaluation must include long-term operating costs as well as first costs. The following factors will play a role in determining value far into the future:

- Speed to market and cost reduction will continue to be pushed, to satisfy shareholders.
- Facilities must adapt faster and at a lower cost.
- Real scrutiny of time and research dollars will determine some assignments of actual research space.
- A company can now buy science. There is a proliferation of small labs serving large companies.
- The downsizing of companies and departments continues. The size of in-house engineering departments is going way down—services are outsourced.
- Corporations are taking a harder look at the entrepreneurial sectors of their companies. They recognize that these sectors have to be lean, fast, flexible, and very innovative.
- Universities are getting into research and development (R&D) projects.
- The requirement to balance institutional budgets may affect research funding, driving buildings to higher populations and lower construction and operating costs.
- R&D is considered the new wave of economic development.

THE LABORATORIES FOR THE 21ST CENTURY INITIATIVE

The U.S. Environmental Protection Agency (EPA) and the U.S. Department of Energy (DOE) have launched a new, voluntary initiative to improve the environmental performance of U.S. laboratories. The Laboratories for the 21st Century (Labs21) initiative is focusing on improving the energy efficiency of the national's laboratories. As laboratory energy efficiency improves, Labs21 will focus on even more aggressive pollution prevention goals and strategies unique to each type of laboratory.

The primary guiding principle of the Labs21 energy and water focus is that improving the energy efficiency and environmental performance of a laboratory requires examining the entire facility from a holistic, or comprehensive, perspective. Adopting this perspective allows laboratory designers, operators, and owners to improve the efficiency of the entire facility rather than improving the efficiency of specific laboratory building components. As Labs21 practitioners understand, improving the efficiency of individual components without examining their relation to the entire system can eliminate opportunities to make other more significant efficiency improvements.

As currently envisioned, Labs21 will focus on the following five activities:

- Creating a national database of current environmental practices, including energy and water consumption data for a variety of laboratory types. The data can be used to compare laboratory performance.

- Negotiating voluntary goals for laboratory environmental performance, including energy and water efficiency goals, with each potential Labs21 participant.

- Providing training or other opportunities to exchange technical information.

- Establishing partnerships with interested Labs21 participants.

- Promoting the Labs21 initiative.

Other benefits of the Labs 21 approach include lower laboratory utility and operating costs, reduced health and safety risks, improved facility management, reduced greenhouse gas emissions, elimination of waste and other inefficiencies, improved community relations and lower insurance premiums.

Case Study 1: National Vehicle and Fuel Emissions Laboratory

The Environmental Protection Agency (EPA) has adopted the Labs21 perspective for its facilities and is anticipating some significant cost savings and environmental benefits as a result. For example, EPA's 150,000 sq ft National Vehicle and Fuel Emissions Laboratory in Ann Arbor, Michigan, has required 2.5 MW of electricity, consumed energy at a rate exceeding 700,000 Btu per GSF, and consumed 31 million gal of water annually at a cost to the taxpayers of more than $1 million a year. EPA is implementing mechanical modifications at the facility that are estimated to reduce annual electrical demand by 68 percent, reduce energy use per GSF by 66 percent, reduce annual water consumption by 80 percent, reduce the annual utility bill by 74 percent (for a savings of more than $800,000 per year), and provide a simple payback on the contractor's capital expenditure of less than ten years.

Based on the expected successes of this project, EPA is retrofitting several other laboratories with very different user profiles, energy costs, and meteorological conditions and is predicting comparable savings.

Case Study 2: North Carolina State University College of Engineering Chemical and Materials Science Engineering Building

The building is 155,000 GSF, with 40 percent of the building for wet labs and the remaining 60 percent for classrooms, dry labs, and offices. The project was in the middle of design development when the experts met with the architects and engineers to discuss design options to improve the quality of the building, maintain the initial construction budget, and reduce the long term operational costs. The following is a list of design decisions that have been made to provide the university with a laboratory facility that focuses on sustainable design:

- Change to a task/ambient lighting system in offices and faculty lounges, reducing lighting levels from 70 foot-candles direct to 30 foot-candles ambient lighting, with appropriate task lighting. The associated heat load can be reduced from 2 W/sq ft to 0.75 W/sq ft (approximately 30 foot-candles, resulting in a reduced need for cooling).

- Light fixtures parallel to the outside wall will allow for each row of lights to be controlled by the sensors more efficiently. Natural light should go to a depth of two to three times ceiling height into the labs. The light fixtures in this area should not need to go on during the day.

- Provide a photo sensor that will automatically turn off the fixture if it senses that there is enough light in the space. This will be used in all non-wet lab spaces and 10 ft along the outside wall of the wet labs.

- Occupancy sensor for all spaces except the exit light requirements.

- Offices along the exterior walls should have dimmable ballasts or a three-position switch (off, 1 lamp on, 2 lamps on).

- Exterior and interior light shelves can help bounce the light 30–45 ft into the space. The shelves are generally more cost effective if integrated into the design of the window wall.

- Specify a simple fixture to justify the costs because pendants generally will cost more than the lay-in type even when taking into account the energy cost savings.

- Specify different glass for each façade based on the solar impact. Also consider different glazing for windows that are used to see out versus the clerestory windows that allow light into the space.

- To reduce leakage of air, avoid butt joints in exterior wall construction. Do not count on caulk to seal the joint. Detailing of windows is important to minimize butt joints and reduce air leakage.

- Consider using natural convection to exhaust air in the atrium; this may eliminate the need for a separate air handler.
- Study the possibility of fiberglass windows. They are less expensive than aluminum and reduce energy cost.
- Use light color roof with a reflective coating to reduce heat gain and energy costs. This is a big energy saver.
- Propose 3 in. for wall insulation instead of 2 in.
- Roof insulation at R-19 is probably sufficient. The building generates a significant amount of heat because of the amount of equipment, which means it is better for the heat to go through the roof. More insulation in the roof can actually hurt, raising the cost of cooling the building. This will need to be verified by energy calculations.
- Eliminate microbial growth in HVAC system. Always try to eliminate any drip pans and areas where water can collect. The biggest problem is usually at the cooling coils, which are wet all the time. Ultraviolet lights can be used to kill the microbial growth, but the lights are expensive and difficult to maintain.
- Combination sashes are not necessary for fume hoods because heat buildup from the equipment (not the number of fume hoods) drives the number of air changes through the labs.
- Construct the skylight with clerestory windows that allow indirect light into the building.

Case Study 3: University of Minnesota Molecular and Cellular Biology Building

This is a 243,000 GSF building located on the University of Minnesota's East Bank campus. The energy cost was estimated at $1,406,353 per year at code level. For the facility, Northern States Power Company developed a DOE-2 model (a sophisticated energy performance simulation program). The following is a list of issues that resulted from the study, in which the design team was involved:

- Heat recovery saves the most dollars because of the large amount of heat required and the relatively high cost of University of Minnesota steam; it

SUMMARY OF THE DOE-2 ANALYSIS		
Design Issue	Annual Energy Savings ($)	Peak kW Savings
Heat recovery	309,933	8.0
Lab VAV	140,662	108.4
Chiller/motors	46,348	403.4
Variable speed drives	39,843	218.4
Decreased fan static	28,812	176.5
Glass selection	12,744	26.0
Daylight dimming	10,241	131.1
Occupancy control VAV	8,273	13.8
Lighting controls	6,176	64.6
Lighting design	5,990	66.9
Daylight step	4,235	51.5

saves relatively few kW however (8.0 peak savings), as most of the savings are in heating energy ($309,933 annual energy savings).

- Improving the chiller efficiency saves the most kW (403.4), as well as a relatively large amount of energy dollars ($46,348).

- Variable speed drives, decreased fan static, daylighting, and lab variable air volume also show strong kW savings potential (218.4) but relatively less dollar savings ($39,843).

The DOE-2 study is very helpful in identifying the best investment paybacks. The study has identified the possibility of reducing annual energy costs by $613,257 (a 44 percent reduction from the estimated $1,406,353 per year).

BIBLIOGRAPHY AND REFERENCES

PRINT

American Institute of Architects, Center for Advanced Technology Facilities Design. 1999. *Guidelines for Planning and Design of Biomedical Research Laboratory Facilities.* Washington, D.C.: American Institute of Architects.

Arthur, Paul, and Romedi Passini. 1984. *Wayfinding: People, Signs, and Architecture.* New York: McGraw-Hill.

ASHRAE Handbook. Atlanta, Ga.: American Society of Heating, Refrigeration, and air-conditioning Engineers. Since 1996 the handbook has consisted of alternately issued volumes with subtitles *Fundamentals, Applications, Equipment,* and *Systems.*

Braybrooke, Susan. 1993. *Design for Research: Principals of Laboratory Architecture.* New York: John Wiley & Sons.

The College and University Science Facilities Reference Book. 1998. Orinda, Calif.: Tradeline, Inc..

DiBerardinis, Louis J., et al. 1993. *Guidelines for Laboratory Design: Health and Safety Considerations.* New York: John Wiley & Sons.

Earl Walls Associates. 2000. *Laboratory* (a newsletter published by Earl Walls Associates). May.

Furr, A. K. 1995. *CRC Handbook of Laboratory Safety.* 4th ed. Boca Raton, Fla.: CRC Press.

Hain, W. 1995. *Laboratories: Briefing and Design Guide.* London: E & FN Spon.

Haxton, Bruce. 1999. *Facility Management Journal,* March/April.

Institute of Laboratory Animal Resources (U.S.), Committee on Care and Use of Laboratory Animals. 1985. *Guide for the Care and Use of Laboratory Animals.* Bethesda, Md.: U.S. Dept. of Health and Human Services, Public Health Service, National Institutes of Health.

Mayer, Leonard. 1995. *Design and Planning of Research and Clinical Laboratory Facilities.* New York: John Wiley & Sons.

Miller, W. L., and L. Morris. 1999. *Fourth Generation R & D: Managing Knowledge, Technology, and Innovation.* New York: John Wiley & Sons.

National Institutes of Health, Division of Engineering Services, Office of Research Services (Farhad Memarzadeh, principal investigator). 1996. *Methodology for Optimization of Laboratory Hood Containment Using Computational Fluid Dynamics Modeling.* Bethesda, Md.: National Institutes of Health.

National Science Foundation. 1992. *Planning Academic Research Facilities: A Guidebook.* Washington, D.C.: National Science Foundation.

National Science Foundation, Division of Science Resources Studies. 1996. *Scientific and Engineering Research Facilities at Colleges and Universities.* Arlington, Va.: National Science Foundation.

——————. 1998. *Research and Development in Industry: 1995–96.* Arlington, Va.: National Science Foundation.

Ruys, T. 1990. *Laboratory Facilities.* Vol. 1 of *Handbook of Facilities Planning.* New York: Van Nostrand Reinhold.

WEB SITES

Sustainable Design

American Council for an Energy Efficient Economy (ACEEE): www.aceee.org/

American Institute of Architects, Committee on the Environment:
www.earchitect.com/pia/Cote/home.asp

American Society of Heating, Refrigerating, and Air-conditioning Engineers (ASHRAE):
www.ashrae.org/

American Solar Energy Society (ASES): www.ases.org/

Center for Renewable Energy and Sustainable Technology (CREST):
www.solstice.crest.org

Center for Resourceful Building Technology (CRBT): www.montana.com/crbt/mis.html

Consortium on Green Design and Manufacturing: euler.berkeley.edu/green/

Energy Efficiency and Renewable Energy Network (EREN): www.eren.doe.gov

Federal Energy Management Programs: www.nrel.gov/femp/

Illuminating Engineering Society of North America: www.iesna.org

The Labs21 initiative: www.epa.gov/labs21century

Lawrence Berkeley National Laboratory, *A Design Guide for Energy-Efficient Research
Laboratories:* ateam.lbl.gov/Design-Guide

U.S. Department of Energy, Center for Sustainable Development:
www.sustainable.doe.gov/

U.S. Environmental Protection Agency, Office of Administration and Resources
Management: www.epa.gov/oaintmt/

U.S. Green Building Council: www.usgbc.org/

Vivarium Facilities

Association for Assessment and Accreditation of Laboratory Animal Care International
(AAALAC): www.aaalac.org

National Academy of Sciences and the National Research Council, *Guide for the Care and
Use of Laboratory Animals*: www.nap.edu/readingroom/books/labrats
Includes the current (1996) edition of the *Guide,* used as a standard by the AAALAC.

U.S. Department of Agriculture, Animal and Plant Health Inspection Service (APHIS):
www.aphis.usda.gov
APHIS is responsible for vivarium facilities under the U.S. Code of Federal
Regulations.

U.S. Government Printing Office and the National Archives and Records Administration:
www.access.po.gov/nara/cfr
Includes the Code of Federal Regulations regarding APHIS.

INDEX